The Modern Catholic Novel in Europe

Twayne's World Authors Series

David O'Connell, Editor

Georgia State University

TWAS 841

*To My Mother
and the
Memory of My Father*

Contents

Acknowledgments

I am happy to have the opportunity to express my deep gratitude to a number of people who have aided me, directly or indirectly, in writing this book. First, to Rev. P. Anthoni Raj Sampathkumar, currently ministering for Missions Africaines, whose friendship and spiritual interest in the project encouraged me to undertake it. Then to my colleague and friend, the late professor Maurizio Vannicelli, so missed by many of us at Holy Cross, whose keen intelligence and strong literary interests aided me in my analysis of a number of authors studied. To my niece Rebecca Graves, a young scholar whose expert reading of and hands-on editorial assistance in preparing the final draft made for a dramatically improved text. To David O'Connell, leading authority in the area of the Catholic novel, who assisted me in every way in undertaking and completing the work. To Alfred Desautels, S.J., my colleague at Holy Cross, whose close reading of the text was invaluable. To my students of the Holy Cross course Modern Religious Novelists, whose enthusiastic and insightful reading of many of the works and authors presented in the book never ceased to be a vital means of inspiration and sustaining force. And, finally, to the college for its generous faculty fellowship to allow me sufficient time to complete the work.

Prologue

The Catholic novel is in many ways a literary phenomenon belonging to the past—one that at present constitutes primarily a subcategory of the modern novel. Such, at any rate, is the conclusion of several notable critics. For example, in an article published in the 2 December 1984 *New York Times Book Review*, Richard Gilman, a respected drama critic and earlier a convert from Judaism to Catholicism, remarked that "the religious spiritual novel is in some sense only a memory."[1] He goes on to describe the Catholic fiction that for a considerable time strongly dominated his literary tastes and played a decisive role in his conversion. The authors of these works were, he says, mostly French—Léon Bloy, François Mauriac, and Georges Bernanos—but he also cites Graham Greene, whose 1940 novel *The Power and the Glory* he refers to as "the first contemporary novel I'd read that dealt with the idea of sin, with human weakness at a level deeper than the psyche or ordinary morality. It was the only fiction of our time that I knew in which something you would call the soul—not the heart or the psyche—and the body contrasted one another" (Gilman, 7). Rereading such classic Catholic novels as Bernanos's *Diary of a Country Priest* (1936), Mauriac's *The Desert of Love* (1925) or *The Viper's Tangle* (1932), and Greene's *The End of the Affair* (1951), Gilman found that, though still powerful and moving, these works were now marred by "contrivances, flaws, arbitrary endings, rhetorical interventions, and the attempts by the author to play God." In explaining the reasons for his new reservations, he acknowledged that his own drift to unbelief had been a principal cause and a factor more important than the novels themselves. Yet he also maintained that there had occurred a "seismatic shift" causing the works to be regarded as critically flawed and this was because it was no longer part of the culture of our age to believe that the drama of sin, damnation, and salvation lies at the heart of the human condition (Gilman, 58).

A far more substantive appraisal to reach somewhat similar conclusions is the important collection *Crossroads: Essays on the Catholic Novel* (1982), by Albert Sonnenfeld. Offered as "an elegy for . . . an apparently dying form in a time of radical change for the Church and for those who saw the drama of Catholic salvation as material for modern fiction,"[2] the essays reflect on the full range and production of the Catholic novel from the "Golden Age"—

the 1920s to the 1950s—and then from the Second Vatican Council (1962–65) to the end of the 1970s. Sonnenfeld's point of view is from the outside—that is, as a critic who does not share the beliefs of Catholics. Not granting to the works the theological urgency or exclusivity that they generally purport to contain for believers, Sonnenfeld is primarily concerned with "the informing mythopoeic structure or generative symbolic system" presented in them, "where the principal and decisive issue is the salvation and damnation of the hero or heroine" (Sonnenfeld, vii). From this perspective they seem as works of art to resemble "the power, if not the glory, of the stained-glass window" or an impressive artistic achievement of a vanished age. And despite his grave reservations about several aspects of this genre ("it can be seen as arrogant, often filled more with hate than with love"), he still grants it "the grandeur of a great struggle and the endurance of great Renaissance sculpture" (xix).

In his essays Sonnenfeld provides ample and valuable references to modern and contemporary novels of European and American Catholic authors (Greene, Bernanos, Mauriac, Heinrich Böll, Flannery O'Connor, and Mary Gordon in particular) to substantiate his thesis that, as far as the Catholic faith is concerned, the "age of theology" has yielded to "the age of clinical psychology" (Sonnenfeld, xi). In its turn the Catholic novel, mirroring the postconcilar changes in attitudes and beliefs in the Church itself, has become primarily concerned with psychological and more human themes and problems. As Sonnenfield sees this transformation, the older, theologically laden plots have gradually been replaced by those depicting or at least suggesting the loss of pristine, orthodox Catholic faith in the face of the overwhelming manifestations of the absurd as the dominant condition of modern life.

Another significant commentary on the genre has been provided by several of David Lodge's essays in *The Novelist at the Crossroads* (1971).[3] A well-known critic of the contemporary novel and himself a prominent practitioner of the Catholic novel in the post–Vatican II period, he has in the essay "Fiction and Catholicism" both defined the genre and anticipated a number of the reservations raised by Gilman and Sonnenfeld. Dealing specifically with Graham Greene, Lodge turns his attention to one charge in particular that critics have leveled against the Catholic novel: that its plots are sometimes rendered unbelievable and obscure to those not of the faith through reliance on elements of Catholic doctrine and worship. Though he focuses on the novels of Greene, Lodge is obviously addressing the Catholic novel as genre and works not written for apologetic or proselytizing ends. He grants that Greene has used in the creation of his artistic universe many Catholic articles of faith—for example, "that there is such a thing as mortal sin, that Christ is really and truly present in the Eucharist, that miracles can and do occur in the 20th Century" (Lodge 1971, 88). Granting the presence and use of such matter, Lodge nevertheless insists that in their appraisal of Catholic novelists critics would do well to follow the wise dictum of Henry James: that artists must be granted the right to use their ideas, their artistic vision, their donnée as their inspiration directs them, and that the proper role of critics is to comment on the use that authors have made of their donnée through an evaluation of the craft of their work (Lodge 1971, 88).

In offering these observations Lodge seems to have been motivated by a common prejudice that he believes has long been advanced by a number of modern critics against the Catholic novel. This prejudice is, for Lodge, crystallized in the case of George Orwell, who claimed that since any kind of ideological orthodoxy is inimical to the creative process, Roman Catholicism, through authoritarian control of its artist-believers, has by and large not produced first-rate novelists, and of "the handful" that one could name, most had not been "good Catholics" (Lodge 1971, 89).

Using James's sensible critical principal as his point of departure, Lodge grants that Greene indeed makes frequent use of Catholic symbolism to create his "metapoesis." Yet in doing so his intention, Lodge insists, is not to proselytize or to present "a body of belief requiring exposition and demanding categorical assent or dissent" but to see his fiction as "a system of concepts, source of situation, and reservoir of symbols . . . to dramatize intuition about the nature of the human experience" (Lodge 1971, 89). Hence, Lodge contends, Catholicism as a system of dogma and laws is not in or by itself an adequate key to understanding and interpreting the meaning of Greene's works, and these are, Lodge argues, as accessible to most readers as any other works of art that possess a unique vision and aesthetic patterns. These Catholic novels can therefore be appreciated as authentic pieces of literature above and beyond the doctrinal or confessional elements of faith contained therein.

What Lodge says of Greene can, I believe, be applied to the other novelists I present in this study as "Catholic," and a good number of these (Mauriac, Julien Green, Graham Greene, and Heinrich Böll, for example) have in fact adamantly shunned for themselves the nomenclature of "Catholic novelist" and have insisted that as artists they possess their own angle of vision and unique literary universe. Ultimately they view themselves not as writers consciously writing novels with specific "Catholic" content but as Catholics who happen to be novelists. François Mauriac has perhaps best explained the intention and intellectual disposition of Catholic novelists who are creative artists in their own right: "Being a Christian," he says, "my Christian beliefs dominate my novels, not because I want to make propaganda for Christianity, but because it is the deepest part of my nature. . . . I am a Christian first and last, which means a man responsible to God and to his conscience for the epoch he lives in . . . he has been put here to play a certain role among his fellow men. He *is* engaged; it isn't a question of deliberately engaging himself."[4]

Though Catholic novelists of Mauriac's persuasion to varying degrees draw poetic and thematic material from their common Catholic experience and belief patterns, it does not follow that the forms their literature takes should be declared problematic and unbelievable to readers not of their faith or, as Gilman has suggested, even marred by artistic attempts to "cheat" through the use and intervention of Catholic dogma and symbolism. Rather, criticism of the works of Catholic novelists (and of all novelists for that matter) should be based on how they use their artistic vision; in no way should it be colored by a critic's possible bias against a particular belief structure or philosophy of life. All novelists imbue their works with a moral vision from which we can discern some value statements on the human condition. (Albert Camus, Jean-Paul Sartre, Samuel Beckett, and André Malraux are, after all, as much intent on addressing issues of ultimate concern as any Catholic novelist.) Hence the work of the critic is not to attack ideology but to assess the manner in which it has been artfully presented.

In his preface to a 1987 translation of Mauriac's *Viper's Tangle* David Lodge describes how this famous novel represents for him "a classic example of the genre." "It has," he states, "all the ingredients: the idea of the sinner 'being at the heart of Christianity' (Péguy's phrase), the idea of 'mystical substitution' (Marie's self-sacrifice), the implied criticism of materialism, the tireless pursuit of the erring soul by God, 'The Hound of Heaven' in Francis Thompson's famous metaphor. Yet it is also a novel that has proved readily accessible and deeply rewarding to authors of various religious persuasions or none."[5]

As we shall see, Charles Péguy's concept of the central place sinners hold in the spiritual life of the Church is at the heart of virtually every Catholic novel and is axiomatic in every plot. One of the implications that can be immediately drawn from this dictum is that the Church's special concern must be for the sinner, for without sinners the drama of salvation cannot play itself out nor can Christ's redemptive mission be fulfilled. Yet the sinner can even be said to have a privileged role in the sacramental life of the Church; Mauriac and Greene have in fact been criticized frequently and severely by good Catholics on just that score— for seeming to imply in their works that sinners are closer to God than pious, practicing Catholics. Indeed, both authors do suggest throughout their novels that because they acknowledge their sinful nature, sinners are more honest, hence more open, to grace and less likely to be blinded by forms of pharisaism.[6]

The theme of "substitution" that Lodge next refers to is a concept first suggested by Fyodor Dostoyevski and actually introduced into the Catholic novel by Léon Bloy in *The Desperate Man* (1886). In its simplest form this term means the offering of one's life for another, following Christ's example. In Mauriac's novel of greed and willful hatred, the protagonist, Louis, the spiteful old man who tries to revenge his family for the cold, manipulative treatment they accord him during his life, is granted conversion of heart at death's door chiefly, we are made to understand, as the result of the offering of self that little Marie, his daughter, had made years before on her own death bed. A similar offer to exchange one's life (and in this instance, even one's salvation) for a loved one is exemplified in the whiskey priest's acceptance of death and damnation for the salvation of his illegitimate daughter in Greene's *The Power and the Glory*; and the curé d'Ambricourt's acceptance of responsibility for the ultimate destiny of the souls of Chantal, her mother the Countess, and his fallen-away priest companion is a similar application of the theme made by Bernanos in *The Diary of a Country Priest*.

God's pursuit of the sinner who resists the power of grace is another staple of the Catholic novel. As a component it represents an amalgamation of two elements: God the relentless hunter stalking his quarry (as portrayed in the Francis Thompson poem "The Hound of Heaven") and Pascal's "hidden God," who operates behind the scenes using mysterious and obscure paths to bring the often hardened sinner back to the fold. As we read in Pascal's *Pensées*, "God being thus hidden, a religion which denies that God is thus hidden is not true; and every religion which fails to declare the reason why fails to teach. Our religion does all this: '*Vere tu es Deus absconditus.*'"[7]

A corollary to these themes is the Pascalian/Augustinian tenet that the fulfillment of love, which is our greatest desire, can never be satisfied by other human beings or by the things of this world. Human beings, nevertheless, strive to find a substitute for this kind of love, often through the misguided use of such natural instincts as power and domination over others, the accumulation of worldly goods, and sexual pleasure. Yet all of the passions and energies exerted to these ends are bound to fail because all ineluctably thirst after a love that can only be found in God. As Saint Augustine expresses this concept in the celebrated passage from his *Confessions*, "Our souls are made for Thee, O God, and they are not content until they return to Thee."[8] Pascal further describes all earthly strivings for happiness as representing essentially multiple and never-ending patterns of diversions—futile rounds of activities vainly used as kinds of drugs to allow us to endure our ennui or to mask and even deny our divine origins and ultimate destiny (Pascal, 174–82).

Lodge's useful summary of major thematic material used by the Catholic novel has, of course, been preceded by far more detailed and systematic descriptions of the genre. One of the best of such works is Conor Cruise O'Brien's 1951 study, *Maria Cross: Imaginative Patterns in a Group of Catholic Authors*, which, more than 30 years after publication, is still regarded by many as the most sustained and successful attempt to identify and synthesize patterns and themes used by the major Catholic novelists of the genre's Golden Age. O'Brien dedicates separate chapters to Léon Bloy, Graham Greene, Georges Bernanos, François Mauriac, Evelyn Waugh, Sean O'Faolain, Paul Claudel, and Charles Péguy. In the final chapter, "Maria Cross," he attempts to establish "vertical connections" and "convergent lines" linking the patterns of the whole group to discern, if possible, "an imaginative pattern which is peculiarly receptive of Catholicism."[9]

O'Brien concludes that the Catholic novel, in all its variant forms and expression, can basically be characterized as extreme reaction against the modern world and all its manifestations. (This judgment is graphically summed up in Péguy's pithy axiom *"Le monde moderne avilit"* [The modern world debases].) Much resembling the "wasteland" point of view of T. S. Eliot, modern Catholic novelists thus both bemoan the fallen state of their society and lash out against the perceived causes of this sad state of affairs. The stance taken by these authors toward modernity's de-Christianized institutions and anemic value systems O'Brien describes as consisting of "multiple forms of exile"—exile not only from historical factors but as a mental state in itself. Such exile includes (1) exile from childhood or the paradise of childish innocence, meaning our compulsive desires to re-create or return again to that state of childish innocence which is equated with an opening to grace, conversion of soul, and salvation (Bernanos, for example, declares throughout his essays and novels that the essential requirement for salvation is to return in spirit to the child we once were); (2) exile from a new kind of humanism—"the natural man" of Auguste Comte, Charles Fourier, and scientism, or that naturally innocent robot and ersatz angel in whom the spiritual complexity of the human is denied (Catholic writers revel in their biting characterizations of this "termite man" sunk in materialism, the modern philistine, the merchant degenerate who lives without reference to the spirit); and (3), closely allied to the preceding, is the exile from reason itself—a condition characterized by a violent attack against Enlightenment heresies of all kinds: rationalism, Voltairianism, the notion of progress, and the "terrible" political legacy of democratic and republican principles inherited from the French Revolution (i.e., the theories and ideologies of nineteenth-century liberalism and economic policies). Antidemocratic in varying degrees (with Bloy, G. K. Chesterton, Bernanos, and Waugh the most virulent), the majority of these novelists describe in disillusioned tones a modern society alienated from its spiritual origins and mired in a "wasteland" where people live out despairing lives (O'Brien, 211–26).

O'Brien also provides a frank treatment of an aspect not often enough or sufficiently investigated or commented on in regard to several of the best-known Catholic novelists: the power that fascist ideals and systems exerted on them. Given their antidemocratic animus and disdain for what they took to be a godless, secular society, some espoused, or were at the very least sympathetic to, political ideas and causes forwarded by fascist groups throughout Europe. Among the most common were the advocacy of monarchy as the ideal form of government, rejection of democratic or socialist ideals, virulent prejudices such as anti-Semitism, the justification of mob violence to bring down the governments of the left, and flirtation with or even outright support of the totalitarian regimes in Germany, Spain, and Italy (O'Brien, 222–24). O'Brien finds many examples of right-wing or even fascist themes in the works of Catholic authors. For example, throughout his novels Bernanos describes France and French society as existing in a final stage of dry rot. He perceived this dissolution to be the consequence of the de-Christianized forms of political and social institutions that had taken root as a result of the displacement of the Christian/chivalric code of honor from a distant period of belief going back to the Middle Ages. Another striking example (from the modern end of the scale) is Léon Bloy's impassioned and emotional indictment of the evil of present-day capitalism. For him, money in modern societies represents nothing less than the blood of the poor worker everywhere victimized by greedy bourgeois masters. In his literature Bloy speaks in increasingly virulent terms of the Second Coming of Christ, when the evil exploiters will be punished and the poor exalted in a kind of apocalyptic destruction of modern political (i.e., democratic) systems.

Along with this hatred of modernity O'Brien identifies as the central theme or conflict shared by all Catholic authors a tension between flesh and spirit, with both terms presented as warring elements in a dualistic view of human nature. The flesh is the principle of corruption (figuratively presented as a kind of ghoulish presence lurking in the lowroads of base temptation); the spirit, symbolized by the Cross, is located at the moral "heights of a human landscape." Hence the drama of every Catholic novel portrays to varying degrees the fierce encounter between the two, and the point where they converge is the physical moment of Christ's crucifixion when, as a redemptive victim, He took upon Himself the weight and sins of the world (O'Brien, 209–10).

If the Catholic imagination is thus "permeated" by these two conflicting elements, O'Brien finds that most generally the fictional clash is embodied by the physical encounter of the male protagonist with a female persona (a kind of Eve whose other face is Mary). "Woman is the Cross," says Bloy, and O'Brien uses the statement as the key to an understanding of the works. As vessel of sin and salvation, the female is at the very heart of the drama of salvation presented in the fictional universe of these Catholic novelists. Woman thus combines the roles of seductress (symbolizing the Jansenist thorn of sexuality) and spiritual mother, whose capacity for suffering and redemption raises up all sinful creatures (O'Brien, 230–43).

In his 1929 essay *God and Mammon* Mauriac gives a cogent explanation of the end to which characters are developed in this conflict of spirit and flesh. As he puts it, the role of the novelist is to "apprehend the whole of human nature" by describing the struggle in a human heart. The character or protagonist created for this purpose thus "becomes beautiful at the cost of a struggle against itself," and this struggle should not stop until the bitter end—or until the evil that the beautiful character has had to overcome is subdued. In this process one sees the goal of the novelist Mauriac succinctly describes: "The reason for the existence of the novelist on earth is to show the element which holds out against God in the highest noblest characters . . . and to light up the secret source of sanctity in creatures who seem to have failed."[10]

In terms of form and narrative technique the Catholic novel does not share the modern prejudice against authorial comment in fiction, and because the narrators in novels by Greene, Mauriac, or Bernanos, for example, often illuminate the motivation of characters with direct commentary, it is fashionable to accuse these writers (and Catholic novelists in general) of authorial "manipulation"—of creating puppetlike characters. In his celebrated 1939 diatribe in which he attacked Mauriac on just these grounds, Sartre wittily declared that since He controlled the destinies of his creatures, God could not be a novelist in any proper sense of the word; nor for that matter was Mauriac, because presumably unlike Sartre, he played God in deciding on the ultimate destinies of the characters in his literary universe.[11] The truth of this charge in regard to Mauriac or Catholic novelists in general is far from being decided, and it is not at all certain that philosophically committed authors like Sartre have not themselves been guilty of the same process, despite their adamant claims that they have granted their characters total freedom for self-definition.

There are other significant areas in which the Catholic novel differs from its contemporary manifestations of the genre. As David O' Connell points out in his 1990 study of the contemporary Catholic novel, and in particular of the French writer Michel de Saint Pierre, Catholic novelists have generally never adopted the fashion of the *nouveau roman* "with its emphasis on *chosisme*, characterized by the minute description of physical detail, and its strident attacks on the traditional novel that tells a story in a conventional manner," and, he wryly observes, for that reason "they have not inflicted what the French call '*terrorisme intellectuel*' on young, aspiring novelists."[12]

If, conversely, Catholic novelists eschew the minimalist techniques of the *nouveau roman*, they are far from being slavishly realist in their depiction of the "real world." Rather, they in fact represent a tradition once removed from the mimetic techniques of such great modern realists as George Eliot, Gustave Flaubert, Anthony Trollope, and Roger Martin du Gard, whose "signs" of reality mirror for the most part the natural or social mores of their fictional characters without penetrating the surface of things.

Catholic authors, in contrast, portray the divine presence in the world as it is reflected in the operations and actions of the human. Although they utilize realist techniques in their portrayal of human life (Mauriac, Waugh, Bernanos, Sigrid Undset, and many others, for example, give minute description of locales and abundant commentary on social mores), they are impatient with a methodology or ethical view that accepts the real, palpable world of the senses as ultimately sufficient to itself. They want instead to convince the reader not of the recognizable, ordinary world but of one that is extraordinary—the spiritual universe wherein the interdependence of good and evil is played out in a time frame of eternity.

In such a scenario the plot is always God-centered, and the visible world is not seen as distinct from the spiritual but as a sacramental manifestation of it. Nothing in the world is arbitrary, and every event or action has its place in the Divine pattern. This in turn is not evident in any particular moment but has its own system of justice and providence, which can only be understood sub specie aeternitatis. And in this framework not only good deeds but even sin provides potential for salvation.

Such, then, in its broadest terms, is the outline for the kind of Catholic novel written in the first half of the twentieth century. In order to better understand the particular configurations in form and theme it would take in the works of the most important Catholic authors of the modern period, it is necessary to chart briefly the genesis and development of the genre in the century preceding our own—hence Chapter 1.

Chapter One

Origins and Development in Nineteenth-Century France

The Catholic novel in Europe as we know it today originated in French literature of the nineteenth century. Originally part of the neo-romantic reaction against Enlightenment philosophy and the anti-religious doctrines of the Revolution, the Catholic novel attained fruition and became an accomplished literary form spearheading the *renouveau catholique*, or Catholic literary revival . This literary movement contained in its ranks a number of brilliant writers (Bloy, Péguy, Huysmans, Bernanos, Mauriac, Claudel, Jacques Maritain, and Jacques Rivière, to name the most important) who reached maturity at the century's end or during the decade of World War I, and it essentially took the form of a strong, even violent, reaction of these French Catholic writers against the doctrine of positivism that had gained preeminence in French political and cultural circles in the last third at least of the nineteenth century. In fact, positivist ideas and theories propagated by an elite cast of philosophers, scientists, literary critics, and writers (Auguste Comte, Ernest Renan, Claude Bernard, Emile Durkheim, Hippolyte Taine, Guy de Maupassant, and Emile Zola) had penetrated all areas of French thought, education, literary theory, and the politics of the left to become a kind of "official" cultural philosophy.

In the first half of the century such committed Catholic writers as Chateaubriand, Joseph de Maistre, Jean Baptiste Lacordaire, and Hughes-Félicité de Lammenais had inveighed against the rationalist, atheistic, secular philosophy of man and the state that they considered the legacy of the hated French Revolution. In trying to create an intellectual climate conducive to a national return to the Catholic faith, these authors targeted as the enduring enemy the ideas of the Enlightenment personified in the unholy trio of Voltaire, Rousseau, and Diderot—Voltaire because of his mocking, skeptical spirit so inimical to Revelation; Rousseau for his dangerous "religion of the heart" that divorced ethics from Christian dogma; and Diderot for his avowed system of atheistic materialism so brilliantly presented in his dialogues.

1

Chateaubriand dedicated his monumental artistic apology of Christianity, *The Genius of Christianity* (1802), as a means to link together the "luminous" Christian civilization of the Middle Ages with the pristine, natural beauty of the New World, both to be incorporated in the aesthetics of the romantic revival. The extremely conservative Catholic political theorist and pamphleteer Joseph de Maistre denounced throughout his essays, and especially in *The Pope* (1819), the Satanic nature of the French Revolution, which he viewed as a deliberate rejection of God and His Church by the French nation. He made an impassioned plea for the restoration of French Catholicism with strong Ultramontane persuasions, or a church whose primary allegiances would be to the pope in Rome as vicar of Christ and ultimate source of religious legitimacy. Two Catholic priests, the Abbé Lammenais and the Dominican Lacordaire, dedicated their efforts to bring back to the Church the peasantry and working classes who had been alienated by the Church's strenuous opposition to the republican ideals of the Revolution. They proposed an entire program of liberal reforms—universal franchise, laws to protect labor, the alliance of the clergy with the people through charitable associations, and concerted efforts to improve the substandard living conditions of the poor in France.[1]

These liberal ideals and concerns for social welfare were adversely affected by the turmoil of the 1848 insurrection, which, through its violent anti-clerical attacks, turned the clergy and middle-class Catholics against these reform measures. The events of 1848 also inaugurated a full-scale return of the bourgeois to adherence to the Church as an institution now favorably viewed because of its opposition to worker violence—hence a bastion of support for law and order and the rights of the ruling class. The French Catholic Church was even more solidly turned to the right by Pius IX's "Syllabus of Errors" of 1864, which constituted a virtual declaration of separation from the ideals of progress and modernity and a total rejection of democracy as a political system.

The prosperous Catholic bourgeoisie did not of itself, however, provide major opposition to the positivist ideas that dominated the Second Empire. This may seem surprising, since the distinguished positivist scholars, scientists, historians, and critics made no bones about their belief that the science of "observable facts and mathematical observations" would reveal the true world and make forever obsolete metaphysics, theology, and religion of any kind. No doubt the marked advance of industry and mercantile interests fostered during Napoleon

III's regime fully satisfied the interests of the now wealthy and conservative middle-class Catholics who had returned to the Church.

It is rather from the ranks of writers that the reaction to the positivist cultural domination arose. These literary figures, highly idiosyncratic characters in their own right, could be variously described as latter-day romantics, decadents, Satanists, and dandys, and though their literary forms and styles differed greatly, they wrote to affirm the absolute freedom of the individual (especially as it pertained to themselves as artists) and to break free of the constraints of biological and environmental determinisms that, according to positivism, defined each person. For these writers the battle lines were clearly drawn between the apostles of "science" and the artist defending freedom of thought and the cultivation of the individual genius and uniqueness. And the spiritualism of religion, the reality of the soul, and the spiritual dimensions of the human—which the positivists denied out of hand—became for them both an agenda and first line of defense.

The major figures among these defenders of the spiritual include Charles Baudelaire; Fyodor Dostoyevski, who had enormous influence on French and, for that matter, all European novelists who came after him; and certainly the Catholic novelists Jules Barbey d'Aurevilly, Léon Bloy, and Joris-Karl Huysmans. I also include in this grouping Charles Péguy, the essayist-poet whose writings provide a kind of inspirational bridge between the writers of this earlier period with the Catholic novelists working after World War I.

Charles Baudelaire

At the core of Baudelaire's poetic vision is his celebrated theory of the "two postulations": "There is," he proclaimed, "in every man at every hour two simultaneous postulations: one toward God, the other toward Satan."[2] From this theory he developed the essential moral and spiritual dynamics of his major poetic opus, *Les Fleurs du Mal* (*The Flowers of Evil*) of 1857. The poems of this collection (and primarily those included under the rubric "Spleen") emphasize the strong attraction that Evil (under the guise of beauty) exerts on humans, to the detriment of Good. Baudelaire ultimately portrays himself (and his mirror image, the "hypocrite reader, my alias, my brother") as mired in sin, trapped in a fallen world, and exiled from the Eden of childhood innocence—the lost paradise that can never be regained and, more tragically, cannot be forgotten.

As a result of the fall, Baudelaire describes the human condition in Platonic terms: through the power of Satan, our human vision is obscured. We see "through a glass darkly," as if the windows through which the soul views the world have been dirtied by the weight and burden of our physical bodies. To transcend this fallen condition and as a means to attain a heightened vision of reality, Baudelaire offers an artistic universal analogy in the celebrated poem "Les Correspondances." Serving as a manifesto of his poetic vision, the poem, as implied in its title, proclaims that visible, tangible reality seen by the eyes of the body is merely a pale reflection of a higher spiritual wholeness, and it is the role of the poet as artist to decipher these inaccessible forms through a kind of synesthesia—concentrated attempts to scramble, as it were, the modes of knowing conveyed by the five senses. The poem offers synthetic approaches to a heightened sense of knowing through diverse kinds of sensory fusion (and of such elements, for example, as music, incense, colors, and softness of flesh), with the result being new and heretofore unimagined realities.[3]

Baudelaire's artistic principle provided nineteenth-century decadent writers with an aesthetic system allowing them to counter the all too real and ugly reality that the positivists presented as the only valid world. Moreover, for Catholic novelists, and in particular Barbey and Huysmans, Baudelaire opened the door to a spiritual universe of good and evil, to the essential duality of the human person torn between the opposing forces of God and Satan, and to the human experience of the drama of sin and salvation.

Fyodor Dostoyevski

It may perhaps not be initially obvious as to why Fyodor Dostoyevski should be included in a chapter dedicated to the precursors and initiators of the Catholic novel in France. Though influenced by Western realist writers (Dickens, Balzac, and Flaubert in particular) during his lifetime, Dostoyevski became a strong advocate of pan-Slavism and gradually came to detest the literary and social influences on Russian culture and thought by what he regarded as the decadent West. He was also a bitter critic of Catholicism—a form of Christianity that he accused of having effected the ultimate betrayal of Christ's message by establishing a corrupt travesty of the original Church. ("The Grand Inquisitor" episode of his novel *The Brothers Karamazov* constitutes his clearest indictment of the Roman Church.) Yet through the innovative thematic content and profound psychological analysis of the soul with which he imbued his works, Dostoyevski provided nothing short of a radical change in the realist form of the European novel, and through this process he would become in very real sense the spiritual father of all forms of the modern Catholic novel.

In his famous psychocritical essay on Dostoyevski, André Gide pointed out that Dostoyevski was the first European novelist to place the relationship of the individual and God at the heart of the novel. Before Dostoyevski, Gide explained, "the novel with but rare exception concerns itself with relations between man and man, passion and intellect, with family, social, and class relations, but never, practically never between the individual and his self and with God."[4] It is this God-centered plot that would therefore distinguish Dostoyevski's genius from all the great nineteenth-century realist novelists in the West. The dominant French variety of the novel—crafted by Balzac, Flaubert, Maupassant, and Zola—had ignored the spiritual dimensions of the soul in favor of brilliant analyses of psychological temperaments and milieux studies. As a result there had been a shriveling effect on the importance of the spiritual dimensions of humans and a virtual denial of the reality and even the existence of the soul. Dostoyevski changed all of this. As Dostoyevski's contemporary Eugène de Vogüé wrote, "No one has carried realism to such an extreme point. He depicts real life but soars above reality in a superhuman effort toward a new consummation of the gospel."[5]

Indeed, Dostoyevski was tormented all his life by the idea of God, and this struggle is the basis of all his thinking and writing. He continually asked, What are the consequences of the existence of God for the world, for man, and for human action in history? How can evil and suffering be explained and made acceptable from a theological point of view? In short, How can the existence of God be reconciled with the fall of man, sin, injustice, and suffering?

At the very center of his literary universe, in all his plots, Dostoyevski portrays man, much as Baudelaire had, as an enigmatic figure, demonic in his penchant for evil yet angelic in his inexhaustible thirst for justice and goodness. The essential drama of any human life he saw as fundamentally moral in nature and taking place (as a kind of war) in the soul of an individual torn between angelic and demonic "postulations." He is one of the first novelists to dramatize the reality of evil in human life (as the effect of Original Sin) and the fallen nature of human beings and their nostalgic yearning for childlike innocence and spiritual regeneration. His novels are the first to depict in a spiritual dimension the moral sufferings of the poor and oppressed.

Dostoyevski sharply rejects any notion that human beings are ruled from without by a kind of "iron necessity" or system of determinism. Rather, he sees us as moral beings who must choose between good and evil, and he believes that true human dignity is to be found in the pursuit and use of freedom. In the 1864 novella *Notes from Underground*, for instance, Dostoyevski seeks both to affirm the importance of freedom and to destroy the fiction that man is primarily a reasonable and sensible being who can be molded or programmed by social systems. Instead he illustrates through the violent character swings of the "underground man" that human nature includes in itself all possibilities and forms of conscious and unconscious existence, and rationality satisfies or represents only one part of our nature. Like this volatile protagonist, human beings can will their own happiness or destruction, can refuse to be defined in reasonable terms, can work against their own genuine interests, and, in short, are terribly free to be what they will.

Mired in his naturalist, dog-eat-dog world of motivation, the underground man lives in a subhuman world of hurt or be hurt; he never arrives at the level on which he can desire to be open, to love, and hence to find a way out of his terrible, walled-in existence. As the work suggests, however, such a path is within his reach were he only to open himself to the immediate reality of "the other."

In *Crime and Punishment* (1866) Dostoyevski creates a protagonist several steps advanced from the underground man, here a young and idealistic student at the moral crossroads of life. Yet Raskolnikov (meaning literally "cut in two") is also depicted as being mortally wounded by forms of Western thought symbolized as a kind of plague. In a very real sense the doctrines of utopian atheistic philosophers have vitiated his soul, and, despite his belief in God, Raskolnikov takes on the role of the man-God, plays Providence, and commits murder in the name of distributive justice. He kills a useless "old louse" who he feels should be sacrificed for the good of the wretched, whom she treats with gross injustice, and for social progress in general.

After he plays God and murders his odious landlady, Raskolnikov is forced to engage in a tremendous struggle with his conscience and to accept the need to acknowledge his crime before God and humanity. In the process, the novel grippingly portrays a repudiation of the notion that we can ever take a human life for a good purpose, hence the rejection of all pragmatic political activism not grounded in love and respect for the other.

Dostoyevski uses the theme of suffering as the means of the spiritual regeneration of the sinner Raskolnikov (whose sin is dealt with as a form of demonic possession). Convicted and punished by human justice, it is only after the most intense spiritual and physical suffering in the Siberian prison camps that he is able to spiritually recognize and renounce his crime. In the famous scene of reconciliation, he kisses the violated earth, whose harmony he has destroyed by murdering the old woman, and thus makes peace with God and all living beings. For only by renewal of union with his fellow human beings can Raskolnikov come face to face with his own conscience and accept once again the message of Christ's Gospel.[6]

Barbey d'Aurevilly

The first self-proclaimed Catholic novelist who proudly identified himself as such was Jules Barbey d'Aurevilly. Scion of an old and impoverished Norman family, ferocious critic of the Revolution and the Republic, and notorious dandy, Barbey first was known as a colorful storyteller delving into the folklore of the Cotentin region of Normandy for his Gothic tales. He experienced a sincere conversion to Catholicism, at the age of 37, and reverted to the faith of his childhood. After that point he became a celebrated polemicist, novelist, and literary critic whose writings were marked by his deep Catholic convictions and attacks against positivist republican ideas.

Much could be said about Barbey's importance as a literary critic. He wrote one of the most perceptive reviews on Baudelaire's *Les Fleurs du Mal* and clearly saw this poet's spiritual dimensions long before most, and he predicted Huysmans's oncoming *crise religieuse* and conversion to Catholicism in a review of Huysmans's *A Rebours*. Yet it is Barbey's fictional work that interests us primarily here. His novels and short prose pieces were strongly influenced by Balzac and Walter Scott. He therefore gave his characters considerable psychological depth and placed them in situations revealing hidden, dark passions not differing significantly from the Gothic/romantic tradition exemplified by these two mentors. Barbey brought to his examination of the deepest recesses of the human heart another decidedly religious dimension that he felt was different and that he proudly described as an essentially "Catholic" vision of reality. In the preface to the 1858 edition of his novel *Une vieille maîtresse* entitled "Catholicism in the Novel," he insisted that "Catholicism has nothing prudish, pedantic or unsettling in its treatment of passions. It leaves that to the false virtues of well-manicured puritanism." And with this sound moral vision, Catholic authors have, Barbey insisted, not only the right but the duty to expose "the disorders and slavery of passion." Unlike the *libres penseurs* such as Rousseau, Georges Sand, and Flaubert, Catholic novelists do not fall into complicity with moral relativism or depravity and never permit themselves to say "that good is evil or evil is good." Nor do they flirt with "perverse doctrines" such as Rousseau's belief in "the sincerity of the heart" as principal judge in matters of morality, or Sand's social views derived from "the universal goodness of human nature" (and implicit denial of the Fall). In what therefore becomes a manifesto of sorts, Barbey in effect declares it the right and duty of Catholic writers to compose using their own special moral vision, which is derived from their faith.

Barbey was a prolific writer (his critical pieces and prose works fill almost 30 volumes in *Oeuvres complètes*). He wrote five major novels, among the best known of which are *Les Diaboliques* (1874), *Une vieille maîtresse* (1851), and *Un prêtre marié* (1865).

In entering Barbey's literary space, the reader is quickly drawn into a moral universe teeming with sin, transgression against the laws of God, morbidity, and striking forms of reversibility, or expiation on the part of the innocent for the salvation of sinners. In short, many if not most of the thematic components of the Catholic novel described above are already in place in Barbey's works. *Une vieille maîtresse*, for example, dramatizes in religious terms a fatal sexual attraction that seems only to be understandable if placed within the framework of the Catholic dynamics of salvation and damnation—in particular, of base passions contesting with those of the spirit for the possession of the soul of a sinner.

In the novel Ryno de Marigny, a handsome young Norman aristocrat with a well-deserved reputation as an accomplished womanizer, ends a 10-year liaison with his aging mistress, Vellini, in order to marry the beautiful though totally innocent and inexperienced Hermangarde de Polastron. Vowing to break decisively with this and any other past affairs, Ryno commits himself to connubial fidelity and a return to the practice of religion. In the wings, however, there remains the remarkably drawn femme fatale, the old mistress Vellini. Described alternately as a Spanish demi-sorceress who practices the rites of Zahari, an androgynous person, and a Chimera, she is further adept as a *voyant* and can, for example, conjure up at will the spectacle of the decomposing body of Ryno and the grave site in which he eventually will lie. Remarkably ugly (hence strangely beautiful) and serpentine in movement, she has managed to initiate and gradually enslave her lover in "a paradise of sensual delights" to which his body has now become conditioned.[7] As she again enters his life, the novel portrays the violent and blind fall from grace of Ryno and his return to the former debased state.

Barbey shows strong Jansenist inclinations in describing the enslaving power of sexual passions and asserting memory's strong attachment to them as reasons for Ryno's virtually total inability to break the hold of his former mistress. Though he strongly loves his wife, "it was his past that he had in excess . . . and which, in his heart, mounted like the sea on a beach that it had left" (*Une vieille maîtresse*, 528).

Despairing of his ability to remain faithful to one, Ryno then tries to play the role of the bigamist to two "wives." Unable to live in either of their worlds, and wracked by guilt at the pain he has caused his wife, Ryno becomes a dead soul, and the novel ends with the theme of decomposition prefigured in Vellini's vision of her dead lover. Luring him into her "Devil's tomb" she clearly becomes a diabolic influence, a reincarnation of the Serpent in the garden, who, by sexually entrapping him, has taken possession of his soul. Aware of his moral state, he knows at the end that he will never again experience peace of any kind, and his heart is compared to "a scorpion bent upon itself and unable through blows given to cause its own death." In short, he now knows through the heart-rending pains of his being "what the Holy Books described as the diabolical possession of souls" (*Une vieille maîtresse*, 508).

In what is perhaps Barbey's most anguished and psychologically complex work, *Un prêtre marié*, the problem or vice exposed is that of apostasy and abandonment of priestly vows. Leaving the priesthood during the chaotic period of the Revolution, the brooding Abbé de Sombreval commits the further sacrilege of marrying. He thus takes on himself the moral opprobrium of the married priest and worsens his sinful state twofold for, as a pious confrère describes the renegade's situation, "a fallen priest is a great sinner who can raise himself up by relying on the law that he has misused, but a married priest corrupts the very concept of law by taking on one in the very shadow of the other through which he has fallen into sin; by embracing this other law [marriage] he then imprisons himself in a fortress state of sin."[8]

When Sombreval's wife dies in childbirth, the drama of the work revolves about the life and ultimate fate of Calixte, the girl born of this sacrilegious union. Returning to his former Normand estate with his baby daughter, the widower becomes famous through his research in quest of a magic elixir. Clearly a Satanic force, Sombreval is both a Lucifer (fallen angel) and Faust figure (in the quest of a scientific absolute). His daughter becomes his foil in that she is irresistibly drawn to religion, despite her father's determined efforts to keep her totally ignorant and removed from all religious influences and knowledge of the faith. She of course is converted and lives the life of a saint or even angel who goes on to suffer intensely for sinners, particularly her father, whom she now sees as monstrous in his total unbelief. When she is stricken by a fatal tetanus poisoning and accepts her imminent death, she says, "I am my father's expiation" (*Un prêtre marié*, 1083).

Calixte was courted and passionately loved before her sickness by the romantically drawn Néel de Néhou, whose pale blond countenance conceals a tempestuously passionate nature. He pines away at the death of Calixte, fulfilling his self-appointed role of one fated not to survive the death of the beloved. But before he dies he must witness the terrible specter of Sombreval, who, refusing to accept the death of his daughter, exhumes her from her grave and tries with all his "scientific" powers to resuscitate her. Failing this he drags her body away with him while cursing God as the agent for Calixte's death ("God, Oh how I disdained him up to now as a false idea; but if he could exist, at present I would hate him like an executioner" [*Un prêtre marié*, 1178]). As Sombreval leaps to his death by drowning, he still clasps her inert form. So heinous are his ultimate betrayal of his vocation and hatred of God that even the angelic intercession of his daughter and her offering up of terrible suffering for him are not, Barbey suggests, sufficient forms of expiation. Sombreval remains, then, a kind of fallen angel, terrible and even overwhelming in his transgression.

Justly called the father of the French Catholic novel, Barbey opens the door in his fiction to the Catholic universe of sacramental forms, hell, religious transgressions, expiation, and the enormously difficult route to salvation. Through his somber Jansenist vision of human nature as wounded by and often prey to the power of the flesh and base passion, he depicts a fallen world where God is indeed hidden, seemingly arbitrary in His dispensation of grace, and more than a little vengeful in the punishment of sinners.

Léon Bloy

Léon Bloy began and continued his career as a novelist and polemicist under the tutelage of Barbey. In fact, Bloy constantly referred to the latter as "*le connétable des lettres*" ("commander-in-chief of letters") and willingly performed as a kind of self-appointed secretary to Barbey, supporting his mentor in all literary ventures. Bloy was a violent man, a self-styled "Prophet of the Absolute," whom Jacques Maritain would compare to "a fire-stained and blackened cathedral," and one who advised Maritain and his wife, Raïssa, always to "place the invisible before the visible, the supernatural before the natural."[9]

Bloy's spiritual and intellectual itinerary began with the ritualistic *crise de foi* and subsequent return to the Church so common to the young writers and intellectuals in mid-century who had before been believers in the doctrines of positivism. First a radical atheist in his earlier years, Bloy attributed his return to the faith (in 1868 at the age of 33) to his association with the recently converted Barbey and to the intellectual influence of Joseph de Maistre, whose works he had begun to read at this time. De Maistre's influence in particular caused him to become a violent critic of the French Revolution—and all that this represented—as well as a passionate advocate of papal infallibility and the dominant spiritual role that he believed the popes, through the Catholic church, should play in the affairs of the world and destiny of humanity.

Bloy's conversion did not initially put to rest his strong sensual nature, and he still had to wrestle with the "demon of the flesh" in the years that immediately followed. It was at this point in his life that he met and rescued from the streets the prostitute Anne-Marie Roulé, for whom he quickly developed a strong sexual attraction and whom he also labored to convert to Catholicism. This conflict between sexual passion and the zeal to convert the woman he loved consumed him during the five years he was involved with her. She converted one year after she had met him and then became for him a mystical and saintly "seer" who validly prophetized the impending end of the world and the imminent coming of the Kingdom of God. Anne-Marie also seemed at this time to have surpassed her mentor in progress made in her spiritual life, and Bloy attributed his own painful progress through a period of spiritual dryness to her example and powerful intercession through prayer. He endured what was perhaps the worst crisis of his life in 1882 when Anne-Marie passed from mystical seer into a state of insanity and had to be committed to an asylum. His initial reaction to this horrible occurrence was that of flight—a long retreat at the Grande Chartreuse near Grenoble with the intention of possibly becoming a Carthusian Monk. Told soon after his arrival by a spiritual advisor that he did not have a vocation, he returned to Paris to begin a literary career launched in 1886 with the publication of his first novel, *Le Désespéré* (*The Desperate Man*). The work was a total commercial failure, selling only a handful of copies, and it received not the slightest critical commentary.

Le Désespéré could be regarded as an early prototype of the Catholic novel that would be written several decades later (by Bernanos, Greene, Mauriac, and others), containing as it does the basic themes and religious concepts at the heart of this literary genre. In the novel Bloy records in fictional form his anguished, impoverished, and unhappy existence with Anne-Marie Roulé. She becomes the character Véronique, and Bloy is Caïn Marchenoir, an aspiring writer. They both act out their drama of salvation in a secularized, hellish Parisian society as ardent Catholics in a Church that, as an institution, has abandoned the teachings of its founder and, as Bloy describes it, has thereby placed Christ "back in His tomb."[10]

The spiritual struggle of the two protagonists is depicted as a battle to overcome the destructive tugs of their strongly sensual natures and thereby succeed in their vocation to become saints. Through Marchenoir's totally devoted attention and concern, the former prostitute Véronique succeeds in living in the same spiritually exalted state, the narrator suggests, as Saint Teresa of Avila; and she is, in fact, a holy Carmelite living outside of the convent. Totally self-sacrificing and intent on helping Marchenoir overcome his sensual desires for her, she offers up her singular beauty by selling her hair and most of her teeth. Through these extreme expedients and her holy life Marchenoir, though still sexually tormented, is finally able to live chastely with her through the period of her tragic mental and physical breakdown and until his own untimely death (he is run over in the street when returning from the asylum to which he has had to commit her).

As Marchenoir and Véronique go through their day-to-day existence of poverty and deprivation, Bloy mounts violent attacks against a debased Christian society that has been impregnated and totally corrupted by the mercantile spirit of modern society and the unctuous hypocrisy of the bourgeois *bien pensants* (good-feeling, conservative Catholics). The clergy is depicted as a group of mostly mawkish, weak-kneed cowards who bastardize and dilute Christ's message and spirit to placate the grasping ambitions of their bourgeois masters. In this environment only the poor, through the scandalous treatment accorded them by the rich, attest to Christ's suffering for humanity and His promise of redemption. The wretched and unjust condition of the poor, in fact, is constantly used as a barometer by Bloy to measure the total lack of spiritual values adhered to by the bourgeois ruling class.

In this framework Marchenoir and Véronique are presented as authentic Christians, born and existing outside of their element in a modern age that worships only material things. Modernity allows them neither the risk nor joy of serving in any exalted cause. In earlier times, Bloy asserts, the vocations of saints, heroes, or soldiers would have offered a means to support Christian ideals. The present, however, has put in the place of honor the person of the grasping and vulgar merchant or business type (and a strong anti-Semitic theme in the novel suggests that the most avaricious of these new "heroes" are Jews [*Le Désespéré*, 203–205]).

As he finds himself more and more victimized by a society entirely hostile to his religious convictions, Marchenoir becomes a kind of latter-day prophet who invokes God to come back as an avenger to punish and destroy the bulk of those who pretend to believe in Him since, almost without exception, they have lost the salt or savor of authentic faith. Christ, Marchenoir believes, will return in the role of a stern judge to deliver the poor from their captivity at the hands of men of power and wealth, and the Kingdom of God will thus be vindicated and brought to fruition through a violent and bloody apocalypse that Marchenoir foresees as imminent.

The second phase in Bloy's life (after the dark and tragic period reflected in *Le Désespéré*) was immeasurably enhanced by his meeting with Jeanne de Molbech, the daughter of the celebrated Danish poet, Christian de Molbech. This Protestant woman from a privileged class ultimately converted to Catholicism, became his wife, and courageously took on his horribly impoverished existence. Bloy had by now absolutely abandoned himself to God's will, which he interpreted as the life of a mendicant trusting totally in God's providence. Considering himself a plaything in God's hands but also His prophet, Bloy even more bitterly continued to lacerate the bourgeoisie for the pious fraud that was their faith. But more positively, he now regarded his life to have special meaning as a kind of expiation (through his and his wife's misery and suffering) for other victims unknown to them.

Bloy's second novel, *La Femme pauvre* (1897; *The Woman Who Was Poor*), is the complete expression of this concept of mission and one containing a more mature Catholic vision as well. Certainly not abandoning his vitriolic attacks on modernity and Catholics of his day, he would stress in the novel the doctrine of the Communion of Saints—or the interdependence existing among those called to be members of the Church (both the triumphant in Heaven and those still suffering here and now on earth). By thoroughly exploring the social and religious implications of this doctrine, Bloy would more specifically develop the theme of interresponsibility (or reversibility), through which all human actions—good, bad, or indifferent—are never performed in a void but profoundly affect countless lives besides that of the doer, thereby creating a mysterious affinity between souls.

La Femme pauvre is essentially the relation of the life of a modern-day Mary Magdalen who becomes a saintly woman of the poor living in the urban metropolis of Paris. Clotilde is first seen in her youth as potentially degraded by her impoverished and corrupt family background. Her mother, a vicious religious hypocrite, lives with a drunken, debauched lover who has repeatedly attempted to sexually abuse the young girl. In her first amorous experience Clotilde is seduced by the first man—a nonentity in every way—for whom she had felt genuine affection. He promptly abandons her, and she lives for a time in a state of moral and physical destitution, feeling herself to be damned. Nevertheless, she is favored during this period with a recurrent vision—the depiction of Christ in the glorious, resurrected form in which He appeared before Mary Magdalen, which to the young woman seems to be a gesture of forgiveness.

Through a fortunate turn of events Clotilde is befriended by the somewhat notorious Parisian painter Pélopidas Glacougnol, to whose atelier her mother has sent her to model (while insinuating to the painter that her daughter, like most models, was corrupt and welcomed sexual advances). Recognizing almost immediately her natural goodness, modesty, and unusual intelligence, Glacougnol makes her rehabilitation his project and sets her on the path of her own spiritual development. Introduced to a group of his professional friends, she meets her future husband, the good and self-effacing Léopold, also an artist but, unlike Glacougnol, unsuccessful and virtually unknown. The early years of their marriage are lived simply and happily in a kind of genteel poverty that is not degrading. Then their lives are enmeshed in tragedy as they must cope with inhumane situations that seem virtually beyond human endurance. Forced by worsening economic conditions to move to a fetid, filthy slum apartment, they lose their infant son when he physically cannot survive the squalor. Then Clotilde must endure the persecution of her neighbors, whom Bloy describes as odious harridans of a dehumanized Parisian underclass who revile her out of spite and envy (presumably because of her virtue and her heroic, even uncomplaining, acceptance of the same poverty that has totally debased them).

Léopold dies in an act of heroism as he enters the burning Opéra-comique theater to save the lives of those desperately trying to escape. Clotilde had, in fact, foreseen this act in a vision replayed for her many times in her life. She now understands that this is a sign that she too must sacrifice her own life on earth for others in order to be united with her saintly husband. Leaving what little she has she spends the rest of her life alone on the streets of the *quartiers pauvres*, a kind of holy mendicant, a pious bag lady who, with serene detachment from the often unsettling events around her, ceaselessly prays for others. She thus represents for Bloy all that is holy in the state of poverty, and her life represents for him the only certain way to remain uncontaminated by the greed and vulgarity of the modern world. The novel ends in a moving description of her last days and relates through her words the ideal that allows her to persevere in this state to the end: "She returns to her immense solitude, in the midst of these streets crowded with people." "There is only one sadness," she says, "and that is not to be saints."[11]

Joris-Karl Huysmans

If Bloy made of the Catholic novel a virulent attack (expressed in apocalyptic terms) against a modern fallen world and a de-Christianized society that abused the poor, Joris-Karl Huysmans imbued the genre with an aesthetic sensibility (and supporting symbolic forms) derived from his profound belief in and appreciation for the Catholic faith and its liturgy. A contemporary of Bloy, and sharing the latter's admiration for Barbey, Huysmans was of a very different temperament. A decadent similar in outlook to Baudelaire and an amateur of the arts, he at first aspired to write essays of art criticism. Though equally critical of his century, he never shared Bloy's messianic vision and was uncomfortable with the latter's violent jeremiads and angry, contorted prose.

Huysmans's involvement with Catholicism could better be described as a long odyssey to belief pursued and intensely experienced in the deepest part of the self. He is also remarkable as one of the best representatives of a nineteenth-century "lost generation" of artists and writers. Along with other decadents or searchers of an absolute (Baudelaire, Paul Verlaine, and Auguste Villiers de l'Isle Adam, to mention a few), he rebelled against the limitations imposed on human nature by the positivist doctrine and its stepchild, the literary naturalism of Zola, Maupassant, and the Goncourt brothers. Yet as a young man he was first a disciple of Zola, a member of the Médan group, and contributor of perhaps the best novella—*Sac au dos*—in the 1880 collection *Soirées de Médan*, which included works by Zola and the younger writers belonging to his most intimate literary circle. And indeed the influence of Zola is heavily apparent in Huysmans's novel *Les Soeurs Vatard*, which he dedicated to his mentor one year before the publication of the Médan collection.

This novel relates the sentimental life of two sisters, Céline and Desirée, young seamstresses of the Parisian working class. The novel stresses the flat, boring existence they lead and revels in minute, realist descriptions of the interior of workshops, the transportation system, cheap restaurants, and scenes of the few leisure moments the workers enjoy. It relates as well their banal sentimental life and desperate efforts to grasp a modicum of happiness in their dull existence.

Soon after this work Huysmans would radically change his literary perspective and abandon the average, gray "slice-of-life" dimensions of the naturalist novel. This change was chiefly the result of a deep spiritual malaise that Huysmans and his contemporaries experienced during the collapse of French society (the Débâcle of 1870) and the strong attraction that popular forms of Schopenhaurean pessimism exerted on the young intellectuals and aspiring writers of the period. With his 1874 novel *A Rebours* (*Against the Grain*) Huysmans in fact gave what Zola himself would later call "a terrible blow to naturalism."[18] In the novel he created a literary character who would incarnate the restless striving of the decadent spirit for all subsequent generations to come. It was also a work that revealed its author to be himself in the final stages of a spiritual crisis that would, as Barbey so perceptively claimed in a thunderously positive review, lead him "to the foot of the cross or the barrel of a pistol" (quoted in *A Rebours*, 246).

The aristocratic protagonist of *A Rebours*, Jean des Esseintes, is the aesthete par excellence who pursues his quest for new experiences over increasingly decadent terrain, to arrive finally at the brink of moral and physical collapse. He becomes a kind of burnt-out case as a result of having consumed his intellectual and vital energies in the most exaggerated and bizarre ways imaginable. Initially he flees with hatred and disgust the vulgarity of modern society (tyrannized, he claims, by the tastes of "butchers wives" and sundry merchants) and secludes himself in anchorite fashion in his impregnable country estate. Here he exists "against the grain" in every manner possible: living a nocturnal existence, he reduces his life to the experience of dreams and hallucinations and exercises the Baudelairean system of correspondences in his thirst to experience strange and unknown forms of reality through altered and bizarre uses of the five senses.

As a consequence, des Esseintes turns away from anything that is palpably real and only aspires to express the vague, the undefined, and the imprecise. He thus becomes a prisoner of his own intellectual and physical excesses and is described by the narrator as "having descended to the very depths of a bottomless pit . . . where there grew rampant forms of the monstrous flowerings of human thought" (*A Rebours*, 117). Faced with the inevitable collapse of mind and body wrought by his existence "against the grain," des Esseintes confronts a seemingly impenetrable wall and a despair that he cannot at this stage of his existence overcome. Yet as he returns to a more normal life in Paris he at least regrets that he has no moral anchor or form of belief. His last recorded works take the form of a prayer to the God in whom he does not yet believe for all "homeless ones" like himself: "Lord, take pity on the Christian who doubts, on the skeptic who would fain believe, on the galley-slave of life who puts out to sea alone" (*A Rebours*, 241).

Des Esseintes's moral breakdown also symbolically marks a decisive step toward Huysmans's conversion. Before this should occur, however, he would have to write the novel *Là-bas* (*Down There*) in 1891. In this work he exorcised his strong attraction to evil (as manifested in the various forms of Satanism rampant in nineteenth-century France, which strongly appealed to the sensibility of romantics and decadents like himself). Thus *Là-bas* represents an approach to faith through the back door—that is, first through fascination with Satan and only afterward to God. It also allowed Huysmans to develop aesthetic theories that would radically transform the kind of novel he would write after his conversion.

The novel's protagonist, Durtal, is an older, wiser, and more philosophically disillusioned des Esseintes, who has lived long enough to transcend the sensual turmoil and violent passions that had tormented the younger decadent. Durtal shares, however, des Esseintes's hatred of the modern world, in which there is no aristocracy of the soul, and he also lives in isolation. Yet he has advanced from the latter's more exotic tastes and has developed pronounced aesthetic interests in Catholic art and liturgy, especially the forms these have taken in the Middle Ages (Gothic architecture and the plain chant, for example).

The structure of Huysmans's novel (strongly suggestive of that used decades later by Sartre in *La Nausée*) is one of a narrator who is researching a biography he plans to write. Here Durtal spends his days in his study reading and commenting on the ancient chronicles dedicated to the life of Gilles de Rais, the notorious Bluebeard of the fourteenth century whose atrocities and cruelty are still legendary. Durtal is also in the pursuit of a literary style or form that will allow him to combine the natural and spiritual elements of soul and body, the spiritual and the physical, and hence provide an escape from the excessive emphasis on biological and physical determinism found in the confining theories of Zola and his followers. Durtal discovers an artistic representation of this yet-to-be realized literary form in the painting of the *Suffering Christ*, by the fifteenth-century German primitivist Matthaeus Grünewald. In this work (the famous retable of Issenheim) Christ's almost naked body is rendered in an extremely tortured and primitive style through which the most severe forms of human suffering and the spiritual reality of Christ mysteriously meet and thereby constitute an aesthetically whole representation of the two realities of body and soul. Durtal would entitle this harmonious fusion a kind of "spiritual naturalism."

Though much of the novel's plot contains a history of Satanism and an explication of major Satanic practices (the Black Mass, sympathetic magic, forms and systems of diabolical possession) current in Gilles de Rais's society and continuing to be used by Satanic cultists in the late nineteenth century, Durtal becomes less and less interested in Satanism and progressively more and more taken by the beauty and force of Catholic sacramental forms and practices. He is finally overwhelmed by what he sees as the Church's power to lead a sinner like Gilles de Rais to a state of true contrition and atonement for the horrible physical atrocities he has committed. How to explain, Durtal muses, Gilles de Rais's radical change of heart when, acknowledging his unspeakable crimes of sadism to the ecclesiastic inquisitors before whom he has been brought, he falls on his knees and asks for pardon and mercy. The answer, Durtal decides, lies in the mysterious interconnection between good and evil, particularly in their highest forms: "There is ultimately only a step between the highest forms of mysticism and the most horrendous manifestations of Satanism. In the great beyond, everything converges to become one."[13]

In the time frame between the appearance of *Là-bas* and the publication of his next novel, *En route* (1895; *On the Way*), Huysmans formally returned to the Church during an extended retreat at the Trappist monastery of Notre Dame d'Igny. As the first novel of his Catholic period, *En route* traces the steps of Durtal/Huysmans's spiritual conversion: his violent efforts to free himself from the strong carnal attractions to which he had previously surrendered, his moral agony in preparing for his confession, the ups and downs he experienced during his long retreat, conferences with his spiritual advisor, and artistic descriptions of how the liturgy was artfully practiced in the monastery. He avows that his love for medieval art had indeed been greatly responsible in creating an inner disposition for conversion (particularly in the tradition of the primitive artists of the German Flemish tradition). He writes long, descriptive passages evoking the beauties of plain chant as it was sung by the monastic choir at Notre Dame and expatiates on such intricate aesthetic considerations as the lapidary symbolism in the seasonal play of the liturgy. The aesthete Durtal thus still very much exists, but he now has for his project the explication of the aesthetics of the Catholic religion, which has become for him the supreme form of human art.

Even the biography of Gilles de Rais is replaced in *En route* by a new hagiographical exercise in which the converted Durtal has become involved: the portrait of the humble, ignorant, and physically repugnant porter he meets at the Notre Dame monastery, Brother Simeon. Now seeing more than the surface of things, the once haughty and arrogant intellectual Durtal finally understands, through his encounter with the saintly porter, the real meaning of spiritual beauty and the truth "that the cultivation of the mind is nothing and the cultivation of the soul everything."[14] Subsequent works—*La Cathédrale* (1898) and *L'Oblat* (1903)—only reveal more strikingly the transformation of Huysmans's artistic style and theory from aesthetic decadence to the evocation of spiritual beauty that contest the dictum that art can be an end in itself. In this respect Huysmans would become in the twentieth century an appealing model for other troubled artists—Mauriac, Waugh, and Julien Green among them—who would take the path of conversion and create in their own literary works a God-centered aesthetics to contest the veneration of art as an end in itself.

Charles Péguy

Though not a novelist, Charles Péguy had a powerful influence on the modern Catholic novel to come. A pamphleteer, essayist, poet, and literary critic; the editor of a once important left-wing journal; and—through his death on the battlefield of the Marne—a national French hero, Péguy is a difficult person to grasp. Of peasant origins yet brilliant enough to rise to the top of the French educational system as a student in the Ecole Normale Supérieure, he ended up, nonetheless, an academic dropout because of a failure incurred in philosophy exam for the *agrégation*. Thus barred from a career as a university professor, he became an ardent socialist and disciple of Jean Jaurès. He opened a socialist bookstore in Paris in 1898 and two years later founded the periodical *Cahiers de la Quinzaine*, which for over a decade would be a very influential voice in all matters of politics, philosophy, education, and national and foreign policy. As editor he wrote many very lengthy (often 200- or even 300-page) essays for the journal.

Having formally left the Church in his adolescence, Péguy was for most of his life a lapsed Catholic. For a number of years socialism became for him a form of religion, yet he eventually lost faith in socialism as an ideology when, as he believed, this ideal turned from a "mystique" to a political system. By this he meant that socialism under the control of inflexible and doctrinary politicians had lost its guiding principles and suppleness of ideas to become instead a narrow-minded and rigid political party. Working from the outside, Péguy for the rest of his life tried to keep aglow the republican principles of justice, charity, and respect for the individual regardless of economic or social conditions. He forged in the process his own mystique—a fusion of social and religious principles that would lead to a kind of "harmonious city" that became his ideal and the end to which he devoted his essays and poetry.

It is Péguy's very personal involvement with Catholicism that would so influence Catholic writers in France and throughout the world. He returned to the Church in 1908 but could not be officially received or practice the sacraments because his wife, Charlotte Baudouin, remained a committed socialist, refusing both to convert with her husband or to have the couple's three sons baptized. Péguy thus knew the pangs of being an outsider in the institutional Church and was, in his own eyes, an example of the kind of sinner who, deprived of grace and the sacraments, could depend solely on the compassion of Christ. He was thus able to put himself in the position of other outsiders who, for a multitude of reasons, were also separated from the institution and who also had to rely exclusively on Christ's mercy and forgiveness. He therefore stressed the special role of the Church (by which he meant not the institutional form but the larger reality of the living and eternal mystique of Christ's legacy of charity) in its relationship to the sinner. Péguy wrote, "The sinner is at the very heart of Christianity. . . . The sinner and the saint, one can say, are two equally integral parts . . . of the mechanism of Christianity. Both are equally indispensable and mutually complementary entities. . . . [W]hoever is not a Christian or competent in the matter of Christianity is someone who does not commit sin. . . . Whoever is literally a sinner . . . is because of this already a Christian. . . . The sinner, together with the saint, enters into the system of Christianity. . . . The sinner holds out his hand to the saint because the saint gives his hand to the sinner. And, both drawing the other, ascend to Jesus in their unbreakable grasp."[15]

With such a view Péguy offered a breadth of vision and an ecumenical spirit that was virtually unique among his Catholic contemporaries. He was first of all a living witness of how the republican and religious traditions of France were not necessarily antithetical but could merge in harmonious justice and charity. He remembered that what he had learned as a young peasant from the curé and the republican schoolteacher often stressed quite similar values. His outsider's position allowed him, moreover, to go a long way in trying to be understood by and to understand Zola, Hugo, and other writers and thinkers also estranged from the Church. He was from the beginning of the tragic Dreyfus affair on the side of Alfred Dreyfus because he was opposed to injustice of all kinds. And though it pained him to be regarded as an enemy of the Church on this issue, he felt that the Church was not the Church if it espoused an unjust cause. He stressed the importance of the poor in the mission of Christendom, the concept of reversibility (or the offering of self for others), and the interdependence of saints and sinners in the mystical body of the Church of Christ; he also espoused a mystical form of patriotism, which had at its center Joan of Arc as France's greatest national hero and saint.

Throughout his life he decried the dehumanized values of the modern age and what he regarded as the cold, unfeeling society based on materialism, which he saw being tragically handed down to subsequent generations through the arrogant masters of the French educational system and its citadel, the Sorbonne. In fact for many students (Raïssa and Jacques Maritain, for example), Péguy's little bookstore situated across the street from the entrance to the Sorbonne symbolized a kind of intellectual challenge and reproach to the reigning doctrines of France's most influential university, and the hope of a spiritual rebirth (R. Maritain, 59).

With such a range of views it is not surprising that Péguy was greatly admired by and influential with writers such as Bernanos, who, despite his right-wing convictions and strong anti-republican views, held similar views—such as the important role of the poor in the Church, the importance of saints and heroes, and disgust for an age that had lost its Christian ideals. Needless to say, he adamantly shared Péguy's disdain for the educational power and ideology of the Sorbonne. For Graham Greene, Péguy offered the model of the left-wing Christian apologist and activist that he himself wished to become. And Péguy's championing of the sinner and his view of a mystical and more authentic church existing outside the walls of the institutional one would become essential thematic components in Greene's fiction. Finally, for other Catholic writers (François Mauriac, Julien Green, Evelyn Waugh, and Sigrid Undset, for example) who would encounter grave personal difficulties on the road to conversion or reconversion within the Church itself, Péguy's belief in a mystique transcending narrow confessional boundaries would become a strong and living inspiration.

Chapter Two

France: Georges Bernanos, François Mauriac, Julien Green, Gilbert Cesbron

Georges Bernanos

In direct literary descent from Barbey, Bloy, and Péguy, Bernanos was a Catholic visionary whose literary universe depicts as its primary reality the eternal conflict between God and Satan. Indeed, Bernanos's world is without meaning unless one takes into account the real presence of Satan, who, as mighty ruler of the vast kingdom of this world, unceasingly works to undermine the grace and power of God to redeem sinful humanity. Like Dostoyevski, whom he very much admired and to whom he is often compared, Bernanos used as the focal point of his novels the heart of man as the battlefield on which is waged a tug of war between God and the Devil for the possession of the human soul.

As a cradle Catholic, Bernanos never seemed to have the need to revert to or renew a faith either lost or somehow compromised. His early education in several Catholic preparatory schools served to develop a staunch belief in Catholic doctrine that would never be shaken. He was not a university graduate nor from a well-off family (his father was a Parisian interior decorator who had achieved a modicum of financial stability as a result of very hard work). After a year spent in study for a law degree at the Institut Catholique in Paris, the young Bernanos left school to pursue an on-and-off again series of involvements in editing and writing for royalist publications.

As a young man Bernanos was politically an arch conservative who directly manifested his opposition to the institutions and policies of the left by ardent adherence to Charles Maurras's fascist Action Française party and its violence-prone political action group of young royalists, the Camelot du Roi. A monarchist who saw God in France's history and its leaders from Clovis to Louis XVI, he considered the Republic and its leaders as representing a non-French entity violating the nation's ancient traditions, and he was anti-Semitic and even for a time fascist in his political and social views. He would have a major falling out with Maurras and Action Française when the movement was placed under papal condemnation. And though he was certainly wrong-minded in the virulence of his anti-republican views, his adherence to such persuasions must be placed in historical context of that violent period of bitter and uncompromising conflict between church and state in France. Bernanos would prove later that he was not a prisoner of the Catholic right when, virtually alone among French Catholics, he condemned in the most bitter terms Francisco Franco's repressive and cruel dictatorship (as he had viewed it while residing in Palma Majorca) and the warm support given the Spanish tyrant by Catholic writers and intellectuals in his own country. He was also among the first to recognize as evil and firmly attack the incipient fascist governments of Germany and Italy.

Despite poor health Bernanos fought throughout World War I in the Sixth Dragoons and was decorated for valor. Wounded in 1917, he read voraciously during his convalescence and was profoundly touched by the works of Léon Bloy. That same year he married his fiancée, Jeanne Talbert d'Arc, a direct descendant of Joan of Arc. Initially having little confidence in gaining sufficient income from a career as a writer, he traveled the byroads of northern France as an insurance salesman. A loner who led a nomadic existence as he shepherded his family (he had six children) from one economically livable locale to another, he spent a great deal of his life outside of France (in Spain and Brazil, for example, where his modest income would go farther). He spent the years of Occupation in Brazil, where he wrote several novels and a number of essays on the evil of the Nazis and in defense of the Free French. An early supporter of Charles de Gaulle, he accepted the general's personal invitation that he resettle in France in 1945. After his reluctant return he predictably again became a critic of the French political parties of all persuasions and resumed his nomadic ways as he settled in Tunisia in 1947. Mortally ill with liver cancer, he was flown a few months later to the American Hospital in Paris for an operation (where he died just after the completion of his final work, *Dialogues des Carmélites*).

As a boy and young man Bernanos was strongly attracted to the priesthood. His spiritual advisor, the Benedictine priest Dom Besse, convinced him after long retreats and consultations that he was not temperamentally suited for this state. Bernanos then began to accept the fact that his burgeoning involvement as a writer (and subsequently a novelist) was a kind of commitment very much akin to the priesthood. As he would later in life declare, "Every vocation is a call—*vocatus*—and every call seeks to be transmitted. . . . The vocation of a writer is often— or rather sometimes—another form of a vocation to the priesthood."[1]

Bernanos also believed that all of his writings were attempts to regain his childhood vision of the world, and he further believed that whatever good there might be in his novels could be traced to the purity and inno- cence of that bygone age: "I'm not sure for whom I am writing but I know why I write. I write to justify myself in the eyes of the child that I was. Whether he has ceased to speak to me or not, is of little importance and I'll never put up with his silence and will respond to him forever."[2] Writing novels, then, was a vocation by which he saw himself as merely an instrument of God's will in the world, and his vocation of writer was his unique way to quest, through a return to the innocence of his child- hood, the state of sanctity ("For having lost my childhood I could only reconquer it by sanctity" [Béguin, 150]).

In his novels Bernanos depicts the modern world as a desolate land- scape where human beings live, for the most part, sunk in a moral tor- por and ennui that he characterizes as a kind of spiritual cancer. Similar in many respect to religious configuration of a the medieval morality play, the Bernanosian novel places the characters in sharply etched spiri- tual categories. First there are the large number of damned or dead souls; then come the souls of the innocent (most often young adoles- cents) preyed upon by sinners and the forces of evil; and in the third cat- egory are a few great saints who, through their lives and sacrifices, contest the power of Satan.

In the category of great sinners and dead souls Bernanos places most often intellectuals—priests, writers, academics—whom he characterizes as fanatical in their lust for power and social preferences. Yet they are already dead, cut off from life, incapable of loving anyone or anything but themselves, and imprisoned in dreadful solitude. A prime example of this famous type is the Abbé de Cénabre of the 1927 novel *L'Imposture*, one of Bernanos's best-drawn tragic apostate priests. A renowned schol- ar, he has secretly ceased to believe and has become glacially indifferent to this loss of belief. He lives in a state of desperate ennui, and with monstrous Satanic curiosity he manipulates and humiliates other souls with whom he comes in contact through his mad obsession to know them as only God can.

Yet the most Satanic of Bernanos's great sinners, Monsieur Ouine, the protagonist of the eponymous novel, shares Bernanos's profession of

writer. As a well-known literary critic/teacher, Ouine is nonetheless con-
sistently described in priestly terms, as an all-intrusive, meddling type
with "ecclesiastical hands"[3] and gestures, who loves the role of moral
counselor to youth. (The name Ouine—in French "oui-non"—suggests
André Gide, whom Bernanos regarded as ultimate pervertor of youth
through his message of moral dilettantism and indulgence in vice.)
Ouine has set himself up in a provincial parish (Fenouille) as a kind of
"priest of dead souls" or anti-priest, thereby contesting the influence and
sacramental role of the young village curé, who is no match for this formidable adversary. Through the years Ouine has emptied himself of any
kind of authentic human sympathy or feeling; all that is left in him is a
fierce pride (masked as indifference), an all-consuming curiosity to pen-
etrate to the innermost secrets of others, and a profound hatred or disgust of the self. This state constitutes for Bernanos the particular form of
sin that cannot be pardoned, since it represents the creature's ultimate
refusal to accept and to love God's gift of self. Sunk in this despairing
life, Ouine is ultimately guilty of debauching and driving to despair the
adolescent Steeny and is heavily responsible for the apparent murder of
a little farm boy, who dies in a moral climate of hatred that replaces love
for others in this now-dead parish. With Ouine mysteriously at the center of this evil malaise, the mayor of the village is then led to commit
suicide, the young curate is driven to despair, and the novel ends with
Ouine's own sordid, solitary, and unrepentant death.

Bernanos's novels *Sous le soleil de Satan* (1926; *Under Satan's Sun*), *La
Joie* (1928; *Joy*), and *Nouvelle histoire de Mouchette* (1936; *Mouchette*) portray *enfants humiliés* ("degraded adolescents") morally or physically
abused by the corruption of adults. These characters represent the
legions of children whose fall from innocence, Bernanos insists, modern
society both strenuously conspires to effect and then at which it
unabashedly rejoices when the abominable end is achieved.

In *Nouvelle histoire de Mouchette* Bernanos attempts to describe, as he
put it, "the desperate awakening of the sentiment of purity in a child
victimized by misery."[4] Here the heroine is the daughter of a brutal
drunkard living in a tiny village of Artois. She is humiliated by her
schoolmates and teacher (she is too old and grown up for her class in
school) and often beaten by her father. Returning home one evening she
meets and is seduced by Arsène, a handsome but totally unscrupulous
village low-life and poacher. Submitting to his rape of her virtue with
"the physical docility of the women of the common people," she realizes
through this act for a short time afterwards a kind of deliverance from

her unloved and humiliated state.[5] Led to despair when she understands that Arsène has no feeling whatsoever for her and ridiculed and reviled by her neighbors when her encounter with Arsène has become known, she falls into a state of despair and commits suicide.

The bleakest of all Bernanos's works, *Mouchette* examines, in almost naturalist terms, the psychology of suicide and the condition of a soul that prepares to destroy itself. The terrible question "What good is life?" receives no reply in the mind of this wretched little creature; hence she regards suicide as her destiny. Still, Bernanos suggests, Mouchette will find God's mercy, since she has been deprived of all spiritual aid and consolation and stands as a victim of unmitigated evil in a perverted world that has stolen her innocence.

The other heroine given the nickname Mouchette is a major character in Bernanos's earlier novel *Sous le soleil de Satan*. Though also a humiliated adolescent, she, however, is not totally abandoned but is aided in her despair by the first of Bernanos's priest-saints, Abbé Donissan. Like the peasant suicide-victim, this adolescent, Germaine Malorthy, also lives in the somber village of Artois. Her father, a wily and stingy brewer, is a shallow freethinker who refuses to give his daughter any kind of religious education. Growing up in a state of religious ignorance and moral solitude, this Mouchette despairs at ever being able to live her youth freely, away from her narrow-minded parents and other inhabitants of the depressing little town she hates so much. Out of defiance and ennui she gives herself to two lovers. The first, the Marquis de Cardignan, is a ne'er-do-well but pretentious country squire who, as a bachelor, thrives on such liaisons and refuses to admit his involvement with Mouchette when confronted by her father. Enraged by his denial and feeling that he has repudiated her love, Mouchette, after a stormy interview, kills her spineless lover with his own hunting rifle. The murder is declared a suicide, and the 16-year-old begins a second liaison, this time with the local doctor who is also a deputy to the National Assembly. Made pregnant by him yet disgusted by his temerity, she tries to shock him by confessing her killing of the Marquis. Refusing to believe the "young schoolgirl" capable of such an act, the doctor drives her to a nervous breakdown; she falls into a state of dementia and is sent away to an institution where she gives birth to a stillborn infant. It is at this point in the novel that Abbé Donissan, the "future saint of Lumbres," enters her life.

Inspired by the life of the eighteenth-century saint Jean de Vianney, the curé of Ars, who was canonized in 1926, Donissan is a young, bull-headed peasant, inarticulate and at first seeming even to be dim-witted.

Yet it is this unprepossessing person who becomes the chosen vessel to perhaps lead the humiliated Mouchette to God and to bring the delicate and intellectually astute vicar, whose assistant he is, to a fuller understanding of and dedication to the priestly vocation. At the beginning of his ministry Donissan is ashamed of his perceived inadequacies: his intellectual density, his clumsiness, lack of refinement, and failure to communicate with the peasants of the country parish. Physically powerful and of a passionate nature, he feels he must scourge his body to control the rebellious flesh. Yet it is this improbable priest who has been chosen to be Satan's foil and to meet head on "the Prince of this world." Bernanos in fact adroitly depicts Satan in human form as a fast-talking horse trader whom Donissan meets on a deserted country road as he goes to an adjoining parish to help with confessions. Though not taking possession of the priest, Satan nevertheless reveals to him the tremendous extent of his kingdom and his power on earth, and he gives him his terrible kiss. Donissan refuses to capitulate and must undergo the experience of seeing himself with all his weaknesses as Satan views every human being. Emerging intact from this terrible vision only through his profound faith, he confronts Satan and vows to hold him as a kind of hostage at the very center of his prayer and spiritual ministry: "I shall pronounce the words that horrify you. I shall nail you to the center of my prayer like an owl or you will promise to give up your tricks against those souls that have been confided to me."[6]

At this point in his life and forever after, the priest must live under "Satan's sun" and endure a never-ending visual awareness of Satan's presence and his power over Donissan's spiritual life as well as the spiritual lives of those for whom Donissan finds himself responsible. He now realizes that he also has been given the terrible power of seeing into the souls of others, to know immediately their spiritual state. Just as after this encounter, for example, he meets Mouchette and immediately recognizes her sinful state and extreme desperation. He succeeds in making her aware that she is not guilty of her first lover's murder ("For at that very moment of his death your will was no freer than it is at present"), and he also somewhat brutally makes her see that, instead of having been liberated (as she believes) by her sin, she was and continues to be nothing more than the plaything of the devil. He tells her, "You are like a toy, like a little child's ball, in the hands of Satan" (*Sous le soleil de Satan*, 161).

Unable to sustain this terrible vision of herself, Mouchette rushes away from the priest and slits her throat with a razor blade. Though he tries to resuscitate her, she dies, and Donissan's life is made a living hell with the knowledge that his actions and words, emanating from his privileged vision of Satan's presence, may well have prompted the young woman's suicide, and that he himself may have played into the hands of or possibly have been used to advance the purposes and advantage of the arch fiend. He commits another monstrously imprudent act when, at the death of an infant child, he in effect dares God to show his power and confound the powers of darkness. He carries the body of the baby to the church and lays it before the altar and for a scant second the corpse seems to move. This seeming miracle turns out to be a momentary illusion, however, and the audacity of his act ends in a public scandal and induces a nervous breakdown for the unfortunate priest.

Sent away by the ecclesiastical authorities for a long retreat during which he recuperates in body and soul, Donissan returns to a new parish. Now more mature and better equipped to minister to others, he becomes, like the curé of Ars, a confessor of souls, renowned throughout the land and literally has to live in his confessional to accommodate the hordes who come for his counsel and absolution. He dies while awaiting penitents in his confessional box, a tortured saint who has witnessed Satan's might but has also been an immense channel of grace for sinners through the sacramental power invested in him as a priest.

Both a commercial and literary success, *Sous le soleil de Satan* catapulted Bernanos to national prominence in France as a Catholic novelist and one who had succeeded in introducing Satan as a character in the novel. It was this unexpected esteem and success that convinced Bernanos to thereafter dedicate himself to a career as a novelist.

Ten years later he published his most renowned literary work and his most moving portrayal of a priest, *Le Journal d'un curé de campagne* (*The Diary of a Country Priest*). When published in 1936 the novel received the prestigious Grand Prix du Roman of the French Academy and caused Bernanos to be regarded in France as the leading (along with Mauriac) Catholic novelist. Written while he was living in Palma Majorca, Spain, the novel derived its inspiration, as Bernanos relates it, from his childhood: "As soon as I take up my pen, what rises suddenly within me is my childhood, from which I draw everything that I write as if from a source of dreams" (Béguin, 173). Bernanos regarded this work not only as his best loved and most intimate creation but also as the one that best presented a microcosm of modern France, on both a spiritual and a temporal plane.

In the village of Ambricourt where the novel takes place we find the essential social groupings of France: aristocracy, petit bourgeoisie, peasantry, and the poor. Also portrayed are the social attitudes and modes of thought typical of each social category. Simultaneously Bernanos offers the spiritual plane and his vision of the state of the Church and its members. Here are included all spiritual dispositions: sinners, the lukewarm and indifferent, tormented souls, heroes, and saints. He adds to this spiritual microcosm his very personal theories on the mission of the Church, its apparent failure to be a major influence on contemporary French society, the scandal of the poor, and his nostalgia for the Christian tradition, now long-vanished, of heroism and chivalry of the Middle Ages. *The Diary* is, therefore, the most broad-based in social and religious themes of all of Bernanos's novels and the best representation of his literary universe. The country priest of Ambricourt and his parish thus constitute the author's most ambitious effort to synthesize his deepest thoughts and convictions on the spiritual and temporal order. And it is in this novel that the figure of the Bernanosian saint (in its most accomplished characterization) must come to grips with and combat the de-Christianized state of the modern world.

In the ensuing struggle between the saint and the fallen world, Bernanos first presents the spectacle of France's modern Catholic Church, which as an institution seems to have gravely compromised Christ's teachings. In the country priest's dialogues with older priests (principally with a genial and far more relaxed De Torcy) and a local doctor, Delbende, who has lost his faith because of the suffering and deprivation he encounters in caring for the poor, Bernanos interjects his very personal reasons for this sad state of affairs. The seeds of this modification are to be found, he maintains, during the Renaissance, when the Church did not protest the formation of the laicized pagan state (which has since evolved into the nation-state). In the process the Church lost both its spiritual authority over the faithful as well as its potential to inspire Christian patterns of life through a mystique of sacrifice and honor (exemplified in a Joan of Arc or a medieval knight). Today there exist no causes to which Christians can devote themselves totally. What remain as "titulary gods" in the modern period are "bankers" and bourgeois business types.[7]

Incapable of understanding any spiritual absolute, the triumphant bourgeoisie have thus manipulated their religion to justify and even honor the accumulation of material goods, and the clergy have not only gone along with but have accepted these principles. In fact, a fashionable and learned canon from the deanery of which the country priest is a member staunchly defends the greed and grasping nature of these "faithful Catholics" as representing the very soul of the French Church. This older, compromising priest then goes on to praise the lower-middle classes (which he calls "the backbone of the French Church") for their greed and love of gain, and Bernanos even has him laud members of this class as being "hard as nails in their dealings with the poor. Modern society is their creation" (*Diary*, 66).

These callous remarks allow Bernanos to expatiate on what is perhaps the novel's most important theme, the one to which he constantly refers here and in all of his writings as the "scandal of the poor"—the demise of the spirit of poverty in the modern-day Catholic Church. Bernanos makes it clear from this and frequent other notations in the country priest's journal that the poor will always be the touchstone for the authentic spirit of Christianity. The poor are the children of God, and poverty has been a privileged state since Jesus Christ embraced it more than 2,000 years ago. The efforts of modern technology to somehow do away with "this filthy state," moreover, will never succeed; they will in fact be always with us as witnesses to the betrayal of the Christian spirit by the bourgeois classes.

Bernanos's major charge against the bourgeoisie is not principally that they have refused to give of their substance (though this is often the case) in aiding the poor but because they have succeeded in infecting the latter with their own materialism, lack of faith, and passion for profit. Noblesse oblige has been corrupted and obliterated from memory at the hands of the modern merchants and industrialists. And in the grinding misery of the poor—a misery permitted and accepted by society—there resides the clearest proof that a nobility no longer exists in either the social or moral sense, for what is left of the old French aristocracy has become morally like the bourgeoisie in the abandonment of its sacred duties and obligations. Thus we are now presented with the sad spectacle of a gravely compromised Christian society in which the dominant *bien pensants* assume a social pose behind which the loss of any form of authentic faith is barely concealed. The resulting hypocrisy manifests itself in what the curé d'Ambricourt discerns as the tragic reality of modern times, the "fermentation of a Christianity in decay" (*Diary*, 3).

To combat this state Bernanos puts in place the little parish priest of Ambricourt who cannot view these spiritual realities without anguish. For him, the scandal of the poor and the need to minister spiritually to them

induces not a state of despairing complacency; rather, the sole justification for the inequality of the supernatural conditions for salvation is the
need to take risks. Yet though he constantly risks all and gives totally of
himself, he nevertheless feels increasingly powerless before the heart-rending spectacle of the apathy of his flock and the de-Christianization of his
parish. Viewing the town from a distance one evening he says, "And this
village was my parish. It was my parish and I could do nothing for it. I
saw it sadly sink into the night . . . to disappear. Villages don't scramble
to their feet like cattle at the call of a school boy. And yet, last night, I
believe a saint might have roused it" (*Diary*, 2).

Yet through the diurnal jottings or entries that we read in the
priest's journal it soon becomes apparent that, despite his anguish at
what he feels to be his gross inadequacy as a priest, his life of total
renunciation and dedication exerts a prodigious effect on both his
parishioners and the village itself. Many of the inhabitants, long mired
in habits of vice, react violently to the presence of this man with the
face of an emaciated adolescent, and by his mere presence he unwittingly destroys the equilibrium or compromise between good and evil
that the latter have maintained in their spiritual life. The purity of the
priest creates a kind of transparency by which others, through contact
with him, are immediately allowed to see the spiritual condition of
their own souls.

Though he generally fails in any kind of practical administrative venture in the decaying parish, the country priest nonetheless works miracles in the lives of the few parishioners who open themselves to him. The
proud and reclusive countess, for example, cannot for long conceal from
her parish priest, whom she at first ridicules and treats as a naive child,
the abominable condition of her soul. She admits that for more than 20
years she has lived with an intense hatred of God because of the death of
her infant son. She has also sealed herself off in hatred from her own
family, despising her weak and adulterous husband, and her only daughter, whom she jealously spites for taking her husband's side, or so she has
imagined it. And to the priest she now reveals her imminent plan to
force her daughter to leave home, knowing fully well that Chantal, an
extremely troubled adolescent, not only would never return but would
in fact be lost to the family.

In a dialogic duel (worthy in dramatic intensity of any created by
Dostoyevski) the priest, no longer the insecure peasant before the local
aristocracy but the simple and direct instrument of God, is able to

plumb the depths of the woman's hate-filled soul. With words that shock him because of their eloquent power and that seem to come from an unknown source in the deepest part of himself, he evokes for her a terrifying vision of sin, "that seed that pollutes the very air that we breathe," and he reveals to her the real nature of that hell for which, for 20 years, she has been preparing: "Hell is not to love any more, madame. Not to love anymore. That sounds quite ordinary to you. To a human being still alive, it means to love less or love elsewhere. To understand is still a way of loving. But suppose this faculty that seems so inseparably ours, of our very essence, should disappear. Oh, prodigy, To stop loving, to stop understanding—and yet to live" (*Diary*, 163).

Gradually the countess renounces her rebellion against God and becomes willing to be reconciled with the death of her son and the marital infidelities of her husband. She makes a full confession to the priest and attributes his victory over her to his childlike simplicity, and the priest himself is astonished at his ability to "give what we ourselves do not possess, oneself." That night the countess dies in her sleep, and the priest senses intuitively that her death marks the beginning of his own final trial (*Diary*, 180).

What follows is nothing less than a kind of persecution-crucifixion of the priest by his parishioners and a ferocious personal battle with despair when he learns that he has a terminal illness—cancer of the stomach. The count, unable to abide the priest's spiritual influence over his wife even after her death and fearful of what she may have disclosed in her confession, spurs on the animosity of other parishioners who fear and resent the priest's spiritual influence. All the forces of evil thus converge about the priest and attempt to hound him out of the parish. As a result he is brought to the brink of despair at his apparent failure in his pastoral duties. When at the same time he learns from a doctor that he will soon die of cancer, everything seems to fall apart. His physical condition fills him with an immense disgust for his own body, and his imagined inadequacies as a priest tempt him to hate himself, since he feels unworthy of God's love and grace.

He will, however, have little time to fight against this form of anxiety. On the same day he receives the diagnosis he stops to visit a friend of his seminary days (now a defrocked priest) who, though he denies it, is living in a genuine state of spiritual despair. Mortally stricken during the visit and forced to remain in the dark, depressing apartment of his friend, the curé d'Ambricourt nevertheless spends his dying moments trying to nudge the former priest to face up to his situation. He also tries to console the illiterate woman with whom the latter is now living and mentally torturing (by accusing her of being largely responsible for his infidelity to his vows and berating her as culturally not worthy of him). Deprived of legitimate access to the last rites, the curé d'Ambricourt asks his friend to hear his confession, and when the latter protests his unworthiness, the country priest dies in his arms saying, "Does it matter? After all, everything is Grace" (*Diary*, 299).

In the last recorded entry of his journal the priest indicates that he has surmounted the temptation to self-hatred and despair. In the final analysis he has attached, he now sees, too much importance to his own "miserable shell" by entertaining such prideful thoughts. Reconciled to his death, he writes (after the consultation with his doctor), "How easy it is to hate oneself. True grace is to forget. Yet if pride could die in us, the supreme grace would be to love oneself in all simplicity—as one would love any one of those who themselves have suffered and loved in Christ" (*Diary*, 296).

This novel, Bernanos's masterpiece, is one of fiction's finest renditions of the autobiographical journal and provides as well an unsurpassed portrait of a modern-day saint. One of a "race that God himself has put in motion and that cannot cease to function until everything has been accomplished" (*Diary*, 256), the priest confounds the forces of evil in the natural and supernatural order through total fidelity to God's will for him. His naïveté, rather than undoing him, becomes the principal arm by which he overcomes everything and everybody. As a mediator between God and human beings, the country priest incarnates Bernanos's ultimate hope that the modern, de-Christianized world can be saved through the prayer and suffering of those who, seemingly weak and ineffectual, are in reality immensely powerful through the total gift of self they make for others out of pure love of God.

Though not a novel, Bernanos's last literary production, *Dialogues des Carmélites* (1948; *The Carmelites*), should be briefly mentioned here. The work, a rewriting in dramatic form of Gertrud von Le Fort's novella *Die Letze am Schaffott* (*The Song at the Scaffold*), is both his most personal work and his memento mori. Bernanos saw the major character, Sister Blanche of the Holy Agony of Christ, the weakest and most fearful of the sisters, as symbolically embodying his own agony as his death approached (he finished *Carmélites* on the same day he was admitted to the American Hospital in Paris, where he died six weeks later). Blanche, the youngest member of the community and in perpetual flight from her chosen destiny to die with the others, finally and courageously accepts martyrdom not because she gains courage but because she mystically assumes Christ's agony and near despair in Gethsemani ("where human anguish never before or after has been experienced at such heights").[8] Blanche ("the mystical prisoner of the Holy Agony") prefigured Bernanos's hope of reconciling human weakness and the anguish of dying with unwavering faith in God. For Bernanos, *Carmélites* was a prayerful meditation by which he could confront death without despair.

François Mauriac

François Mauriac, one of France's greatest modern novelists and recipient of the 1952 Nobel Award for Literature, had also achieved, at the time of his death in 1970, universal recognition as the preeminent Catholic writer and novelist of his age. Born in Bordeaux of solidly middle-class parents who between them owned huge tracts of pine forests in the Gironde, Mauriac was during all his professional life financially well off. All his life, too, he remained close to his Bordeaux origins, and his works are inseparable from this area of pines and vineyards, where most of his characters live or have their family roots.

Having lost his father when less than two years old, Mauriac was raised in a family of five children headed by his extremely religious mother, to whom he was devoted and who would always have a strong influence on him. The family atmosphere has been characterized as warm, protective and piously Catholic, even Jansenistic in its emphasis on strict religious observance of duties and a moral code stressing sin, guilt, and the potential dangers of worldly pleasures. This strict approach to religion was strengthened by the education he received as a young boy in the Catholic school run by the Marianite Fathers in Bordeaux. Hence, as Mauriac later would describe it, he was early on inoculated with the "vaccine" of an austere Catholic religious formation and had the kind of temperament on which this "inoculation" took. And even as an adolescent he realized that he would never be able "to escape from Catholicism, . . . to leave it or re-enter it." Adherence to this faith was, he believed, his own particular destiny (*God and Mammon*, 20).

Yet following his religion was never an easy matter for Mauriac. Of an extremely passionate nature (and apparently inheriting much of his father's freethinking temperament) he was both attracted to and repelled by the demands of Catholic morality and practice. What for many of his critics best explains his troubled state of mind is an essential and enduring conflict between the concepts of "nature and grace," and it is perhaps this very duality and resulting tensions that best account for the distinctive contours and dimensions of his literary universe. To understand the terms of this struggle we must briefly deal with the major intellectual influences that shaped Mauriac's religious and moral vision.

Among his major influences Mauriac records first Huysmans, whose religious/aesthetic vision corresponded markedly with his own profound love of Catholic liturgy as a young man. Then there was Jean Racine, the seventeenth-century dramatist for whom Mauriac wrote a famous psychoanalytic essay-biography, *La Vie de Jean Racine* (1928). Racine received passionate attention because Mauriac viewed him as a veritable counterpart of himself—that is, as a Catholic writer who has been raised in a Jansenistic environment of "high tension." Moreover, like Mauriac, Racine in his own day had to work out his destiny as a vulnerable man torn between the tug of the flesh and the call of the Divine. The nineteenth-century poets Verlaine and Rimbaud, whose quests for the absolute brought them beyond the boundaries of sin and repentance, also served as important literary models. But above and beyond the others, it was Pascal who became and remained Mauriac's principal mentor throughout his life.

Pascal was also the subject of one of Mauriac's biographical essays, *Blaise Pascal et sa soeur Jacqueline* (*Blaise Pascal and His Sister Jacqueline*), here presented as a man of passion and a genius who knew fully well, even at the pinnacle of success, that he would have to overcome his pride in knowledge and pleasure of society. Mauriac had also early been inspired by Pascal's life and conversion, which convinced him "that there could always be a voyage of discovery within revealed truth" (*God and Mammon*, 25), and his fiction resonates with many of Pascal's major themes: the "grandeur and misery" of the human condition; the intuitive way of thinking and knowing about God ("*esprit de finesse*") rooted not in the intellect but in the heart; the notion of the hidden God and His mysterious channeling of grace; the need to wager everything on the probability of His existence; and the inability of human love to satisfy the cravings of the human heart.

Like Pascal, Mauriac was a Christian humanist who opposed Montaigne's ideal of the cultivation of the purely natural self as the highest good. This fact explains Mauriac's conflicts and debates with André Gide, who, as a self-styled modern disciple of Montaigne, preached a doctrine of openness (*disponibilité*) and the cultivation of the self as the moral end of life. Like Pascal, Mauriac accepted natural man as the point of departure and the enhancement of human qualities as only part of the goal of developing a morally whole person. Rather, his ultimate concern was for human beings seen as part of a Divine plan and called to a higher order. Hence human beings had first of all to overcome their physical nature in order to fulfill their spiritual destiny. And Mauriac describes the resulting conflict as a fierce battle between "Cybele," the classical deity that incarnated the beauty and pleasures of nature (or the physical world), and the Divine call to go beyond the limitations of the flesh governing one's lower nature.

Mauriac uses the mimetic technique of the realist to describe in concrete terms the universe and environment in which his characters are born and live out their destiny. He is carefully attentive to the dynamics of heredity and temperament in the individual's ability (or lack thereof) to adapt to his or her society. Yet to this initially naturalist portrayal of human character he adds such vital spiritual dimensions as the reality of the Fall and the resulting attraction humans have for sin and evil in their weakened state. He finally situates his plots in an eternal time frame in which human motivation and conduct are seen as part of a Divine pattern or Providence. He characterized his artistic intentions as follows: "I make the Catholic universe of evil palpable, tangible, pungent. The theologians offer us an abstract idea of the sinner; I present him in flesh and blood."[9]

With this technique Mauriac explored how his characters become "beautiful" or not through their struggle to overcome the domination of the primary temptations of the natural order. These can be summarized by using as points of conflict the categories of power/domination, possessions, and pleasure. For any one of these, if not controlled, can become ruling passions (or even forms of monomaniacal obsessions) that stand in the way of grace and cause the loss of one's immortal soul. Such passions lead, in other words, to a rejection of the Cross ("We are born prisoner of our cross. Nothing can tear us from it" [*God and Mammon*, 39]), and to follow the Cross demands dying to the natural order and responding to the will of God. Each individual must confront or refuse this fact, with the terrible consequences of salvation or damnation depending on what choice is ultimately made. Through a portrayal of the concrete Mauriac's novels describe the obscure, even invisible, action of grace in the lives of individuals who, caught in the web of their fallen nature, struggle to respond to the call of the Divine.

Mauriac's early works of the 1920s are dark and somber pieces depicting characters driven or victimized by unhealthy obsessions and seemingly unable to control their destinies. In the 1922 novel *Le Baiser au lépreux* (*The Kiss for the Leper*) Noémi d'Artiailh, a beautiful and pious young woman, is forced by her greedy family to contract a disastrous marriage solely for financial reasons. Her husband, Jean Péloueyre, a sickly young man suffering from tuberculosis (but of an immensely wealthy family), has from the start been physically repugnant to her; he, on the other hand, is passionately in love and, for a time, prevails upon her to fulfill her "marital duties." Soon made aware of her physical disgust for him and not wishing to subject her any longer to the torture of intimate contact, he heroically sacrifices his life for hers (he leaves the Bordeaux region for Paris and aggravates his sickness by frequent exposures to a friend terminally ill with the same disease). The young woman, in the meantime, is courted by a local Don Juan, a young doctor to whom she is very much attracted. Fully aware when her husband dies of his sublime sacrifice for her and convinced that "every path except renunciation is closed to her," she refuses to follow her passions and forsakes any hope of happiness.[10]

Aside from the Jansenistic theme of inescapable fatality so essential to the novel, Mauriac also strongly indicts the bourgeois mentality of this family of Catholics who, with the active support of friends and clergy, conspire to ruin the life of a young person solely to protect the interests of the all-powerful family cell. The hypocrisy and venality of this class became a primary theme in all of Mauriac's subsequent fiction.

The novel *Génitrix*, published a year after *Le Baiser*, is a remarkable study of the power of a mother from this Catholic middle class to totally dominate her son. Refusing to relinquish her jealous attachment to him after his marriage, Felicité Cazenave maliciously convinces her son Ferdinand that her mortally ill and neglected daughter-in-law (who has been aware of the older woman's hateful animosity) , does not need further medical care. The resulting death of the younger woman represents, however, a temporary triumph from the grave over the murderous intentions of Felicité. The son now venerates the memory of his wife and loves her as he never did in life. In the long run, however, ties of blood and family possessions win out, and when the old woman dies her son soon becomes virtually possessed by her and spends the rest of his life as a recluse in his mother's house, aping her miserly ways in his tight-fisted and frugal management of the family's substantial properties.

Like *Le Baiser au lépreux*, *Génetrix* is a study in family domination. Felicité has such a sense of property that she views her son and everyone around her as mere extensions of herself and her vital interests. Like the young couple in the first work, Ferdinand and his wife are victims, and the mother is the executioner whose crime is justified by protection of family interests. And as in *Le Baiser*, the possibility of free choice is not available to these victims as a means of avoiding their fate.

These two brief novels, classical in their study of a limited number of characters who represent "types" dominated by single psychological obsessions, were soon followed by works of more ample scope but enveloped in a similarly somber moral universe. *Le Désert de l'amour* (1925; *The Desert of Love*), *Thérèse Desqueyroux* (1928), and *Destins* (1928; *Lines of Life*) elicited strong attacks on the part of Catholics against what they considered to be Mauriac's excessively dark and pessimistic view of human nature and his mordant satire of and apparent contempt for "good" middle-class Catholics. He also was attacked by some French critics (and notably André Gide) as having established a kind of moral complicity (neither expected nor worthy of a practicing Catholic) with the sinful world through a now unmistakable predilection in his novels for themes or situations of moral baseness (usually involving sexual matters). It was argued that in professing such sinful matters to be part of the fallen world and yet manifestly reveling in the use of such sinful matter as major components of his plots,[11] Mauriac, as a practicing Catholic, seemed to want to have his cake and eat it too. Mauriac did not take these charges lightly and in fact underwent a very difficult spiritual and artistic crisis at the close of the 1920s.

Indeed, the claims of sin-charged plots suggesting more than a little authorial relish for such situations, as well as the constant evocation of a dark, hopeless, and repressive moral climate seem to be sustained systematically by the novels Mauriac wrote during this period. Yet at least two of them, *The Desert of Love* and *Thérèse Desqueyroux*, are unquestionably among his acknowledged masterpieces while the third, *Lines of Life*, is important in eliciting Gide's specific charge of Mauriac's

moral complicity with evil (which he delivered to him in the form of a
"J'accuse" epistolary statement so well loved by French intellectuals
through the ages).

Lines of Life narrates the aimless career, amorous adventures, and violent death by auto accident of the young man Bob Lagave. Charming,
manipulative, and morally corrupt, he uses his attractiveness (and his
body) to advance his career and interests. When he comes to spend a
vacation with his grandmother, who lives as the servant of a wealthy
Bordeaux family at their summer estate, he encounters once again Paule
de la Sesque (whom he has met socially in Paris) and falls in love with
her. From a prominent Catholic family, Paule is a good catch for the
impoverished young man but also represents for him, as he begins to see
it, the kind of woman for whom he could change his amoral way of life
and thus start to make something of himself. Certainly, marriage to her
would allow him to disengage himself from the fast and decadent set to
which he has been attached in Paris. In order to pursue his project (and
to meet the young woman on an acceptable social level) he realizes that
he has to have at his disposal the facilities of the opulent summer house
(and not the very modest quarters of his servant grandmother). Elisabeth
Gornac, the mistress of the house, a wealthy, pious, and widowed 50-
year-old who is very much involved in the maintenance and development of her considerable properties and financial investments, allows
Bob the use of her property, primarily because of the affection she has for
his grandmother, but also because she becomes taken with his charming
grace and personality. She is even willing, after a point, to use her considerable influence with Paule's family in forwarding the young man's
courtship of Paule.

Bob's project is upset, however, by the untimely arrival of Elisabeth
Gornac's decidedly unpleasant and even detestable son. The worst kind
of repressed, pious bigot, he maliciously relates to Paule (for her own
moral welfare, he claims) stories told about Bob in Paris (that he is a
prostitute serving both men and women and a scheming parasite to
boot). Manifestly seen as an unhappy and unfilled person through this
unseemly show of hypocritical malice, Pierre Gornac is a foil to Bob
Lagave's physical (and potentially moral) beauty, and he is presumably
jealous of Bob's attractiveness and exceptional propensity to enjoy the
pleasures of the world. Favorably disposed up to this time by Bob, Paule
is understandably troubled by Pierre's charges and precipitately leaves
the summer house for Paris. Suspecting that Pierre has been responsible

for Paule's departure, Bob confronts him, and when the latter unctuously reveals what he has told her, Bob brutally assaults him.

Elisabeth Gornac covers up the scandal, and though increasingly troubled, she allows Bob to remain at the estate. But he, now in a state of moral and physical abandonment akin to despair, takes to drink and decides to renew his association with the perverted influences of his past life. In an extended conversation with the half-drunk young man just before he links up again with his fast friends from Paris, Elisabeth is forced to admit to herself the violent physical attraction that she feels in his presence. Then Bob leaves for Paris with friends who drop in on him, and is killed in a violent auto accident. Elisabeth Gornac suffers a complete loss of control at Bob Lagave's funeral. Here she seems to rebel against the narrow and constricting religious practices that have held her captive and starved her affections during all her life. And she ridicules her moralizing son who tries to convince her of her error. So abusive is she of his pretensions to piety that he himself undergoes a kind of moral awakening, sees his hypocrisy for what it is, and commits himself to a life in the African mission (presumably in this way to work out the guilt for his part in Bob's fall and death). The work introduces several of Mauriac's favorite themes: the sudden (and destructive) love of an aging woman for a young man, the young man as prodigal yet disposed to grace through passion, and the ugly repressive nature of the pharisaical "good" Catholic. Finally, the title presents the major theme of the heavy influence and weight of encounters or "interferences" on the path of life. The same kind of Jansenistic fatality seen as operative in the earlier works seems, finally, to again control the destinies of characters who cannot overcome their nature.

Le Désert de l'amour is a far more explicitly Catholic novel than previous ones because of its emphasis on the real possibility of grace touching the souls of spiritually tormented individuals. It also deals with human love as the central passion and not simply human beings overcome by greed or possessiveness. The novel begins with Raymond Courrèges, a 35-year-old playboy who is preparing for another night of diversions in a Paris bar. A well-known womanizer in the Paris club circles, he unexpectedly meets here a woman from his past, whom, we learn, he has always held responsible for having put him on this road of sexual dissipation. And when Maria Cross, now middle-aged, enters with her husband, Raymond is thrown back in memory to his adolescence in Bordeaux. In particular there surges up that day more than 17 years ago

when he swore to avenge Maria Cross's traumatic rejection of him in his
first attempt at seduction through the conquest of other women.

With its structure from this point on consisting of a series of flash-
backs, the novel recounts the triangular sentimental patterns that had
linked together the prominent medical doctor Paul Courrèges, his tormented adolescent son, and the weak but sympathetic "kept woman" in
her mid-twenties, who is Maria Cross. A widow and with an infant child
to support, she had gradually become the mistress of a rich but totally
amoral benefactor, the Bordeaux businessman Victor Larousselle. Doctor
Courrèges meets her when he is called to care for her ailing child. Falling
helplessly in love, he continues to be in touch with her after the death of
her child and imagines that there might exist between them deep sentimental affinities that would lead to a relationship. She never sees the
doctor, however, in any other light than as a kindly older man devoted
to her professionally, and she is frankly bored with his presence.

Desperately lonely and still very much afflicted by the death of her
child, she develops an ambiguous attraction to a young *lycéen* with an
"angelic face" who regularly travels on the tram that she takes returning from the grave site of her son. Raymond Courrèges inspires in her
confused feelings such as pure maternal love, which she transfers from
her dead child to him, but also something more suspect because it is
prompted by the grace and charm of the very physically attractive and
sexually aroused young male that he proves to be. For Raymond, there
is much less ambiguity. Noting her strong attraction for him and
learning very soon that she is the famous Maria Cross, Bordeaux's
notorious "kept woman," he regards her simply as a sexual challenge.
After she speaks to him on the tram and establishes contact, she
imprudently invites him to her house (on the pretext of showing him
pictures of her dead son whom Raymond supposedly resembles), and
during his second visit he tries to take her sexually by force. When she
rejects him with horror and disgust, he is so wounded and humiliated
that his whole life will be spent in avenging this "disgrace." Deeply
troubled by her perceived complicity in Raymond's overture and her
general feelings of guilt, Maria attempts suicide after his angry departure by throwing herself from a window. Attended by Doctor
Courrèges, whose piously Catholic wife tries to dissuade him from
going to the aid of "that woman," Maria, in a delirious and semicon-
scious state, conjures up the vision of herself and others like her who
are lost "in the desert of love." With this vision she touches on the
deep theological content of the work as she reveals her anguish at

never having been able to satisfy her deepest feelings of love with any earthly object. In this state she aspires, she says, to "not loves but a single one . . . of a being we can reach, possess but never in the flesh—by whom we are to be possessed."[12] In short, she expresses the Augustinian/Pascalian view that regards all earthly love as a mere shadow of a higher reality, the love of God for creatures.

In their association with one another, all three characters thus fall into this "desert of love," since the satisfaction of physical desire that each holds for the other has its roots to a great extent in sexual desire. There can be, in this configuration at least, no satisfactory fulfillment. The doctor lives out his sterile, loveless life to the end, still unable to divest himself of the foolish hope that some kind of physical love might have been possible between him and Maria. The son never forgets the humiliation and plays it out sadistically in the seduction of women. Maria eventually becomes the wife of the man whose mistress she was. Now a banal, married woman, she exists far below the exalted state of understanding during her "epiphany."

As Conor Cruise O'Brien has pointed out, Maria is the "cross of flesh" on which both father and son have been crucified in their quest for love; she has at the same time, through the prompting of grace in her life, been the vessel of another kind of love that is eternal. At the novel's end both father and son seem still to be imprisoned in this desert. The father will soon die, never having been emotionally fulfilled, and Raymond will continue to act out that sterile mime of seduction. Hence neither will attain solace unless he turns to that being waiting in the wings whom the author describes as "He Who unknown to them calls from the deepest part of their being to draw them from this burning tide" (*Le Désert*, 243). Whether they have escaped from the desert or prison of human passions through response to supernatural grace is thus left unanswered.

Thérèse Desqueyroux is the first of a four-part cycle of works dedicated to Mauriac's most famous literary characterization, Thérèse. This character seems to have been inspired to him by the real-life situation of a woman in the Bordeaux region who, in a trial achieving considerable notoriety, had been convicted of poisoning her husband. In the foreword to the novel Mauriac alludes to his character as potentially a modern Saint Locusta (a notorious poisoner living during the reign of Nero who repented her sins and became a saint). But he would decline, he states, to depict Thérèse in a redeemed state because of the outrage that this would cause among his readers, who, accepting the Fall and its consequences "in our torn and twisted natures," would nevertheless raise a cry

of "sacrilege."[13] The famous quotation from Baudelaire in the preface—
a prayer invoking God's pity for the mad and monstrous among human
beings (since He as their Creator alone understands their nature)—prepares the way for the novel's disturbing characterization of a great sinner
who might also be regarded as having similar potential to become a
saint.

In its most simple terms the novel represents another portrayal (and
perhaps the darkest) of the failed marriages of convenience contracted by
the prominent middle-class families of Bordeaux. In this case Thérèse
marries Bernard Desqueyroux, brother of her childhood friend Anne, in
a carefully negotiated match. She herself is in fact far from indifferent to
the economic advantages of the project, and with a peasantlike love of
the land, she rejoices at the acquisition of more than 2,000 acres of pine
forest that her family gains through this union.

From the start, however, the marriage proves to be an unmitigated disaster for her. This young, intelligent, sensitive woman finds herself
trapped and suffocating in the narrow confines of bourgeois life and conventions that make up her husband's household. (The novel uses many
images of confinement, both man-made and natural, to indicate Thérèse's
essential condition as prisoner of bourgeois complacency and cruelty.) Her
placid husband gradually reveals vulgarity, egotism, and brutality (especially in lovemaking) that soon make Thérèse tragically aware that she
never knew what kind of person he was before the marriage, nor did he
know her. Of radically different temperaments and interests, they are
therefore trapped in what becomes for her an unbearable situation. As a
woman in a traditional provincial household, she has none of the outlets
of escape granted to men (she cannot, for example, go hunting as her husband does, following his only passion). Nor can she as a woman develop
her considerable intellectual and artistic talents on the outside.
Motherhood (the birth of a daughter) leaves her strangely unfulfilled; in
fact, she is regarded by the family as a *"mère dénaturée"* ("an unnatural
mother") because of the indifference she shows to being with and providing care for her child. Totally alienated from the family circle and consumed by a despairing ennui, she soon comes to the very edge of a
physical and mental breakdown and seriously contemplates suicide.

At this point she is led to fill the emptiness of her life with a project
that is Baudelairean in its fervent inclination toward the "postulation to
evil": the slow, systematic poisoning of her husband with doses of arsenic
added to a prescribed drug. This would constitute an attempt to overcome her ennui with something new, and she later admits that she per-

formed the crime principally to see the dull, complacent features of her husband "light up with a flicker of anxiety" or with some other authentically *human* emotion (*Thérèse*, 110).

When her attempted murder is detected by the family, for reasons of its reputation the members do not bring formal charges against her. Instead, she is consigned to a life sentence of seclusion by them, and on her return from the trial she has to live in total isolation (she is locked in her room, must take meals by herself, is deprived of the cigarettes to which she is addicted, and, aside from the appearance-saving attendance at Mass each Sunday with her husband, is abandoned).

Embarrassed by her physical decline and haggard appearance (when friends of the family arrive unexpectedly to visit), her relatives are forced to relax her "life sentence" and finally agree to allow her to take up another existence in Paris with the conditions that she give up her daughter and never again live in Bordeaux. In the final pages of the work, Thérèse, recently delivered from the prison of the family cell, is seen seated alone at a sidewalk café in the capital; here she ruminates over the overwhelming possibilities for a new life: "It is not the bricks and mortar I love, not even the lectures and museums, but the living human forest that fills the streets, the creatures torn by passions more violent than any storm" (*Thérèse*, 115).

Not mediocre like the pharisaical members of the family that conspired to destroy her, Thérèse is a sinner—and perhaps a great one—by her mystical attraction to evil as a means to transcend her suffocating existence. Through her grand, passionate nature she is also potentially a saint because she risks all and dares go to the very limits of her being in striving to attain an absolute. The biblical expression "The violent bear it [salvation] away" is perhaps a most appropriate citation to describe her potential for redemption, if not sanctity. And Péguy's "sinner at the center of Christianity" is, of course, also axiomatic to her state. Yet whether she will accept the grace that seems to lie just beyond her visible reach is another question and one Mauriac again leaves moot.

The Viper's Tangle, the first novel Mauriac wrote after his spiritual crisis of the 1920s, reveals that he had taken to heart the charges of having perhaps relied excessively in these earlier novels on plot situations that were morally perverse (especially in regard to their treatment of sexual matters) and that the works themselves had been painted in a too dark and pessimistic light. In this later novel he chose as the ruling passion acquisitiveness (and by extension the sinful desire to dominate and control others through one's possessions), and though the essential struggle between grace and natural depravity remains, there is now far more emphasis on the individual's free choice in resolving the struggle. And more significant is the fact that the novel is the first in which Mauriac would depict the actual triumph of grace revealed in the conversion of a life, even if this occurs at death's door. The novel is also a far more ample social commentary, and in it Mauriac provides his most extensive and biting portrayal of the degenerate and pharisaical state of Catholicism as practiced by the bourgeoisie.

The novel is written in the form of an epistolary journal by a miserly and extremely wealthy old man, Louis, who lives alone in his country estate. Sitting in his bedroom, a semi-invalid with a serious heart condition, he passes his time writing a letter to his wife, Isa, in which he gleefully declares his intentions to disinherit his children. Meant to accompany his will (to be sent after his death), the letter becomes an extended journal in which he pours out the bitterness in his heart and charts the reasons for and progress of his 40-year estrangement from his wife and family.

In the letter/journal Louis reveals himself to be essentially an outsider in his family circle. In spiteful tones he records what he sees as the humiliated and loveless existence that he has led at the hands of the powerful Fondaudège family, with whom he became involved through his marriage to Isa. This ruling family of the Bordeaux bourgeoisie had tolerated him as son-in-law only because of the enormous wealth that his peasant mother had amassed in forest property and vineyards, but they would always view him as socially unacceptable. Having been forced to live an unhappy childhood climbing the social ladder and preparing for a legal career, Louis had never known a happy existence until he met Isa. For a brief time (during courtship to the first weeks of marriage) he experienced the intense happiness of being in love and assumed that his wife felt as strongly as he did. One night as she lay in his arms, however, she imprudently recounts in nostalgic terms her memories of a handsome young man of her "own" class whom she had very much loved and wanted to marry. Because it was rumored that individuals in his family had died of tuberculosis (thus making him unreliable in providing the necessary progeny) the family had ruled him out. Isa, as Louis now understood it, had thus taken him as a regrettable necessary choice (for though socially prominent, the Fondaudèges were short on money). He was therefore not beloved by her but simply represented a kind of economic destiny.

From this early point on, Louis's role in the family was one of confrontation as he resisted his wife's attempts to make him submissive to her own creeds and beliefs. Naturally freethinking and agnostic, he resisted any attempts to support or be assimilated into the faith to which the family gave lip service. Hence there began an intense duel between Isa and Louis for the affection and loyalty of their five children. In this rivalry Isa held the upper hand and constantly screened and protected her children from the negative influences of her nonbelieving spouse. Louis is perceptive enough to realize that by controlling the affections of her children Isa was in fact punishing him for his refusal to be integrated into the belief structure and mores of her all-powerful family, even though he genuinely was not disposed to believe. Yet for his wife, control of the children (and not belief) would seem to have been the essential issue in this duel of wills. Louis, however, very craftily pays her back in kind. Extremely wealthy through his legal practice and astute investments on the Bourse, he nevertheless gives his wife and family only minimum support and keeps them dependent on his largesse. For since they have denied him love, so he will refuse them what he possesses in abundance: money. Indignant at his withholding what they consider to be their just due, the children (but not his wife) live with ill-concealed resentment as they impatiently await his death and the possession of their inheritance.

Such is the unhappy state of affairs and disposition of the old man in the early stages of the journal. The introspective effort required in its writing, however, gradually opens him to a greater level of understanding about his state of mind and spiritual condition. Though he would like to continue to feel sorry for himself by thinking he has been unloved throughout his life, he is forced to concede that this is not true. Two members of his family, had, in fact loved him very much. The first was his youngest daughter, Marie, who had died in childhood. Despite her mother's attempts to wean her away from him, he recalls how she had clung to him and prayed for his conversion. In fact at the moment of her death she had expressed the wish "to die for Papa," and this gift of the self for another (the theme of substitution or reversibility) is skillfully presented in the text as a dominant force effecting Louis's eventual conversion. Whenever he thinks of the child he is deeply moved, and he recognizes and regrets his own hardness of heart. Marie creates a kind of magnetic field through grace applied to his salvation, which allows him to distance himself from his hateful and vengeful attitudes. Another member of the family, his nephew Luc, who possesses a kind of natural goodness and is untouched by the calculating, self-interested motivations of the family, also sees a different side of his uncle and sincerely loves him for what he sees as the latter's propensity to give unselfishly and to love unconditionally (traits he alone seems to elicit in Louis's otherwise hardened nature). When Luc is killed in the war, the old man grieves inconsolably as if for his own son.

Louis's progress from hatred to love also mirrors a major change in perspective that Mauriac brilliantly forces the reader to adopt. The theme of the "viper's tangle" is, for at least the first half of the novel, symbolic of the deplorable condition of Louis's heart, clogged and filled with mindless hatred against others whom he lumps together as the cause of his unhappiness. Louis, of course, views the "vipers" as the members of his family and does not acknowledge his own bitter, spiteful state. When his wife suddenly dies, the scales fall from eyes and he is suddenly aware that he has lived for all the wrong reasons, that he has never really loved material possessions but has simply grasped on to them as means to dominate and torture those whom he detests. He is able to deliver himself of hatred, and here the term "viper's tangle" becomes inextricably associated with the members of the family itself. Throughout the years, while giving pious lip service to their faith, they have denied their father their love and thought only of their material possessions. Louis realizes that his own hatred for Catholicism and the way Catholics practiced their faith had been based on the fundamental misconception that the way his family had practiced religion had anything to do with the authentic version. He had actually, he now realizes, "loathed and detested the caricature and mean interpretation of the Christian life which I had deliberately chosen to regard as the essence of the religious mind, in order that I might feel free to hate it" (*Viper's Tangle*, 198). In comparison to his family, the so-called pagan freethinker seems in hindsight always to have possessed a far more acute and genuine religious sense (in his quest for love and fulfillment) than most members of his "pious Catholic" family, whose hostage in hateful disbelief he had long been.

In the very little time that is left to him, Louis begins to live unfettered by worldly possessions. He divests himself completely of all but the necessary means to live in his country house by allowing his frantic children to tap into their vast inheritance before he dies. Their venality and continuing uncaring attitude toward him now justifies the transference of the "viper" metaphor to the family cell. Mired in their own materialism, they are unable to imagine that a their father could have been touched by a spiritual experience or a change of heart.

Louis takes under his wing a granddaughter, Janine, whose abandonment by her wayward husband had placed her in family disgrace. She lives with him in his estate and receives from him attentive care and even spiritual counsel to allow her to face up to her situation. He is mindful now of having the chance to transfer to Janine the love and devotion that his daughter Marie had bestowed on him. Also, he strongly feels the all-pervasive presence of Marie during these last days when he undergoes a definitive conversion of heart. Shortly after receiving the sacraments one morning he dies while writing in his journal and being overcome, as he puts it, with "a Love whose name at last I know, whose ador . . ." (*Viper's Tangle*, 199). And it is left to the reader to decipher this unfinished declaration of love.

In reading the journal after Louis's death, the family members are convinced that these pages offer evidence that the unpleasant old man was really insane in his last moments. Janine alone understands the reality of her grandfather's conversion and response to grace and the fact that, as she informs them, "a great light shone upon him during the last days of his life." And she herself is awakened now to the perverse kind of religion practiced in the family circle. She says of the members, "Where our treasure was, there were our hearts also. We thought of nothing but the threat to our inheritance. . . . All our strength was employed in keeping our eyes fixed on material things, while Grandpa . . . where his treasure was, there his heart was not" (*Viper's Tangle*, 208).

The novel represents Mauriac's greatest achievement in re-creating the way of grace in a soul. As he has said of the magnitude of such a task, "Nothing is more elusive in human life than the finger of God. It is not that it is not visible, but its imprint is so delicate that it disappears as soon as we try to capture it. God is inimitable, and He escapes the novelist's grasp" (*God and Mammon*, 80). Though the actual moment and manner of "imprint" is veiled, the metamorphosis of the hardened, bitter sinner Louis is depicted as he transcends his grasping acquisitive self to turn to a love that totally defines and fulfills his deepest desires. God works here within the limits of human freedom to accept or reject grace, and Louis, at the cost of an enormous struggle against the self, becomes the "beautiful character" that he potentially always has been and taps the secret source of sanctity hidden almost to the very last. In the dozen or so novels that he would write after *Viper's Tangle*, Mauriac never surpasses in depth or artistry this account of a soul's being overcome by

Divine grace; nor did he ever create a more psychologically convincing character than that of Louis. And for these reasons (as well as those articulated by David Lodge) the novel remains the quintessential Catholic novel written during the genre's so-called Golden Age.

Julien Green

Born one generation after Bernanos and Waugh of American parents, Julien Green is today one of France's foremost novelists and the first American ever to be elected to the French Academy. (Jacques Maritain wrote of him several decades ago, "I find it marvelous that an American should be the greatest French writer of our times" [quoted in Dunaway, 15].) A prolific writer (and still writing today at a very advanced age), he had attained a certain recognition as novelist in the United States during the 1950s. Since then, though his works continue to be enthusiastically received by a small but fervent group of Francophile Catholics, earlier translations of his novels into English have long gone out of circulation and are virtually unavailable for the larger reading audience. He has, however, recently become the subject of renewed critical attention in this country through the publication of what he calls his "Civil War novels." The first of these, *Les Pays lointains* (1991; *The Distant Lands*), has in fact been compared favorably in plot, length, and scope with *Gone with the Wind*, which is not surprising given Green's roots in the American South.

Julien Green was born in 1900 in Paris of parents from the state of Georgia who had immigrated to Europe. His father was an official of the Southern Cotton Company, and his mother was a fiercely proud "daughter of the South." Both wished to escape the social depression of the postbellum period. They chose France instead of Germany as their country of residence because it too had been conquered by an oppressive neighbor in 1870, and its citizens would therefore, they believed, "understand the Southerner." Green was a product, then, of two cultures—that of the antebellum South, to which he has always remained intensely loyal, and that of Parisian society, which he adopted as his own and in which he completely immersed himself both intellectually and culturally. He attended French schools exclusively up through the *lycée* and only went to America for the first time as a student (to the University of Virginia) in 1919. Though he would later spend long periods in the States (and would live there during the Occupation of Paris), he is essentially French, has written his voluminous works in that language, and has always revealed a close affinity with French literary models and intellectual modes of thought.

Green was the last of eight children and the only male. From the start his father, a hard-working businessman, seems to have played a very minor role in the child's formation. On the surface a happy child, Green was in reality very lonely and was brought up in a strict Calvinist family environment. His pious Protestant mother, obviously a victim of religious scruples, inculcated in him a horror of the body—of its natural functions and of sex in general—that would mark him for life. His mother's death when he was only 14 devastated him, and he seemingly never recovered emotionally from the loss.

Two years after this tragedy Julien Green converted to Catholicism. He would later explain that this step had long been prepared for through his earliest religious education (and through such practices as the family reading of the Bible). Catholicism also offered him a means to confront the moral crisis that, he relates, was tearing him apart during this period of his life. Some years later he identified the cause of this turmoil as the "problem of the two realities"—the spiritual and the carnal—and referred it to his personal life as follows: "Am I to be their [these two entities'] battleground to the end of my life? So that is to be my fate, the fate I so often speculated about in my thirtieth year; the particular question that will have been asked of me in this world and that I will have to answer. But in what way do these difficulties differ from those of all human beings? In a great many ways each of us is a special case."[14]

As perceived throughout his writings (and especially in his journal and autobiographies), Green's life from adolescence to old age can be essentially resumed in terms of this moral struggle. As a young convert to Catholicism, he cultivated an intense spiritual life and for a time felt strongly called to a religious vocation as a monk. He records in his journal that at the age of 19, at a very specific moment and for reasons that he could not at the time fully understand, he rejected this call, and the "great refusal," as he refers to this more or less unconscious decision, led immediately to the lifting "of the weight of the Cross."[15] It also prompted him, however, to give vent to a special proclivity he felt to be an essential part of his nature—one that his religious fervor had hitherto forced him to deny.

This special dimension, exhaustively reflected on and explored throughout his journal and autobiographies (and with more distance in his novels), is the moral battle he was to wage against his strong homosexual drives. Through his own admittedly troubled nature, Julien Green becomes in fact the witness to the world of the supernatural and to the warring realities of the flesh and the spirit (as he views the ultimate spiritual situation of every human soul). As a latent homosexual who considered his sexual orientation at the least problematic and at worst sinful, his moral drama as a Catholic came to be that of giving in or not to his nature, and to those physical desires that, if gratified, threatened his eternal salvation. Hence feeling himself to be a pariah (whether or not he would decide to reveal his special makeup), Green as a homosexual would also in his moral solitude become more acutely aware of the universal conflict (between the carnal and spiritual) being waged as well in the souls of the "normal" members of society. As a result, his literature is not limited to a study of his own particular moral situation but dramatizes the universal manifestations of the "two realities" as they affect all human existence, vision, and situation.

In his journal Green early emphasized how important these two warring realities were in the drama of his spiritual life. "There have always been," he says, "two types of men I could really understand—the mystic and the debauchee, because each in his own way flies to extremes and seeks the absolute" (quoted in Burne, 135). As to the presence of sin in human life, Green is convinced of its inevitability in every person. For even as humans yearn naturally for God, "it inevitably happens that the aspiration to the good is simultaneously accompanied by a raging flood of carnal desires" (*Diary*, 106). Yet Green believes that a certain benefit possibly accrues from sins committed, and he tells us that he once even suggested to his spiritual director that "sin gives an experience of life that can be turned to immense advantage, spiritual advantage; that sin educates the individual, is a sort of school where he learns to know humanity; that God allows souls that have lived in sin to escape from and then grow closer to humanity than souls that have never lost their innocence" (*Diary*, 155). And despite the universal sinfulness of human beings, he strongly believes that God's presence and redemptive love are never absent: "Money, sensual pleasure, ambition, success, kill in us all feeling of the mystery that surrounds us from birth to death; yet there arises in every soul an inner voice echoing the words 'You are mine, I shall never let you go'" (*Diary*, 135).

For Green the artist, writing novels is nothing more or less than an extension of life seen as the drama (and risk) of salvation. A real novelist, he believes, creates a relationship of connivance between himself and his characters. And if the characters sin, "he [the novelist] sins too, in a certain way." If his work is to be artistically successful the novelist must also be "caught" in the spell that his book exerts on him, and Green says that "if he [the novelist] is not under the spell cast by the monstrous thing that issues from his brain—for a novel is a monster—he no longer writes novels, he manufactures them." And if the novel is indeed "monstrous," Green is led to ask if "the fact of writing a novel is consistent with the state of grace." He declines the question presumably because he is afraid of the answer, but he is sure that for all these reasons a saint would not write a novel nor a "scrupulous man . . . a great novel." Yet he ultimately believes that perhaps, despite the risk to salvation involved, the role of the writer may be the means of fulfilling a vocation that, though perilous, can be acceptable to God (*Diary*, 158).

As to how he views his novels in relation to his faith, Green has always refused, even bristled, at his possible designation as a Catholic novelist ("The very idea," he says, "appalls me" [*Diary*, 219]). Yet when he considers Jacques Maritain's judgment "that my books were those of a man living on the mystical plane," he concedes that "there lies in all my books a deep uneasiness that an irreligious man would never have felt." And he admits that all of his fiction, though written not to advance or support religious dogma, is nonetheless "essentially religious." And in the most succinct definition he will give of what he means by this appellation, he writes, "The anguish and loneliness of my characters can almost always be reduced to what I think I called a manifold dread of living in the world" (*Diary*, 219).

The spiritual odyssey Green has made since his early conversion is indeed rather convoluted and complex. We learn from his journal and autobiographies that he underwent at least three distinct "stages": first, the conversion to Catholicism and a period of fervent adherence to and practice of his faith; then a falling away in the 1930s during which time he immersed himself in a study of Eastern religions and philosophical systems; and, finally, a "reconversion" to Catholicism in the 1940s—a state in which he still finds himself despite his less than enthusiastic reception of the new spirit and changes enacted within the Church by the provisions of the Second Vatican Council.

From Green's early Catholic period are several "dark" novels—*Mont-Cinère* (1926), *Adrienne Mesurat* (1927), and *Le Voyageur sur la terre* (1927). Then there are several novels of "fantasy" and "magical realism" (as critics have characterized them) that he wrote during his years outside the Church—*Le Visionnaire* (1932), *Minuit* (1936), and *Varouna* (1940). Finally, there are three more specifically Catholic novels written during his return to the Church—*Moïra* (1950); *Le Malfaiteur* (1955), of which he composed a first version in 1937; and *Chaque homme dans sa nuit* (1960). As I have noted, from the beginning of his career as novelist Green has been reluctant to invest his novels with specifically Catholic themes or theological/sacramental elements. He once related to Gide that being labeled a Catholic writer would personally fill him with horror and would even "cheapen religion" (*Diary*, 6). And only *Chaque homme dans sa nuit* uses Catholic dogma or sacramental forms in any significant way as important components in the plot. In the place of these Green's novels almost without exception have as the central theme the need to escape from the prison of the day-to-day. And like Gide, Bernanos, Mauriac, Malraux, Sartre, and Camus, Green pits his individuals against rigid systems of conformism imposed by a bourgeois society that he depicts as dominated by bigots, hypocrites, scheming predators, and the spiritually dead. He peoples his fictional universe with only a few authentically good people and, against this stifling, dehumanized mass, his emotionally troubled protagonists are forced to find some way of transcending or overcoming the sordid reality of the here and now. Whether authentic or false, the means that his characters use are numerous and include such psychological escape hatches as hallucinations, dreams, madness, sexual obsession, violent crimes and transgressions, and (in the novels after 1950) grace, repentance, and reconciliation with God.

Green gives the best example of his psychological universe in his early novels, especially *Adrienne Mesurat*, which earned him serious recognition. Here he depicts the closed universe of a young woman living in a provincial household as suffocating and stifling as any depicted by Mauriac. Consumed by boredom, emotionally starved for affection of any sort, and without any meaningful social or sentimental outlets, Adrienne is also a strong-minded young woman who struggles to overcome her solitude (or, more precisely, her state of spiritual desolation). When from her window she sees the newly arrived medical doctor of the village pass by in his carriage, she experiences a violent *coup de foudre*, imagines herself deeply in love, and nourishes this attachment with her imagination. Through increasingly wild, even grotesque, efforts to attract his attention and make him aware of her feelings, she gradually causes herself to be virtually ostracized from the "good" society of the small town. The doctor turns out to be a plain, sickly bachelor with absolutely no intention of marriage and with not much time to live. Yet through a process of crystallization she transforms him into a romantic "agent of salvation."

Predictably, when Adrienne finally makes him aware of her feeling, he retreats in horror. The broken young woman now falls into a troubled state of near insanity, which has threatened her from the beginning. Before her definitive breakdown (which occurs soon after the doctor's rejection) she had made a wild and sudden flight to another town where she spent the night in lonely hotel room, overcome with anguish, even terror, culminating in nightmares and hallucinations. This experience puts an end to any kind of ordinary existence for her, and henceforth she sees her life in ever more threatening and sinister terms and her destiny as being inexorably worked out under some nefarious power. As the novel ends she is viewed wandering in a state of mental collapse through the dark streets of the town whose inhabitants, for the most part, are unsympathetic and who even maliciously mock her pathological state. The novel is a psychologically brilliant tour de force in its gradual and relentless development of a "ring of fear" that closes in on the woman as she sinks into a "profound night" of madness. Her world of obsession and darkness, described in almost unbearably clear, psychological detail (there is no trace of local color or concrete, realist descriptions of persons or things), is given a palpable and disturbing reality reminiscent of Kafka's anguished universe.

Like *Adrienne Mesurat*, the other novels of Green's first and second cycles of production, as they may be called, contain very few traces of religious themes or solutions. And if they have a religious content, this would be the unmitigated darkness of sin in a fallen world that a pharisaical society worsens through its distortion of Christian virtues. But, as Green suggests, these works may be viewed as having an implicit religious core through their admirable depiction of the "manifold dread of living in the world."

In several novels written after 1950 Green does, however, go significantly beyond the theme of this dark angst common to the human condition by presenting concrete moral dilemmas of a certain kind and within a religious context. In these works he introduces protagonists reminiscent of or who even mirror Green's spiritual struggle and anguished past. These young males, tormented by their strong sexual drives, yearn for an inner purity and regained innocence that seems lost or out of their reach. The reader is tempted to see in their struggles Green's tortuous coming to grips with his homosexuality and the obstacles his sexual orientation placed before the practice of his religious beliefs.

With *Le Malfaiteur* Green plunges the reader into the hellish existence of the homosexual and the tragic situation his sexual orientation creates for him. Green began the work during his thirties, in perhaps the darkest period of his life. Having turned from the protection of his faith, he was living the double life portrayed by his protagonist: by day the intellectual writing his fiction and journal, by night the adventurous wanderer exploring the clandestine *bas fond* of the homosexual world of Paris and the provinces. The novel was not completed until two decades later.

In the preface to the novel Green states that he wrote *Le Malfaiteur* to understand "the tragedy of impossible love, as a woman could conceive of it."[16] In fact, the novel relates the fate of two principal characters: the first the aging Jean Rollet, whose "confessions of an invert" comprise the greater part of the plot, and the second the young woman Hedwige, to whom Rollet addresses the most intimate and lurid disclosures of his secret life in the form of a letter. Hedwige is involved in an "impossible love" with a third character, the perverse Gaston Dolange, a young prostitute and homosexual of whom Rollet is desperately enamored and whose sexual favors he must purchase. Unaware of Dolange's true nature, Hedwige throughout most of the work clings to the hope of interesting the young man who, of course, could never respond to her passion with authentic love. Out of sympathy for Hedwige, Rollet tries to disabuse her of her affection for the latter by exposing him for the cad that he is. The triangular relationship among the three is thus the matter of the plot.

The novel, essentially a bildungsroman, recounts the education and experience of the homosexual, first viewed at the critical stage of adolescence when he becomes acutely aware of his special makeup and has to deal with the shattering spiritual crisis that this provokes in the soul of a fervently religious youth. The novel then goes on to depict the hidden life that the homosexual, as pariah, must construct if he is to conceal his true nature from the "straight" society in which he lives. The world of the "normal"—here middle-class Parisian society—is characterized as cold, hypocritical, self-righteous, and heartless. Only two of its members are sympathetically presented: M. Vasseur, Jean's provider (who adopts him as a boy and in whose household he now lives), a good, religious man who is unappreciated because of his simplicity; and the innocent and compassionate Hedwige, herself an orphan and also a member of M. Vasseur's family.

We learn about Jean's life through the letter (really a full-blown auto-biography) he writes to Hedwige for the purpose of revealing the truth about Dolange, whom she loves obsessively and who, through a sinister kind of charm, preys with great success on victims of his affection like Jean and this young woman. In the context of the letter Jean depicts in the most realistic terms his own coming to grips with his homosexual condition, his departure as a young man from the protective confines of religious belief, and his dizzying descent into the hellish world of nightly homosexual cruising. Seldom if ever in fiction written up to this time have the forays of the sexually driven homosexual been as graphically described as they are in this work. And what proves especially interesting is Green's attempt to illustrate these experiences from the points of view of the different age groups involved in this traffic. In fact, the first man who approaches Jean at the beginning of his nocturnal adventures is M. Paris, his tutor when he was a young boy. Discharged from his functions by Jean's father who suspected his homosexuality, this now pitiful and aging man relates in the most pained and disillusioned terms the kind of life that has been his (and, of course, he prophetically points to what Jean's will also be like when he too arrives at this later stage in life): "I've run after pleasures. You cannot know what these words conceal. To pursue pleasure, the sadness of these endless avenues the length of which we wander all night long, for years and years, the disappointments, the dangers, the loneliness. Put all these avenues of world end to end, and they lead to hell, yes, they make you believe in hell" (*Le Malfaiteur*, 164).

After years of successful encounters while he is physically attractive, Jean indeed comes to the same despairing condition as his mentor, M. Paris. He does not, however, succumb to this tragic decline without strenuously trying to take himself out of this life-style, and in the most psychologically compelling part of the novel, when he struggles most fiercely against his nature, Jean "sees" himself as cut into two warring personas: the first, his spiritual part trying mightily to divorce itself from the tyranny of sexual habits, and the other, the lustful fleshly component of the self hanging on tooth and nail to these erotic pleasures. Of this condition he writes, "This being cut into two parts didn't occur without pain. On one hand a sort of automaton continued to make the gestures and speak the words that habit had taught him; on the other, a mere powerless spectator assisted at these games which now were nothing more than a caricature of happiness" (*Le Malfaiteur*, 195).

Unable to deliver himself from his obsessions and more and more the target of investigation by the Paris police, he flees to Naples and, despairing there of changing his life, commits suicide, though not before his letter has been read by Hedwige. Too innocent to fully understand the kind of perverted life of which Jean writes and still not finally convinced by this testimony of the shallowness and duplicity of Gaston Dolange, she cannot move beyond her obsession. After unmistakable evidence of Dolange's callous disregard for her, she too takes her own life.

Despite their tragic ends, the lives of Hedwige and Jean have, however, been touched by a religious presence and a force akin to grace. Twice in her dreams Hedwige sees a man so humbly dressed that she takes him to be a beggar, and in a dreamlike dialogue that she imagines with the stranger, he asks that she dispossess herself of her favorite things, "her clothing, the modest jewels of this young provincial woman." She finds deep within herself the desire to give more and more, eventually all and thus became completely happy for the first time in her life, "as if an enormous weight was slipping from her shoulders and she hesitated on her feet like an infant who had not yet learned to stand on its feet" (*Le Malfaiteur*, 76). Green discloses in his preface that the unknown stranger is, of course, Christ, but she does not seem to know this. Jean, too, when wracked with despair, is momentarily overcome with the desire to repent for his sins: his faith, however, is inadequate, and he says, "If I had a stronger, more living belief, I would certainly go to confession" (*Le Malfaiteur*, 241). He is, however, still imprisoned by sexual desire, and, much like a character from one of Mauriac's novels, he cannot emerge from his "desert of love." Both Hedwige and Jean seem ultimately to be unable to fight against a certain Jansenistic fatality—she by her temperament and he by his nature.

Moïra, Green's classic study of sexual repression, is also far and away his most popular and best known work with American readers. The action takes place at the University of Virginia, and the novel is to a certain extent autobiographical, fed as it was by Green's memories of his student days there (from 1919 to 1921). The protagonist, Joseph Day, is this time a young, robust, and fanatically religious student from the Virginia hills. He arrives at this sophisticated center of learning armed with a fundamentalist background so restrictive and puritanical that it seems almost a caricature. Though naturally intelligent and sensitive, he is totally unable to deal with the secular and humanistic approach to learning that is in vogue. He cannot, for example, accept as anything but morally depraved the foibles of human nature made explicit in

Shakespeare and in the Greco-Roman classics that he reads in his courses. For him, these literary works are strong temptations to sin through their explicit depiction of vice. He is, of course, a virgin yet at the same time a very passionate, lusty youth whose red hair and powerful physique ill conceal (or not at all) his ardent nature.

Torn between his deep-seated passions and puritanical restraints, he is to himself a living contradiction and a disturbing influence for those whom he encounters, particularly in his harsh denunciations of the free and easy life-style of the students with whom he lives. Unsure as well of his sexual orientation, he seems only vaguely aware, for example, of the motives for the strong, even violent, reactions he feels automatically in the presence of a fellow student, the elegant and sophisticated Bruce Praileau. These he attempts to overcome at one point by almost suffocating the other youth in a wrestling match turned violent. Praileau, aware, it would seem, of the real nature of the violent reaction he elicits with Joseph, is not explicit; he only calls his adversary an assassin and will refuse to have anything more to do with him. Another student, Simon, becomes enamored of Joseph. Filled with guilt and despair at this attraction, he commits suicide without, it would seem, Joseph's being conscious at the time of the unfortunate youth's passion for him.

Because Joseph is so different from the other students in rejecting sex of any kind (he even strongly professes to disdain the natural interests in sexuality common to them), his fellow students soon come to regard him as a paragon who must be brought down to their level. In effecting what becomes a project they enlist the aid of Moïra, a young woman known on the campus for her sexually relaxed morals. She is the daughter of Joseph's landlady and he has even slept in her bed on one occasion when she was away and when the boardinghouse was overcrowded. Grossly depicted as dressed in scarlet, with her mouth "red as an open wound," she is, as her name suggests, the sexual fate against which Joseph's puritanical innocence and resolve will be helpless. She agrees to go along with the "prank of the students" and is voluptuously present in his room one evening when he returns from class. Her resolve to seduce him lessens, however, the more she talks with him, and, touched by his naïveté and natural modesty, she decides not to continue the game and to leave him in peace. Joseph, however, becomes powerfully aroused by her physical presence in his room and seduces (or rather sexually assaults) her before she is able to leave. After a night of sex he awakens to see Moïra asleep at his side. Filled with guilt and overwhelmed with the desire to destroy the "cause" of his fall from grace, he kills her, buries her body, and flees from the town as a fugitive. His conscience will not, however, allow him to abandon the scene of the crime; he returns and reconciles himself with Praileau, who has arrived on the scene to help him escape. Joseph now understands the true nature of his feelings for the latter and, before his apprehension by the law, sends him as a final message the words "It was not possible." He clearly repents his terrible crime and refuses any longer to escape apprehension and punishment, which, the narrator states, "were part of his destiny."[17]

Green presents Joseph Day as a sinner who no longer hopes for salvation and accepts eternal damnation for his act. But he also strongly suggests that Joseph is not totally guilty or responsible because he is the victim of a pernicious religious formation. Moreover, he has been infected with one of the worst elements of this kind of religion—a form of angelism that taught him to despise his body and reject the reality and needs of his physical nature. To what extent, then, is his obsession for Moïra of his making and can he in these circumstances be seen as having given any real moral consent to this killing of another human being? Green, of course, provides no clear response to this moral conundrum, and at the novel's end the reader is left in the same moral limbo about the guilt and salvation of the protagonist as often is the case in a work of Mauriac or Graham Greene.

Green completes his trilogy of religious novels with one that is clearly Catholic in its reference to and use of religious symbols and doctrine. In *Chaque homme dans sa nuit* the protagonist is a confirmed heterosexual and practicing Catholic (though, it would seem, far from a good one). Wilfred, a lowly shirt salesman in a large department store in a city of the American South (Charleston), leads a life of sexual indulgence in one-night stands with women who find him irresistible. And although he seems to make little attempt to avoid the temptation of seeking out these easy conquests in the seedy bars he frequents, he still clings to the outward practice of his faith (he goes to Mass each Sunday and regularly to confession, knowing that he will inevitably fall again into the same sins). Though he vaguely regrets his being a sinner, he cannot break out of the habits of the flesh, and he certainly cannot resolve the tug of war between the "two principles."

Wilfred's situation changes when he meets Phoebe, the wife of his well-off cousin, James. This intelligent and spirited young woman is not like the other easy prey he is used to meeting, and he develops for her an idealized love that will not allow him even to think of seduction. Her trust and genuine interest in him as a person further disarm him, and he ultimately comes to realize that adultery, for him as a Catholic, is a sin that he must no longer commit. We are therefore to understand that Phoebe has become a spiritual catalyst allowing Wilfred to control, if not transcend, his purely sensual involvements of the past.

Yet even before having met her, Wilfred has had a kind of spiritual influence on people that continually surprises him. People seek him out for religious counsel as if he were a lay priest. His uncle, who eventually leaves him a substantial fortune, confesses to Wilfred on his deathbed as having had the same kind of weaknesses of the flesh that assail his nephew, and the young man is astonished to hear himself take the part of spiritual director and to use the words and authority that only a priest would have on such momentous occasions. Wilfred also baptizes a young friend, Freddie, and plays a major role in the spiritual lives of several others. For example, Tommy, a younger fellow worker in the department store, takes Wilfred for his role model and out of admiration follows the same sensual life-style that he knows to be that of his friend. And much to Wilfred's dismay, though initially a practicing Catholic, Tommy leaves the Church to plunge into a life of dissipation because of what he seems to believe has been Wilfred's tacit encouragement all along. Finally Max, Wilfred's sinister alter ego, tries to tempt him to seduce Phoebe because he foresees the latter's approaching conversion and feels his own involvement with Wilfred threatened by it. A male prostitute strongly attracted to Wilfred, Max regards the latter's spiritual rehabilitation as a palpable indictment of his own debauched life. No longer hoping to change his own fallen state, he will therefore do every thing in his power to keep the object of his affection in a similar degraded condition. A dark presence and kind of fallen angel, Max therefore works actively for the damnation of the souls of others.

These multiple relationships move Wilfred from his state of egotistical pursuit of pleasures to that of thinking of the effect of his own acts on others. He learns painfully that the bad influence he has unconsciously and inadvertently exerted on Tommy proves Dostoyevski's dictum that we are morally responsible before God for everything that we do; that his sins have corrupted the very air Tommy breathed. And he goes beyond the knowledge of this fact to enact a sacrifice of his life for others. Though aware of Max's violent nature and hopeless desire for him, he returns, shortly after refusing the latter's sexual advances, to the male brothel where Max lives, drawn there by an overwhelming desire to comfort him in his despair. Maddened by sexual desire for Wilfred and seemingly compelled to destroy what he cannot possess or control, Max

fatally shoots him. His death seems almost immediately to push Max
toward God, for when Wilfred falls to the floor, Max cries out, "Say you
forgive me. Say yes for the love of Christ." And barely able to respond,
Wilfred murmurs, "Yes."[18]

In addition to this bare plot summary it should be pointed out that
Green's narrator also gives careful attention to the inner life of Wilfred
and to the movement and motivation of conversion he is undergoing.
Again Green uses the device of *dédoublement*, or splitting of the character
in two, here through the creation of two voices. There is first the ordinary voice of Wilfred, the "man of the flesh" and sinner. At pivotal
points during his religious odysseys, this is contested by the voice of his
spiritual part. For example, just after Max has openly propositioned him
for the first time, Wilfred feels compelled by a strange force to enter a
church and to kneel before the Eucharist. Here a voice that seems to be
that of another person and yet emerges from his own lips confronts him
with his guilt and lack of repentance for his sins. Believing all along that
his sins against the flesh were the prime causes for his alienation from
God, he is instead led to a higher plane, to the realization that the greatest of all sins are those against charity: "Suddenly, he thought of Max; he
had lacked charity toward this terribly unhappy person. 'I got angry
with him,' he said, as if he were already talking to someone else. 'I was
lacking in love'" (*Chaque homme*, 371).

Rushing out of the church to return to Max, Wilfred foregoes the
opportunity to confess his sins, as his "voice" had counseled. Green thus
makes Wilfred a sinner-saint in Péguy's mode, who gives up his own salvation for that of others. Writing in his journal shortly after completing
the novel he is explicit on that score: "I have made it clear that the salvation of Wilfred is probable, at the very least. . . . Wilfred had the treasure of faith that he has kept in spite of everything" (quoted in Burne,
133–34).

Chaque homme dans sa nuit is thus the Green novel that presents the
author's most optimistic view of the possibility of salvation. As he tells
us later, he had borrowed his title—translated as *Everyone in His
Darkness*—from a line of Victor Hugo's poetry. For Green, this meant
that "the life of each of us has a direction that escapes us . . . and we nevertheless move in a stifling darkness toward peace" (quoted in Burne,
133–34).

With this novel Green seems to have evolved from the dark,
Jansenistic universe of sin, guilt, and immovable weight of destiny press-

ing down on his characters which is the backdrop of most of his previous fiction. Though he certainly did not then believe that a definitive victory of the spirit over the lower nature was attainable or even possible, Green does not end up in despair. God, he now seems to imply, guides His creatures mysteriously through the unique course that every human life will take, and, as he writes in a journal entry composed just as he completed *Chaque homme dans sa nuit*, "each human being is a path that leads to God." This evolution from the earlier days of dark *"inquiétude"* to a large measure of trusting hope lying at the end of Green's anguished quest seems reflected in the respective fates of the protagonists of the three "Catholic novels"—men who are seen to progress from sinful obsessions, transgressions, and despair to conversion and redemption through the sacrifice of self for others.

Gilbert Cesbron

Cesbron was born a generation after Bernanos, Mauriac, and Green. As such he is a transitional novelist whose work serves as kind of bridge between the classical form of the genre and what the Catholic novel would become in the years after Vatican II. During his life he was a journalist and served for an extended period as production manager for Radio Luxembourg. He became a very popular Catholic novelist and *engagé* writer. In his 15 or so works of fiction he explored the most pressing social issues of the day, ranging from juvenile delinquency, the care given to homeless children in state institutions, the harsh and lonely life of adolescents in the *lycée* system, the sufferings of cancer victims, euthanasia, the issue of torture and violence perpetrated on the suffering victims of the Algerian War, and the plight of, plain, unloved people in a society surfeited with false and erotic standards of human attractiveness and desirability. Not happy, like his predecessors, with the designation of "Catholic novelist," he preferred the title of "witness" before the problems and injustices of contemporary society. As a Christian, Cesbron perceived Christ's presence not in the cosmic sense of Pascal's "hidden God" but as incarnated in all the human beings he encountered in life. "For the witness in the midst of the world," he writes, "the shortest route from his soul to God passes through others." And the witness uses as his most powerful arm in this active involvement human love, without which life is impossible. "As soon as I cease to love," he goes on, "I cease to be."[19] With this imperative of love, he envisaged the role of a Christian as ever a kind of counterweight, in active commitment against all kinds of injustice and suffering inflicted on human beings of every political, religious, social, or racial designation.

His most famous novel, *Les Saints vont en enfer* (1952; *Saints in Hell*), deals with the phenomenon of the worker-priest movement in France in its early phases. The work describes the day-to-day career and involvement of a Father Pierre in one of the wretched working ghettos of Paris. Living in the worker's slum of Sagny, the priest combines the Herculean tasks of full-time factory worker with those of the caring pastor for his very heterogeneous and unorthodox "flock" of poor and exploited workers, believers and nonbelievers, Communists, battered wives and children, prostitutes, sleazy landlords, drug providers, arrogant and sympathetic members of the clergy, and heroic and saintly people, both clergy and lay, who offer up their lives for the well being of those forced to live in terribly disadvantaged circumstances.

Facing impossible odds and a lack of material, Pierre runs the mission with the help of the saintly Madeleine, who devotes her life to this charismatic endeavor. He approaches his task as a human being on exactly the same level as those to whom he ministers. He adopts their impoverished life, speaks their rude and direct language, and participates in their political organizations and syndicates as just another worker. His ministry as a priest has none of the separateness afforded by living in a parish rectory and asserting the clerical power to which the "traditional" priests in the area still cling. And he has neither the time nor the disposition to divide his life neatly into the categories of "active" and "contemplative" but is all things to everyone at any time or place during the day. Yet it is from just this commitment that he deepens his own faith and love. In fact, the longer he is at the mission the more he is struck with how much he has learned spiritually from the workers and the fraternal caring that they naturally give to one another. "They still didn't know the Gospel," he muses at one point, "but already they live it." And of these tragically de-Christianized people he says, "It is we [the priests] who must be converted by them."[20]

With its strong stress on the importance of charismatic openings and the necessity of good works replacing intentions, *Les Saints vont en enfer* is a valuable document in tracing the demise of the spirit of triumphalism in the Catholic Church at this time. Here the goal is to find God in others, not the other way around. Charismatic living and giving, cooperation with all political parties, fraternizing with sinners, standing up to political injustices from every side, and finding the focus of charity not in

the traditional parish structure but literally on the streets all seem har-
bingers of Catholic activism as it develops after Vatican II. The Mass, for
example, while still very important in the novel as the central communal
act to bring all together in mystical union with Christ, is given secondary priority whenever Pierre must help others in trouble: for example, when he rushes from the chapel to save the boy Etienne, almost
beaten to death by his drunken father, or to try to find Jean, his friend
and valued helper, whom he knows to be in a despairing state and whose
suicide he tragically cannot prevent.

In fact, Cesbron mirrors this disparity between the triumphal and
evangelical frames of reference in a dialogue he creates between Pierre
and the cardinal archbishop who, displeased with Pierre's active partici-
pation in political meetings co-sponsored by the Communist party, has
decided to replace him in the mission. Defending the spirit of the enterprise, Pierre describes it to the cardinal as "a fraternity, a form of disin-
terestedness, a growing love. It is the Gospel being lived . . . oh the rest
will come later, Ah Your Excellence, the district is alive." The cardinal
counters with the objection that the workers are lacking in obedience,
that if left alone they would nominate one of their group to be their
ministers (as was the case in the primitive Church): "We are not the
primitive church, the Archbishop said firmly. . . . [W]e are the Roman
Catholic church." Pierre responds, "And apostolic." The cardinal counters, "And Catholic, and apostolic Roman. Our strength resides in unity
and obedience." To which Pierre quickly retorts, "Our strength resides in
Christ; and our only reason for being is to spread his love and example"
(*Les Saints*, 347).

Despite his disaffection with the views of the hierarchy and clerical
power structure, Pierre remains faithful to his church, and when forced
to leave Sagny he chooses to be a worker priest among those who presumably suffer the most—the miners in the northern part of France. For
him, this also constitutes a return to his roots, since it is in this area
where, as the son a miner, he first received the inspiration to follow a
vocation of service to others.

As a sociological study the novel is rich in detail of the mission of the
worker priest and the difficulties entailed in bringing the de-Christianized
working classes back to the Church. Yet the novel also continues the use
of important features of the traditional Catholic novel. It is first a life of a
modern saint who, like Christ, is betrayed by religious authorities, suffers
the agony of Gethsemani, and is crucified on the cross of rejection by his
Church. Cesbron also introduces the theme of miraculous intervention in

an action by Pierre who, in this respect, is reminiscent of Bernanos's rough-hewn saint, Abbé Donnissan (though Cesbron's protagonist is not drawn with the psychological depths of the latter). When the boy Etienne, whom Pierre virtually adopts as a son, is mortally wounded by his drunken father, Pierre prays over the dying boy in the hospital: "Extending his arms he wasn't totally aware of what he was doing. In his hands which no longer belonged to him he took the suffering head of the boy." At this point the youth's breathing changes from a death rale to normal respiration" (*Les Saints*, 288).

The novel also portrays the death of the saintly cardinal archbishop (in real life Cardinal Suhard), who, unlike his bureaucratic successor who sacked Pierre for flirting with unsavory "leftist" groups, warmly supports the worker priest missions and constantly laments over the sad spectacle of his de-Christianized flock. The cardinal resembles a Bernanosian saint when, at the point of death, he is described as having a "prolonged tête-à-tête with the little child that he had been," and when, with his dying breath he asks the Father that "not one of these little ones be lost" (*Les Saints*, 308).

Chapter Three

England: Early Catholic Novelists, Evelyn Waugh, Graham Greene

The Legacy of Manning and Newman

The Catholic novel in England is a product of a radically different background and set of circumstances from those that had existed in France. Nineteenth-century English intellectuals and writers were, first of all, from a dominant Protestant culture, hence they were not engaged, as were their French counterparts, in intense ideological battles for or against the social and religious ideas inherited from the French Revolution. In fact, the general reaction of English thinkers and intellectuals to this cataclysm could well be described as conservative revulsion to the turmoil and destructive consequences that followed in it's wake. Moreover, nineteenth-century British society itself was hardly interested in those issues or ideas forwarded by the writers of the *renouveau catholique* in France. After Oliver Cromwell's insurrection, the British middle class had refined a balance of power struck between monarchy and nobility that would eventually make its members increasingly prosperous and content with the status quo in matters of religion and politics. At the heart of this balance was social adherence to Protestantism and the Church of England as the national institution that both justified and defined this system.

Catholics in England comprised only about 10 percent of the population during the nineteenth century, with most of this number being from poor Irish stock. Less than 3 percent of English Catholics were of the noble families, and this almost total disappearance of the old Catholic families that had existed long before the Tudor rejection of Catholicism was mainly the result of the imposition, during the éighteenth century, of the cruel and restrictive Penal Laws. Aimed at tearing the old families from the social, political, and economic life of the country, these laws forbade Catholics to own property, to vote, and to send their sons to Oxford and Cambridge; nor could any Catholic church exist on English soil, aside from the chapels of the country houses of the gentry or in diplomatic embassies. The few educated Catholics surviving these restrictions (identified as "Dissenters") were schooled on the Continent at the English university in Douai, Belgium, or at French or German universities. They were therefore isolated from the English community and out of step with major British intellectual movements and thought.

Unlike French Catholics who, regardless of their political affiliation, shared a common Catholic heritage, English Catholics were isolated and alienated from their own society. Hence they would react against the Protestant establishment and way life that had developed from what they termed the "Tudor Apostasy." And most English Catholic thinkers focused their criticism on English Protestantism itself, which they viewed as having fostered nationalistic, utilitarian, and religiously indifferent culture that had culminated in what they saw as the ugly and materialistic English society of the industrial revolution. These English Catholics, conversely, saw themselves as very different from their Protestant compatriots. For them, England had separated itself from its authentic heritage—the Catholic faith of its ancestors—and in its place had substituted a despiritualized and grossly materialistic society based on mercantile profit. English Catholicism, as its adherents viewed it, had, on the other hand, developed quite separate and distinct cultural and economic attributes and affinities, and rather than being English in its beliefs and tastes, it was culturally more Italian and medieval (holding Rome to be its spiritual center) and fundamentally opposed to the spirit of the industrial age.[1]

For most of the nineteenth century the Catholic position had the excellent fortune of attracting some exceptionally gifted—even brilliant—writers to forward its ideas. There occurred, in fact, a strong Catholic revival in England in the 1840s, initially sparked by conversions from the Oxford Movement, which included such prominent Anglicans as John Henry Newman, William George Ward, Henry Manning, and Gerard Manley Hopkins. Their ranks were augmented by such cradle Catholics as Hilaire Belloc and Lord Acton and illustrious future converts such as G. K. Chesterton, Ronald Knox, and, eventually, Waugh and Greene.

Manning and Newman, converts of the 1840s, were both priests who eventually became cardinals. Each adopted very different positions regarding the forms that they believed Catholicism should assume in England. Newman, perhaps the most brilliant Catholic theologian of his century, essentially converted from Anglicanism (in which creed he was a priest) when he could no longer assent to the belief that the Church of England shared apostolic legitimacy with Rome. As a Catholic priest he wrote a body of theological treatises and essays in which he attempted to graft in a form of Christian humanism the best elements of the Protestant and Catholic theological and intellectual traditions. His ultimate aim was to shape a cosmopolitan Catholic culture, orthodox in its origins yet ecumenical in its application to and dealings with other Christian denominations. Manning, Newman's junior and rival for papal favors, was quite differently disposed. He became the pugnacious defender of an English church much more culturally closed to the intellectual influences of the outside world and very closely allied to the doctrinal interpretations and cultural attitudes of the Vatican. A staunch champion of the Ultramontane position of papal supremacy, a position favored by most English converts, Manning believed that the English Catholic Church should make no accommodation (cultural or otherwise) with the Anglican Church or, for that matter, the rest of the non-Catholic world. Eventually Manning's more narrow view won the day and is mirrored in the vision of Catholic Church triumphant—the essential view of virtually all English Catholic novelists writing from the turn of the century to our own time.

One of the earlier Catholic novels to attain great popularity was *Hadrian VII* (1904), by Frederick Rolfe (or Baron Corvo, as he later called himself). A convert and a rather eccentric character, Rolfe as a young man first studied for the priesthood in Rome at Scots College. Presumably discharged from the seminary for his homosexuality in 1890, he thereafter lived a dissipated life of bohemian wanderings supported by many generous friends and his own occasional efforts (for a time he worked as a gondolier in Venice to pay, it was said, for his procurement of boys). In a series of essays dedicated to him, Graham Greene referred to him as "spoilt priest" with a "painfully divided personality" and as a Satanic figure (one of the few the Edwardian period produced) who, "if he could not have Heaven . . . would have Hell."[2] In this intriguing "novel of genius," as Greene refers to it, Rolfe presents the life of a fictitious English pope, Hadrian VII, who, renouncing all rights of papal sovereignty (including the historical claims to the papal states), sells the art treasures of the Vatican in order to give the money to the poor.

There is in this unevenly written work one passage that is particularly interesting and even curiously prophetic in its portrayal of this new spirit that Adrian brings to his papacy. At one point he appears before

Vatican windows that, up to his reign, had always been sealed and
closed, and against the strong protests of the assembled cardinals he
gives his apostolic benediction, *urbi et orbi*, to the cheering masses assembled in the great square.[3] (We can draw parallels with the actions of
John XXIII, who, when announcing the creation of the Second Vatican
Council, called on the Church to open its windows to the rest of the
world.) Rolfe's work is strongly Ultramontane in its aim to present the
pope as alone holding the moral and spiritual authority to overcome the
materialism of the secular world. Despite its inferior quality to French
Catholic novels written in the same period and its didacticism, the novel
remains of interest as a reflection of English Catholics' disgust at the
ugly materialism rampant in the modern world and their fervent belief
in the papacy as the sole power to respiritualize such a degenerate world.

Belloc and Chesterton

Hilaire Belloc and Gilbert Keith Chesterton were among the most
influential and popular writers of their generation. Both were prolific
(Chesterton wrote more than 200 books and Belloc more than 100),
and both were at the very center of the Catholic intellectual revival in
twentieth-century England. Collaborating in the development of their
intellectual theories and writings, they became popularly referred to as
the "Chesterbelloc," an identification coined by George Bernard Shaw,
because of their joint promotion of a sociopolitical system they would
call "distributism." This system called for a new and equal distribution
of property and wealth and the restoration of workers' control of their
various pursuits (in commerce, farming, and industry) through reinstitution of medieval guilds. "Chesterbelloc" advocated this radical concept as the most effective means to combat proposed Liberal legislation
in Parliament that, the two men thought, was swiftly leading to rigid
state control in the kind of world prepared for by positivist ideas. They
idealistically envisioned, through the reinstitution of the guild ethic, a
return to the democracy of the medieval Free Cities and to a rural kind
of peasant state to be watched over and nourished by the wisdom and
discipline of the Catholic Church.

Belloc is primarily remembered as a historian and political theorist,
and it was he, an English Catholic of French ancestry, who was chiefly
responsible for shaping Chesterton's romanticized veneration for that
spiritually harmonious, just, and happy society that the latter believed
England and Europe had been during the Middle Ages. A more philo-

sophically oriented and trained mind than his bellicose friend, Chesterton became a primary catalyst for the neo-Thomist revival in England through brilliant essays and articles. Both men shared the animus of their Catholic counterparts on the Continent for modernity and all that the terms denoted—statism, secularism, indifferentism, socialism—and both were thoroughly and unrepentantly anti-Semitic in ascribing the evil power of money to the financial genius of "unassimilable" Jewish merchants and bankers.[4]

Though Chesterton converted, much through Belloc's influence, in 1922, the two men could not have been more different in temperament. Belloc was a stern apologist for Catholicism and held all other religions in utter contempt. He especially hated Jewish and Germanic culture and considered only Catholicism to be the mainspring of European culture ("Europe is the faith and the faith is Europe," he wrote). And he held that the Western world would only survive morally by returning to its roots. He also constantly advanced his belief that Catholicism meant implicitly both spiritual and temporal allegiance to Rome. In comparison, Chesterton was by far the better intellect, not doctrinally narrow but in fact a genius in philosophical reflection and disquisition. Loving intellectual encounters and debates, his works are far more open and have none of the bitter, intolerant strain of the proselytizer we find in Belloc. And though he shares many of Belloc's views on the moral and intellectual superiority of Catholic teaching and doctrine, Chesterton attacks his adversaries with mirthful satire and broad gales of laughter at what he regards as the utter insanity of many non-Christian attitudes, when exposed to clear and systematic examination. He was, in short, a genial, humorous apologist exposing what he thought to be error or inconsistencies with rapier-sharp logic and appealing rhetorical persuasion. The sharp differences in temperament and intellectual approach and manner can clearly be seen in the kind of novels each would write.

Belloc's best-known fiction is the 1904 novel *Emmanuel Burden*. Though it is of inferior quality when compared with French Catholic novels of the period, it remains significant because it so well conveys English Catholics' antipathy to the ugly forms of modernity advanced by the Protestant ethic dominant in industrial society. A fictionalized history (somewhat resembling in theme and intention Thomas Mann's *Buddenbrooks*), the novel recounts via a naively admiring and unreliable narrator the life of a London wool merchant, Emmanuel Burden, and his family, who are portrayed as a perfectly modern, upright example of the city's merchant class. Burden's firm exports cheap iron finger rings to

Africa, where they are exchanged for ivory. Hence Burden is regarded by the narrator/biographer as making a healthy and justifiable profit and, at the same time, bringing British civilization to the darkest areas of Africa. In reality the novel is a scathing rendition, a kind of "Fall of the House of Burden," as it charts the family's discarding of religious beliefs to replace them with the Puritan work ethic and the ideal of utilitarian progress and the profit motive. Emmanuel's ancestors had fought for Cromwell in the seventeenth century, and his Christian name, meaning "God with us," is a mocking indictment of the spiritual void in which he and his family live. His line has, in fact, become more and more "burdened" or imprisoned by its economic ambition and success, which the Protestant ethic has sanctified. Despite the admiring support of the narrator, the father is seen, as the work progresses, to have become a pompous, empty, self-righteous man.

Though he is hollow, Emmanuel is not yet corrupt. His son Cosmo, the latest representative of the Burden family, is, however, lacking in moral probity and becomes nothing less than a rake. Through him we see the fall of the family into corrupt conduct and practice. While at Oxford Cosmo has impregnated an innkeeper's daughter, and, forced to buy back compromising letters written to her, must resort to a sinister Jewish moneylender, Mr. Barnett. Through Cosmo's service as confidence man for the Jew, his father is drawn into a swindle involving a scheme to mine gold in an African territory called the M'Korio, which of course does not exist. Placed by his son's intrigue on the board of directors, Burden, through his respectable business reputation, becomes responsible for encouraging the investment of many stockholders who are subsequently ruined when the fraud comes to light (Barnett and his cohorts sell off their stock in the nick of time).

In the end Cosmo's ascendancy indicates that the Burdens, once honest representatives of the English middle class, have shorn themselves of their integrity and are now a corrupting influence on British society. And Cosmo's collusion with Barnett proves that the old virtues of hard work and industry—all that had remained after the loss of religious faith—have been replaced by underhanded business deals concocted with Jewish financiers and equally unscrupulous people. Four years later in the novel *Mr. Clutterbuck's Election* Belloc expanded his attack on the sinister power of Jewish money and influence in English society and charts the rise in public administration of Mr. Barnett, now Lord Lambeth, who has risen to the top of British politics through a corrupt purchase of a title and power.[5] Belloc's bitter indictment of the British Protestant middle class prefigures the more brilliant yet less heavy-handed satirical treatment of British society and mores that will be one of Evelyn Waugh's principal preoccupations.

G. K. Chesterton wrote 15 novels from 1904 to 1936. As a novelist, he intended his fiction to convey his political and social views, and his novels took the form of allegorical satires of the politics and institutions of his day. As a Catholic writer, he invested his works with his deepest religious convictions—most directed at what he believed to be the godless positivist philosophy and direction of the Liberal party and the Fabians. Chesterton, in short, was not concerned with the personal history of a soul caught in the drama of salvation or damnation but rather with more universal political and social issues. His novels therefore differ markedly from the French prototype and from the form the British variety would take a few decades later with Greene and Waugh. Even in his own time he was accused of writing novels short on art and essentially propagandistic in nature and intention. The fact that they are rarely read today would seem to support this view, and it is certainly true that the novels do not present characters or plot situations that are enduring or universal enough to attract the interest of modern readers.

Graham Greene, though much taken with Chesterton and even considering him a kind of Catholic hero, had to admit that the latter was certainly not an accomplished and not even a successful novelist. This was, Greene, asserted, because Chesterton, as a brilliant apologist and man of faith, did not have the temperament to capture the sordid complexities of human nature in the concrete and invest them in fictional situations. For Greene, it was the clear, timeless statement of religious truths with which Chesterton invested his essays (the collections *Orthodoxy* and *Everlasting Man*, for example) that made him a brilliant religious writer and the inspiration to British Catholic intellectuals that he assuredly was. But a major novelist he was not.[6]

Though the major conclusions of Greene's evaluation are certainly true, Chesterton remains important as a novelist who, in the tradition of George Orwell and H. G. Wells, directed his works to illuminating political and social questions of his period in imaginative allegorical form. He also presented most clearly in fictional form a spirit that is all pervasive in the works and attitudes of the Catholic novelists I have examined up to now—and that Albert Sonnenfeld has referred to in his essays as "romantic quixotism."[7] What this expression means can be clearly perceived through an analysis of Chesterton's first and one of his best novels, *The Napoleon of Notting Hill* (1904).

The work is a sharp attack on the gray, monotonous, and unfeeling society that Chesterton felt London, and by extension England, had become. The capital is depicted as having long lost its appreciation for the glory of its historical past, the rich tradition of its boroughs, townships, and guilds; the splendor of its medieval pageantry. There now remains in its place a faceless bureaucracy intent on programming the citizens of the city along utopian lines.

In the novel's introduction Chesteron takes swipes at any kind of prophet who would program human beings or attempt to rein in their natural perversity. "Humanity is," he states, "as a whole changeful, mystical, fickle, delightful. Men are men but man is a woman."[8] The novel proceeds to illustrate this dictum through the narration of the "uprising of Notting Hill." Auberon Quinn, a fledgling barrister (described as looking like a boy), becomes politically active and interested in reacting against this gray society after a chance meeting that he has with the colorful deposed king of Nicaragua, Jean del Fuego. This spirited ex-monarch of a tiny country refuses to accept his defeat as warranted or even justified by modern realpolitik, and he defiantly declares, "Nicaragua has been annexed like Athens . . . like Jerusalem. . . . The Yankee and the German and the brute powers of modernity have trampled it . . . but Nicaragua is not dead, it is an idea" (Napoleon, 26).

Elected king (through an imaginary lottery system), Auberon hatches as a pure diversion the colorful scheme for restoring the London boroughs to their lost medieval finery, replete with provosts, barrier custom houses, halberers, and the entire panoply of medieval pomp. To Auberon's complete astonishment, his suggestion is taken seriously and put into effect by numerous London boroughs. With the idea of self-determination of districts once again in vogue, the residents of the Notting Hill area of London now are prompted to refuse the program of industrial zoning that influential business and financial figures have arranged. They reject in particular the plan to open to road development a small area in and around Pump Street. Opposing the will of this small district, the business powers of the city unite to force the acceptance of the project.

What ensues is a David-Goliath combat as the residents of Pump Hill, under the leadership of Adam Wayne (a precocious adolescent whose hobby is war strategies), conducts a guerrilla war against insurmountable odds. The struggle is viewed as tantamount to the individual's contesting and taking on the totalitarian forces of modernity. The first battle of Notting Hill is won by its defenders through an intricate use of street lamps as weapons. Yet the victory is only temporary—human beings cannot, it would seem, retain the force or purity of intention for long in selfless crusades. Rather, the forces of the "majority," under the pretense of democratic norms, will always crush the will of the people and set up rigidly controlled societies.

Though the forces of Pump Street are defeated and its leaders punished, Adam Wayne presents what is certainly one of the essential points of the work—an eternal hope in the ability of individuals to come together, at least at certain times, to use their collective free will to contest oppression, even if this means force: "Something," he muses, "must break this strange indifference, this strange dreary egoism, this strange loneliness of millions in a crowd. Why should it not be you or I?" (*Napoleon*, 99). Yet Chesterton does not allow this qualified optimism to dominate nor does he suggest that forms of resistance, such as the spirited measures of the inhabitants of Pump Street, will ever usher in utopian societies. Too deeply engrained in human beings, he seems to say, are the negative effects of man's "bent nature"—the result of the Fall—to allow such qualitative leaps or breakthroughs in the workings of human society. This particular view, dramatized in the failed battle of the Pump Street activists against modernity and its tyrannies, is succinctly and frequently expressed in many of Chesterton's essays; there is, for example, the celebrated passage from *Orthodoxy* in which he writes, "I have always maintained that men are backsliders, that human nature tended of itself to rest or not, that human beings as such go wrong, especially happy human beings. The hopeless cause and the happy spectacle of giving all in its defense, for one shining moment seems the best that human beings can achieve in a fallen world."[9]

Evelyn Waugh

Evelyn Waugh shared Chesterton's vision of a fallen world and was equally critical in his attacks on the spirit of the age. His particular genius, however, lay not in writing political allegories or essays and treatises in defense of Christianity. Rather, as a convert totally convinced of the essential truths of Catholicism, he would become a novelist intent on satirizing and exposing the foibles and stupidities of an English society that he viewed as uprooted from its Catholic birthright, bereft of values, and composed of members whom he saw as "flickering shadows without permanence." Because of the sharpness of his social satire, critics have designated him as a modern-day Jonathan Swift. He has also been called a worthy successor of Anthony Trollope through his extensive portrayal of uppercrust English society that continues Trollope's portraits of eminent Victorians. He has also been extolled by Edmund Wilson for being "the only first-rate comic genius to have appeared in England since Bernard Shaw."[10] He was, finally, a Catholic novelist who, from the start of his literary career, suffused his satirical novels with religious symbolism, giving them a depth not found in the brilliant but purely secular forms of this kind of literature produced by eminent English writers from the Restoration period up through the nineteenth century.

From an upper-middle-class family, Waugh was as a young man a high living member of what he would later depict as a kind of lost generation of "bright young things." At Oxford (Hertsford College) he gained the reputation of being a snobbish decadent and was a member of the notorious Hypocrites Club (along with Cyril Connolly, Lord Henry Acton, and Anthony Powell). He has been described as having cultivated during this period the pose of the dandy dedicated to the role of shocking the more pedestrian undergraduates. His increasingly dissipated life as a student forced him to be sent down from the university in 1924 (he would never complete his degree). For the next few years he tried his hand at teaching at a private school (a disastrous one-year experience that inspired the topic of his first novel, *Decline and Fall*) and wrote articles and edited a gossip column for several newspapers. He married Evelyn Gardner in 1928, and her infidelity caused the marriage to break up only a few months later.

Overwhelmed by a sense of betrayal and deeply despondent, Waugh pursued divorce proceedings and began religious instructions with Father Martin D'Arcy, a well-known Jesuit attached to London's Farm Street church. Received into the Church in 1930, he described his conversion as not abrupt but as the result of a longer evolution dating back as far as his prep school days when he had first become interested in Anglo-Catholicism. And though the bitter experience of his failed first marriage was an important factor, he later described his decision to have been made "on firm intellectual conviction but with little emotion." As he further commented, "I look back . . . with wonder at the trust of the priest who saw the possibility of growth in such a dry soul" (quoted in Lane, 25).

After the traumatic watershed year of 1930, Waugh spent the next few years time traveling as a journalist (taking major assignments in British Guiana, Brazil, and Ethiopia). He also wrote copiously on the side (completing four novels and a life of Dante Rossetti by 1934).

When his previous marriage was annulled in 1936, he married Laura Herbert, settled into a large country house (Piers Court), and began to cultivate the style of a country squire, devoting most of time to writing novels, raising a large family, and traveling as a lecturer or commentator (often to the United States).

Critics have designated the novels that Waugh wrote from 1928 (starting with *Decline and Fall*) to about 1940 as representing his most purely satirical works, and some have evinced surprise at what they regard to be the seeming lack of religious themes and content in them, despite the author's subsequent conversion.[11] The other major novels he wrote in this period are *Vile Bodies* (1930), *Black Mischief* (1933), and *A Handful of Dust* (1934). In these novels there is no explicit turning to religion on the part of the protagonists, nor does the Catholic Church intrude into the affairs of what is continually characterized as a totally secularized world where religion has no significant influence in the playing out of the intricate plots. Waugh seems to admit to this omission when, just two years after the appearance of *Brideshead Revisited* (1945), he stated that only with this novel had he begun "to represent human beings more fully, which to me means only one thing, man in relation to God."[12] And he wrote in a diary dating from about this same time that in respect to his newfound religious commitment, "I think perhaps it [*Brideshead*] is the first of my novels rather than the last."[13]

Waugh's earlier novels were in fact more intent on representing in flippant and sometimes cruel terms the basically illogical, stupid, and hollow world that continued to intrigue Waugh and to goad him to give a Swiftian "one lash the more" to the absurd spectacle that he viewed from many angles. But this does not preclude the presence of frequent and strong religious undertones in the respective works. On the contrary, the absence of any permanent values and the depiction of a dog-eat-dog world devoid of sympathy, love, or transcendence of any kind begs the antidote of spiritual belief and consolation. Indeed, Waugh's first intent in this period would seem to have been that of creating an absolute negation of the spiritual beliefs to which he had already given credence and thus of developing a reductio ad absurdum as point of departure for the eventual emergence of spiritual elements and themes.

Each of these novels presents the cases of a certain kind of protagonist, of men and women who float about in a shadowy world where there are no authentic relationships and where love, honor, and loyalty are either debased or nonexistent. The protagonist of *Decline and Fall*, Paul Pennyfeather, is a candidate for Anglican Holy Orders at Oxford as the novel begins. He is depicted as having few if any religious convictions or any knowledge of theology as such, and his talent is to be a well-meaning kind of moral cipher, able to sustain himself by taking on the coloration of the world about him. Regarded by all as a very respectable student at "Scone College," he is suddenly sent down on the charges of indecent exposure (he has been "debagged" by drunken members of the Bollinger Club during one of their bacchic revels). Thrown out of the secure society of the university into a world teeming with heartless, self-seeking opportunists, charlatans, and mountebanks of all stripes, Pennyfeather becomes a modern Candide whom the author will use to expose the base and corrupt society that be believes England has become. When then swindled out of his inheritance by an unscrupulous guardian, Paul has to take a teaching post at Llunaba Castle, where he is told by the fashionable, totally corrupt, and Dickensian headmaster, Augustus Fagan, "to temper discretion with deceit."[14]

Waugh creates a fabulous galaxy of sharply drawn caricatures and hilariously improbable circumstances to elucidate the meaning of the work's title, the decline of British society and mores. Pennyfeather is the conduit through which one sees the moral decay in values and standards in English public (that is, private) schools. Through the ineptitude of the Llunaba chaplain, Prendergast, the school becomes the scene of a needless tragedy. Prendergast, who is plagued by religious doubts, shoots a student, Lord Tangent, in the heel while officiating at a track meet (the boy subsequently dies of gangrene poisoning). Because of the enormous scandal into which the school is thrown by the accident, Paul meets Lady Margot Best Chetwynde (the English pronunciation is "beast cheating"), who arrives to view the track meet with her African-American paramour, a jazz musician, Sebastian Chokey Cholmondly. Agreeing to tutor her son Peter Pastmaster at her monstrous Bauhaus estate (for the building of which she had destroyed a magnificent edifice that dated back to Tudor times), Paul eventually becomes her lover and then is arrested while in her service (she is, it turns out, a drug addict and nymphomaniac who also traffics extensively in the white slave market). Sent to prison, Pennyfeather reveals the bankruptcy of the English penal system (the warden is an exponent of the theory that criminal tendencies can be overcome by aesthetic practices).

At this point Paul witnesses the horrible death of Prendergast, his former Llunaba colleague and now a prison chaplain, who is decapitated with a chainsaw by a manic carpenter whose "authentic" inner voices have urged him to "kill and spare not" (*Decline and Fall*, 239). Margot manages to have Pennyfeather rescued from prison (he is reported dead of an appendectomy). He thus returns to Scone College under a new identity and placidly submits once again to the system without, it would seem, having learned a thing about life or challenging in any way the absurd world he has encountered. Instead, he tranquilly prepares again to stand for Holy Orders.

Vile Bodies is Waugh's portrayal of the "bright young things"—the British equivalent of Scott Fitzgerald's "lost generation." The novel presents the same kind of outrageously farcical episodes as *Decline and Fall*, but it is grimmer in tone, particularly in its conclusion when this lost generation of the Jazz Age suffers the market crash of 1929 and is swept away by the chaos that follows. Waugh peoples the work with sexually promiscuous, urbane, mindless types without honor or moral principles. The young spend their days trying to overcome their desperate boredom. Not really malicious or even ill intentioned, they are essentially selfish and irresponsible. Their dimwitted, stodgy, and amoral parents seem always to be virtually unaware of the existence of these troubled children except when the latter annoy or embarrass them by conduct violating the superficial moral code of their class.

Essentially the novel's plot relates the love affair between Adam Symes and Nina Blunt—young innocents who, through the corrupting influence of their society, have become victims of its permissiveness towards sex. In a direct authorial intrusion, Waugh has his narrator comment, "Like so many people of their age and class, Adam and Nina were suffering from being sophisticated about sex before they were at all widely experienced."[15]

Colonel Blunt, Nina's eccentric father, refuses to approve this daughter's marriage because Adam is not financially secure. The colonel, for whom money is everything, has given over his estate to a Hollywood movie company that is shooting "an all-talk super-religious film." To increase his income, he literally auctions off his daughter to a shallow playboy, Ginger. Almost immediately after their marriage Ginger is called (during the Christmas season) into military service. Nina abandons her husband forthwith and takes Adam to live with her in her father's house. Besotted and lost in his foggy world, the colonel is totally unaware of this exchange. Pretending to be husband and wife, Nina and Adam then celebrate the family yule festival, partake of the Christmas meal, exchange presents, and in the process degrade and make a mockery of traditional family values. World War I is declared soon thereafter, and Adam is sent onto the battlefield. Yet Waugh suggests that in a larger battle that has been waging all along in England and the West, traditional religious and social values have been cast aside. And the novel describes not only a world in which these values have been abandoned but one in which the younger generation has lost—perhaps irrevocably—any significant ties to the past.

In *A Handful of Dust* Waugh presents an even more somber appraisal of Edwardian England—this time specifically attacking the hollow Victorian ideals of the gentry and ruling class. The protagonist, Tony Last, is in fact a portrait of a kind of last Victorian gentleman living out the now useless existence of the country squire. His manor house, Hetton Abbey, is a Gothic monstrosity built in the nineteenth century. It consists of a series of galleries and rooms decorated with a frieze of Gothic text and named for medieval knights and ladies—Iseult, Tristram, Lancelot, Galahad, Morgan, Merlin, and others. Tony's private dressing room is named after Morgan La Fey, and his wife's is ominously named after Lady Guinevere. The Arthurian chamber motif attests, of course, to Tony's helplessly romantic state of mind, and in a larger sense it points to the moral fuzziness of the English gentry fixated on an ideal past that blinds it to the moral bankruptcy of the present.

Tony is married in a loveless match to Brenda, an intelligent woman rendered vacuous by the monotonous routine of the couple's stifling social life—rounds of dinner parties and the entertaining of numerous weekend visitors to the manor. While Tony seems to find some satisfaction—perhaps a tie with his ancestors—from living in the bizarre architectural pile that is the Abbey, Brenda, far more modern in her tastes, prefers the social life of London and abhors both the house itself and the ceremonial life-style that it encourages. Neither possesses any authentic religious belief, but of the two Brenda seems frankly agnostic and mocks her husband's perfunctory Sunday routine of Anglican churchgoing. He attends services, chats afterwards "with the vicar's sister and the people from the village," and has a glass of sherry in the library before Sunday dinner. Brenda is especially fond of teasing him, as the narrator informs us, "whenever she caught him posing as an upright, God-fearing gentleman of the old school, and Tony saw the joke."[16] They treat their son, John, as if he were simply another of the colts they are raising in their stables.

Into this ritualistic existence there enters the social parasite and rank opportunist, John Beaver, who will destroy whatever remains of their marriage. A kind of modern-day Rastignac who lives off the "honey hive" of the rich and well connected, Beaver spends his days on the phone in his London flat trying to cadge invitations to weekend country parties of the wealthy. Enjoying (and abusing) Tony's hospitality at these Hetton weekends, he introduces Brenda to the "smart" London set, seduces her, and thus sets in motion the roles suggested by the novel's Arthurian motif—he the corrupt Lancelot, with Tony an obtusely naive Arthur, and Brenda a bored and willing Guinevere.

As Brenda becomes the captive of London society and now lives weeks on end away from the manor house, the life of the Last family virtually disintegrates. When the couple's son is kicked to death by a horse who has become frightened by the backfiring of a motorcycle (seemingly symbolic of the mechanized cruelty of the modern world), Tony's medieval never-never land is destroyed. Only now made aware of his wife's infidelity and deprived of his son—the only human being who had loved him—Tony is brought to despair. Not only is he unable to reconcile the loss of his son, but he receives no solace from his religion. For a short period he seems to gain comfort through the intervention of a totally demoralized, rich American drug addict, Mrs. Rattery. She introduces him to card games, allowing him to divert his attention and providing him in the process with the alibi that all that occurs in life is the result of chance ("under her fingers order grew out of chaos; she established sequence and precedence" [*A Handful of Dust*, 150]). Clearly a bogus deity masking God's divine order, she tempts Tony to accept the tragedy as one governed by random chance and fatality rather than by divine providence and as a consequence of God's will.

In the aftermath of his son's death, Tony refuses to divorce Brenda and to sell off Hetton Abbey. Instead he runs away and travels in the South American jungles with a strange Messianic figure, the archaeologist Dr. Missinger. At this point the reader understands that now despairing of his English civilization, Tony finds as substitute for his Arthurian ideal of the English gentleman that of the noble savage of the primeval jungle forests. Yet this world (also devoid of belief in God's providence) therefore becomes as ominous to Tony's well-being as the vapid and de-Christianized society of England. In the jungles Tony ends a prisoner in the hands of the sinister Mr. Todd (the word Todd in German meaning "death"), himself an escapee of Tony's homeland. In a finale of unmitigated darkness (in a chapter whose title, "Du côté de Chez Todd," obviously parodies and starkly contrasts Proust's successful voyage backward to the joys and consolation gained through culture, "Du côté de Chez Swann") the now drugged and captive Tony must serve as Todd's slave. In a macabre twist his principal task in captivity is to each day read where, when, and as long as his capricious master desires, the corpus of the novels of that supreme English "voice," Charles Dickens.

Tony's jungle imprisonment is the result of his continual inability to confront reality of any kind and to take moral responsibility for the disintegration of his past personal and family life. The "City of Todd" (that city of pure nature juxtaposed to the Augustinian "City of God") has come to be as equally fallacious as the "City of England." Waugh ends the novel on a sardonic note by linking as subhuman levels of existence the two profane realms of Todd and England. Todd's kingdom remains the uncivilized jungle, and the England of Hetton Abbey has, we find, become a fox-breeding farm managed, in Tony's absence, by the ragtag and disreputable end of the Last family (while the adulterous Brenda lives with her lover in London).

Everything human in the novel has thus fallen into ruin and disintegrated in a world lacking love, commitment, and religious belief. In the end Waugh artfully demonstrates the aptness of the quotation from T. S. Eliot's *Waste Land* that he chose as the novel's epigraph: "I shall show you fear in a handful of Dust." And, just as important, for the first time Waugh had created a protagonist whose predicament and fate make him a genuinely pathetic, even sympathetic, character and not a mere cardboard caricature of a human being (like Pennyfeather or Adam Symes). Though not a "religious" novel, *A Handful of Dust* would seem to have led its author to a satirical cul de sac from which there was no escape except through the light of faith.

Written in the winter and spring of 1944 while Waugh was on military leave, *Brideshead Revisited* represents the way out of the moral morass of the earlier works and shows the way back through the door of religious belief. The novel's subtitle, "The Sacred and Profane Memories of Captain Charles Ryder," suggests the crux of the work's moral drama and dominant theme. The principal protagonist, Charles Ryder, is (as his name implies) a pilgrim-voyager who, through Proustian recollections and dredging up of privileged memories of his past, succeeds in recognizing a divine, or sacred, pattern in God's designs for him. Ryder's drama is also that of the artist in search of this authentic vocation, with much of the work recounting his futile struggle against conforming to the use God would have him make of his art. (He has to learn and accept the basic truth that art must serve God, not man, and that the end of life is not art but God.) As a novel exploring the relationship of art and the artist, *Brideshead* is therefore reminiscent of Joyce's *A Portrait of the Artist*

as a Young Man, but with an entirely opposite evolution given to the protagonist. Unlike Stephen Dedalus, who rejects religion and ultimately
regards its power as a obstacle to his vocation as artist, Ryder's artistic
culmination comes about only after he willingly refuses to use art as an
end in itself and gives himself over to grace so as to find his own unique
role in the divine order of things.

Brideshead is also the saga of an aristocratic English family, the Flytes,
and the workings of grace on its members, who as individuals seem, initially at least, worlds apart each from the other in their particular dispositions to their faith. The devout, "almost saintly" Lady Marchmain lives in
her private apartments in the magnificent country manor of Brideshead. She represents through her dissenter ancestors the "old" Catholic
side of the family that has never apostasized, and she is the last of her line
(her brothers were killed in the Great War). Her husband, Lord
Marchmain, to whom Brideshead belongs, descends from an illustrious
family that had been Catholic for centuries before lapsing to Anglicanism.
He returned to his family's ancient faith when he married his wife, but
after serving in the war he left her and the family to go to live as an exile
in Venice with his Italian mistress. Bitterly estranged, he hates his pious
wife and refuses ever to be in her proximity, whether in England or abroad.
There are four children from the union. Brideshead (Bridey), the elder son,
is a plain, dry, eccentric misfit in society but a devoted Catholic (and a kind
of "spoiled priest"). The elder daughter, Julia, is beautiful, strong-willed,
and rebellious; she is a leading debutante in fashionable London. The
younger son, Sebastian, is a dramatically handsome, troubled neurotic
who, during his student career at Eton and then Oxford, spends his existence in flight from the Catholic influences and atmosphere of family life
his mother had been responsible for fostering during his childhood at
Brideshead. The younger daughter, Cordelia, shares her older brother's
physical plainness and has the same unquestioning loyalty and commitment to her faith, but she has greater propensities toward self-sacrifice
than her siblings and inevitably sees the reality of situations with extreme
clarity.

Brideshead manor is also a major protagonist in the novel. Erected
after the Reformation from the stones of the old (Catholic) Flyte manor,
Brideshead was designed in the baroque style and, as Jeffrey Heath has
pointed out, can be taken for Protestant England itself: "A house of aber-
rant worship and profane love that shelters here and there a few remnants of a better age."[17] Brideshead's interior seems to be further divided
into two distinct areas or spheres of influence: Lady Marchmain's room

and the chapel her husband built for her as a wedding gift, and the rest of the manor. Her room, filled with objects reflecting her personality and pious belief, is set apart from and clashes with the "masculine" atmosphere of the other areas of the house. And the art nouveau chapel seems, in its excessive profusion of colors and forms, an extension of her own rooms. Heath considers Brideshead is this respect as an emblem of schism, a house divided between the Catholic and Anglican sides. Architecturally, he sees it as symbolizing artifice, because the building's origin has been covered with illusory disguises (representing the substitution of the false faith for the true). As he further describes it, "the high and insolent dome" and the beautiful fountain are trompe l'oeils that disguise and distort the purity of the more simple "Catholic lines" of the earlier edifice (Heath, 167–68).

Charles Ryder's spiritual evolution and eventual conversion become inextricably intertwined with the destiny of the Flyte family and the gorgeous emblem that is Brideshead. This process begins with a love relationship that he establishes with Sebastian when both are students at Oxford. A kind of spiritual orphan (his eccentric father, though living, is totally derelict in his role as a parent), Charles spends most of his academic time off at Brideshead as Sebastian's guest. Here he is soon virtually adopted by the Flytes and becomes involved in the intense struggles that are tearing the family apart.

By her stern, uncompromising practice of religion and by what seems to be her unfeeling nature, Lady Marchmain at first seems largely responsible for having created the repressive atmosphere that will eventually cause half of the family members to abandon their Catholic faith and, with this, their own sense of moral integrity. (Lady Marchmain's difficulty seems to stem from the fact that she is "pious without being a saint," as her daughter Cordelia describes her.) First there has been her husband's apostasy, exile from the family, and adultery. In direct revolt against her mother's interdiction, Julia will abandon her faith to pursue a love affair and eventual marriage with the power-hungry and totally amoral Rex Mottram (Waugh's modern man without a soul). The black sheep of the family and avatar of the Oxford lost generation of the 1920s, Sebastian, finds temporary solace in sex, alcoholism, and then a frenzied retreat to North Africa, where he will live out his religious destiny. Brideshead and Cordelia remain solidly in the fold, but both are misfits and not at all integrated in the normal social patterns of their aristocratic peers. Bridey, the failed priest, is almost ludicrous in the extent to which he is out of step with his times and is also totally inept in all attempts at a secular career. After responding to what had seemed a religious vocation, Cordelia leaves the convent and, as another example of a saintly bag lady, throws herself without reserve into religious and social causes (the Spanish Civil War, and later relief work among other displaced people) that keep her far from Brideshead. Yet not surprisingly it is she alone who seems to understand the spiritual dimensions of the drama of grace in which all of the members of the family, and eventually Charles, are caught up.

To dramatize the multiple conversions that will be the result of the onslaught of grace, Waugh uses a thematic device borrowed from one of Chesterton's Father Brown stories, "The Queer Feet." Here having apprehended a celebrated criminal and then releasing him after the goods he had stolen have been returned, Father Brown assures the victims of the crime that the criminal will always be within reach: "I caught him," the priest says, "with an invisible line which is long enough to let him wander to the ends of the world and still to bring him back with a twitch upon the thread" (quoted in Heath, 176). Waugh is, of course, using Chesterton's "twitch upon the thread" as another figurative way to express the "Hound of Heaven" theme (and its correlative, Pascal's hidden God) of the mysterious action of grace. And as the novel unfolds, so too is revealed the divine plan encompassing all the players in the drama of salvation seen sub specie aeternitatis.

The reader views the action of grace as it operates on the various players through the eyes of Charles Ryder. This artist/aesthete sifts through his experiences (which he once saw only with the eyes of the art-for-art's-sake devotee and pagan that he was) with added vision of the Christian moralist he has become. Like Proust's narrator Marcel, he is at 40 in the gray, comfortless period of his life. He has, so to speak, outlived himself in a loveless marriage ending in divorce, a successful career as a "smart" painter of English country houses, and a stormy love affair with Julia Flyte. Returning as part of a military group billeted at Brideshead during the closing days of World War II, his memory is jogged by the sudden resurgence of the beautiful monument, and he returns in memory to his buried past, to be recaptured in Proustian fashion.

The first of Charles's "excavations" of memory is devoted to the halcyon days of his youth. Here he evokes with lush romantic prose the tender recollection of a love affair with Sebastian at Edwardian Oxford and the color of its student life as a backdrop. Now with proper distance Ryder sees the relationship as "high in the catalogue of grave sins," yet he finds its gravity for both of them as mitigated somewhat by "something of nursery freshness about us that fell short of joy." And for his part, he now realizes that the affair was prompted by his earliest search for love, and from it he learned that "to know and love one human being is the root of all wisdom."[18] Though certainly a "profane" love, Charles's brief idyll with Sebastian thus opened the door on the spiritual drama as quest for permanent love that he (and Sebastian as well) will painfully have to undergo in future years.

An alcoholic and near derelict when sent down from Oxford after his second year, Sebastian distances himself from Charles and then leaves the center stage of the novel, and what we know of him from this point on will be mostly related by what has been seen or heard about him. From these sources we learn that he has resisted his mother's attempts to reha- bilitate him and bring him back to family and Church. Instead, wander- ing in a drunken state through much of Europe, he forms a new liaison with another derelict—a seriously ill young German who has deserted the Foreign Legion—and he commits himself totally to being the latter's provider and protector while they both live together. When the young man is imprisoned by the Nazis for resisting mobilization in the Wehrmacht and subsequently commits suicide in prison, Sebastian attaches himself to a monastery in North Africa as a kind of lay brother. Here he lives out his days well loved by all for his acts of charity—a saintly beggar who is plagued to the end of his life by his fitful returns to the bottle.

Spiritually dead after her marriage to Mottram, Julia meets Charles years after during a transatlantic voyage. She is returning from a failed attempt to form another relationship in America, and he, in a similarly despondent/spiritless state, is returning to England and to his loveless marriage from South America (where he has painted "dead works of primitive nature" to augment his now well-known repertory of English country pictures). They begin a tormented love affair in which Julia, through her troubling beauty and charm, seems to become for Charles in later life the sexual counterpart of her brother Sebastian through the vio- lent passion that she arouses in her new lover. This attraction each has for the other is, however, doomed because it stands in the way of the growing influence of the sacred, of the action of grace; this Waugh depicts, in a dream sequence experienced by Charles, as a sudden avalanche of snow that totally demolishes a trapper's cabin on the slope of a mountain (*Brideshead*, 310–11).

When the erring father, Lord Marchmain, returns to Brideshead to die (and in the process to become reconciled to family and faith), Julia is desperately torn between her love for Charles and the weight of her religious upbringing that she has long abandoned but that will not let her live in peace. She is, moreover, increasingly overwhelmed by her sinful state and its repercussions—the guilt caused by her recognition of the grief she has inflicted on her mother, and on Christ as well: "Mummy carrying my sin with her to Church bowed under it and the black lace veil. . . . Mummy dying with my sin eating at her, more cruelly than her own deadly illness. . . . Mummy dying with it, Christ dying with it, nailed hand and foot" (*Brideshead*, 288).

Realizing that she can no longer live with Charles, she leaves him immediately after her father's death because, as bad as she is, she is not bad enough, she says, "to set up a rival good to God's. And she finally recognizes that this grace to do what defies her human desires has been made possible through the intervention and prayers of others who have loved her and have offered their prayers and lives for her: "It may be, she says, "because of Mummy, Nanny, Cordelia, Sebastian, perhaps Bridey—keeping my name in their prayers . . . or a private bargain between me and God, that if I give up this one thing that I want so much, however bad I am, He won't quite despair of me in the end" (*Brideshead*, 340).

Powerless in the face of the "barbaric code" of Catholics that he sees as once again taking hold of Julia and leading her away from him, the still recalcitrant Ryder feverishly attempts to block the action of grace. He centers all his efforts in this regard in strenuously opposing the presence of a priest at Lord Marchmain's death bed because the latter had up to now staunchly refused the consolation of the last sacraments. Julia in a monumental use of her will against the persuasive power of her lover brings the priest into the room, and, before slipping into unconsciousness, Marchmain makes the sign of the cross at the priest's urging to indicate his desire for repentance and acceptance of general absolution for sins of his life.

In admitting that he has lost the match, Charles becomes the last of the players in the drama to be touched by grace; unable to resist a strange power that overcomes him, he kneels at the foot of the bed and, despite himself, says a prayer for Lord Marchmain's conversion. Ineluctably drawn himself at this very moment into the magnetic field of grace, he then agrees to sever his relationship with Julia and, as the spiritual adopted son of Lord Marchmain, becomes the last member of the Flyte family to return to the faith of their fathers. Finally, and only after Charles's conversion, Brideshead, the house divided against itself through religious schism, is "twitched back" to its ancient roots.

In the end Brideshead ceases to represent for Charles Ryder a dazzling triumph of artistic beauty as an end in itself. Freed from its illusive power to beguile, he is no longer moved by the magnificent dome, fountains, and gardens but by something far more humble and "remote" from anything the builders had intended: "a beaten copper lamp of deplorable design, relit before the beaten copper doors of a tabernacle" (*Brideshead*, 351). As Charles's journey ends before the real presence exposed in the chapel, the sacred has triumphed over the profane, and grace has overcome everything in its path.

Brideshead soon became Waugh's best-known and most successful novel. It was a best-seller in the United States (Book-of-the-Month Club selection in 1946), and it remains very popular today chiefly because of a lavish and skillful television adaptation in serial form made under English direction for the Public Broadcasting Service in the 1970s. The novel, however, elicited several negative reviews because of its perceived downgrading of the importance of human love to that owed to God alone, and some critics argued that in their choices the major characters seemed more overwhelmed by grace than as free agents cooperating with grace in the workings of salvation. Edmund Wilson, in particular, castigated Waugh for having, in the case of Charles Ryder, drowned his "hot springs of anarchy" by stifling them in Catholic dogma, and thus for having reduced the intelligent and rebellious spirit of this character to the status of a puppet (Lane, 101). Waugh responded indirectly to such unfavorable secular reactions to his use of religious themes in a memorandum written in 1946, ostensibly for several Hollywood movie producers who were then negotiating with him to turn the novel into a film (Waugh subsequently rejected the project, presumably because he feared that such a version would betray the work's deepest meaning, given the inability of the Hollywood group to appreciate its religious dimensions). "Grace," he stated, "is not confined to the happy, prosperous, and conventionally virtuous. . . . God has a separate plan for each individual in which he or she may find salvation" (quoted in Heath, 188).

Reflecting his deep adherence to the spirit and attitudes of triumphal Catholicism, Waugh would, in the face of adverse criticism, remain adamant that no easy balance could be struck between the demands of secular life and those imposed by the supernatural order of things. Hence Charles's profane love for Sebastian and then Julia, though providing perhaps only temporary happiness, could not in the long run be sufficient. And in Waugh's novels to follow, his characters—similar to those of Mauriac—quest after a love that cannot be fulfilled in the here and now, lying as it does in the province of the hidden God.

Between 1945 and his death in 1966 Waugh continued to write novels in the two modes he followed throughout his career: the primarily satirical works that lash out at the stupidity of modern secular society separated from its religious foundations, and novels that explore serious religious themes such as those examined in *Brideshead*. In this second category Waugh presents such themes as the idea that God endows each of His creatures with a unique identity and purpose that must be discovered and followed out; the necessity for human beings to gain a proper perspective of their lives as part of a divine pattern; the need to distinguish in this life between the illusory and the permanent, the false and the true.

Examples of later works written in a primarily satirical vein are *The Loved One* (1947) and *Love among the Ruins* (1953). The first, perhaps as popular in the United States as *Brideshead*, castigates with cruel, brilliant humor and undeniable accuracy the superficial way that Americans deal with death and dying. Waugh was inspired to write the work after a visit to Los Angeles's Forest Lawn Cemetery (which he termed "a deep mine of literary gold" [Heath, 188]). Never an admirer of America as a culture or political experiment (it was far too "brave new world" for him), Waugh reveled in pointing out in the novel the plastic and dehumanized life-style thriving in a society that, as he believed, denies the reality of the Fall, sin, guilt, and moral anxiety. The vapid, hapless characters who grotesquely try to deny the reality of death by masking it with the bizarre burial habits Waugh discovered divest human beings of all moral responsibility. And these people further fall victim to the illusion that life is nothing more than a pleasant dream without moral or spiritual dimensions. Whispering Glades, the death-defying cemetery, thus represented for him the harbinger of the tasteless, sterile culture and religion being prepared for the rest of the world by the new barbarians of American society (and particularly those living in the avant-garde enclave of California).

Love among the Ruins is Waugh's futuristic vision of society in New Britain. Here the protagonist is Miles Plastic (Plastic Soldier) who lives in a kind of welfare state much like the Orwellian society of *Nineteen Eighty-four*. As prototype of modern man, Miles illustrates the moral decline of the species. The idea of personal moral responsibility has been all but eradicated in him by the "New Law," which postulates that no man is responsible "for the consequences of his work." Miles still retains a certain vestige of personal honor (and a lingering sense of Original Sin). When he burns the prison in which he is incarcerated and chooses to die in the fire, he both asserts his own humanity (or the scrap that is left of it) and attests to the end of an authentically human race. After his demise, only the plastic humanoids of Satellite City remain.

Among the most significant of Waugh's later novels are the three that comprise his War Trilogy, whose title, *Sword of Honor*, was not chosen until 1965. Like *Brideshead*, the work deals with the rejection of false, illusory values and a return to grace on the part of a scion of an aristocratic family. In the first volume, *Men at Arms* (1952), the protagonist, Guy Crouchback, is the last male heir of an ancient Catholic family at whose ancestral estate at Broome there is a chapel, where "the sanctuary light still burns" as it has for centuries.[19] Yet Guy is first seen as a modern "wasteland" figure, disaffected and separated from his roots as he lives abroad in a family villa (Castello Crouchback) on the Italian Riviera. His ties with his religion are functional, his spiritual life is one of "dryness," and his reception of the sacraments sporadic. At the advent of World War II Guy welcomes the combat, evoking as it does for him a kind of crusade against perceived modern powers of darkness, hence offering him a meaning in life.

Before leaving for the war Guy girds himself with reception of the sacraments (though his disaffection remains) and prays before the tomb of Sir Roger of Waybroke, a knight who had participated in the Crusades and whom Guy emulates as a role model for having centuries before participated in an analogous struggle of good against evil. The exemplary figure, whose influence will be crucial (but is at this point latent), is Guy's father, Gervase. He is depicted as a Christian gentleman and humanist who holds a far more sober view of the approaching war than does his son. He in fact sees it in spiritual dimensions as a primarily bloody conflict that surely will bring out the worst in human nature and not one that pits the forces of good against those of evil. He has a larger view of history as part of a divine pattern, and his value system is rooted in faith and a code of family honor. Guy will thus eventually have to decide which of the two (Sir Roger, the warring crusader, or Gervase, the Christian gentleman and family man) exemplifies the more authentic values. He will decide only after having been immersed in the bloody conflict that is World War II.

In *Men at Arms* Guy is temporary trapped in the lotus land of military bravado and pretense. During training camp, which Waugh describes in a comic manner worthy of Gilbert and Sullivan, he reverts to adolescence and seems overcome by the dash and color of being a soldier. The landscape darkens as France falls, and the grim absurdity of war starts to be affirmed. When Guy's brigade is sent to Dakar, he is there persuaded by a fellow officer to lead an unauthorized night raid. Though he adroitly conducts the operation, he is almost court martialed, and here begins the decline in Guy's acceptance of war as an ideal.

The second volume, *Officers and Gentlemen* (1955), presents a brilliant fictionalized account of the British campaign at Crete and the subsequent defeat and rout of all its forces in which Waugh took part as member of a British Commando unit. Here Waugh depicts in no uncertain terms the lack of honor, chivalry, and descent into bestiality that Guy views on all sides as the military operation turns to disaster. The desertion from the regiment of an aristocratic officer, Ivan Clair, whom Guy had regarded as a kind of perfect replica of a medieval knight (though he is in reality an unscrupulous coward), seriously dampens the hope Guy still has to see the war as a chivalrous venture. The only honorable act recorded in the entire conflict is a private one conducted by Guy himself: he buries and prays over the grave of a dead British soldier whose ID tags designate him to be a Roman Catholic. For, as Waugh seems to suggest, only in the personal sphere can honor survive in a conflict that is totally meaningless and bestial. (In fact, Waugh's treatment here of war is very similar in tone and style to the absurdist view of the same presented by Joseph Heller in *Catch-22*.)

The third volume, *Unconditional Surrender* (1961), provides grim examples of betrayal—this time not only of personal honor by men in battle but of political and ethical principles compromised or abandoned by politicians in high places. Transferred to Yugoslavia, Guy becomes an unwitting agent in the betrayal of several Jewish refugees, to whose aid he totally dedicates himself in a personal act of honor. (On the insistence of the Soviet high command, they are handed over by Guy's liaison superior to the Communist partisans who massacre them as potential rivals to their power after the war.) Guy finally realizes through this terrible circumstance that he too has become an agent of evil and executioner of the innocent. Returning from the war, Guy begins the process of atonement and renewal: he refuses to return to the Castello retreat but will live in his father's house at Broome. In a purely selfless act, he remarries his unfaithful wife and adopts a child she has had out of wedlock. When she is killed in one of the last air raids of the war, he marries Domenica Blessington and establishes not a man-centered but a God-centered family at Broome.

Guy's care of little Trimmer (the bastard son) and his devotion to his new wife become proof that Guy has become a complete human being. The role of paterfamilias thus replaces for him the illusory ideal of errant knight in a dubious crusading cause, and the Christian family becomes the one bulwark against the fallen modern world. Such, it would seem, is Waugh's last message (and prescription for himself). And during the last years of his life he lived in the privacy of his huge Somerset country house, surrounded by his large family and maintaining a guarded distance from the fallen world outside.

Graham Greene

At his death in 1991, Graham Greene had achieved in the opinion of many critics the distinction of being the foremost English novelist of his day. With almost 60 years of productivity during an intensely active literary career, he wrote more than 20 novels, four plays, numerous short stories, as well as travel books and two autobiographies. A product of and educated in the most traditional English institutions—the Church of England, Berkhamsted Public School (of which his father was headmaster), and Balliol College, Oxford—Greene in his writings and life continually pushed beyond the conventions and boundaries these institutions represented for him. His first writing experience was as a journalist (for the *Nottingham Journal* after university), and he realized his first literary success with the novel (or "entertainment" as he called it) *Stamboul Train* in 1932.

Soon to be one of the most celebrated of all the distinguished converts from Anglicanism to Catholicism of his time, Greene was received into the Catholic Church in 1926. Although the reasons for his conversion were many, one of the most compelling was the influence of his wife-to-be, herself a convert, Vivien Agrell-Browning. In the first volume of his biography, *The Life of Graham Greene*, Norman Sherry argues that Vivien and her religion offered Greene "an anchor . . . and an excuse for hope in his life."[20] As companion and believer, she provided what seemed for him to be a kind of absolute in the realm of love and belief for which he had been desperately seeking from at least as far back as his prep school days.

In fact, Greene early on had begun to distance himself from the conventions and ideals of the English middle class and against modernity itself. The Anglican Communion in which he had been raised never seems to have been regarded by him as a church with a spiritual foundation but rather as a public and somewhat compromising institution that merely reflected and upheld traditional English mores and values. And well before his conversion he had come to admire what other famous converts had also perceived as the "unnatural" and demanding impositions placed on human life by Catholicism. The Rock of Peter seemed to assure him and troubled seekers like him (Greene had contemplated suicide several times in his early years) that life could having a meaning and that there were real, solid values by which to live.

In one of his autobiographies, *The Lawless Roads* (1939), he states that though Vivien had given him a "pattern of religion," he had from early childhood already been morally disposed to view the world through Catholic eyes. As a young boy forced to board in his father's school, he had become tragically aware of a fallen world, the struggle between good and evil that lay at the heart of human life, and the reality of pure evil existing in everyday life. And he credits Majorie Bowen—whose novel *The Viper of Milan* he read at the age of 14—with having, through the work's villainous character Visconti, first opened his eyes to the existence of real evil. "She had," he says, "given me my pattern—religion might later explain it to me in other terms, but the pattern was already there—perfect evil walking the world where perfect good can never walk again, and only the pendulum ensures that after all in the end justice is done."[21]

In the same autobiography he relates that as a young boy he had divided his existence into two compartments: that of the dormitory in which, as a sensitive and bullied child, he had been required by his father to live and where "one met for the first time characters, adult and adolescent, who bore about them the genuine quality of evil"; and that of the garden of his home adjoining the school, where "one became aware of God with intensity—time hung suspended—music lay on the air; anything might happen before it became necessary to join the crowd across the border. There was no inevitability anywhere . . . faith was almost great enough to move mountains. . . . And so faith came to one—shapelessly, without dogma, a presence above a croquet lawn" (*Lawless Roads*, 14).

Critics have heavily relied on such texts as representing Greene's clearest expression of his essential moral vision of a fallen world wherein are suspended the seemingly irreconcilable elements of evil and grace. The permanence and necessary conflict between the two provided Greene with the dramatic tension for his novels, in which his characters yearn for the consolation of faith while weighted down by sin in an unjust and corrupt world. And this situation, the result of the Fall (that "terrible aboriginal calamity," as Cardinal Newman described it), was for Greene proof of God's existence. Rather than negate one's belief in God, the terribly palpable accumulation of evil and suffering that human beings encountered only confirmed, through universal yearning, a state of order and goodness beyond human understanding. Hence what completed the tragic vision of the fallen world and fully illuminated the "canvas" of human life was the corresponding sense of the mystery of God's existence (only dimly perceived by the rational intellect). For Greene, Pascal's hidden God became, then, the ultimate source of light and attraction, existing beyond the power of the senses yet constituting the point toward which creatures of the fallen world were pulled, despite their natural gravitation to evil.

Greene the novelist would therefore examine fallen creatures caught in their sinful condition. This emphasis on sin in the Catholic novel is, of course, not original to Greene and is substantially explained in the terms of Péguy's "sinner at the heart of Christendom" theory that Greene would frequently weave into his fiction. And, of course, Greene, like Mauriac and others, rejected from the start the idea that he was a Catholic author. For Greene, such a designation would imply (as Newman had earlier suggested in *The Idea of a University*) a sinless literature about sinless man.[22] Rather, Greene wished to be considered as a Catholic who in his fiction created his own special vision of reality—or what critics early on discerned to be his particular universe or, as some called it, his "Greeneland." This term denotes a concretely drawn yet psychologically evocative point in time and place where the human condition seems especially prone to corruption, vice, and squalor. As a journalist Greene traveled to all parts of the world, and increasingly he preferred to use as sites for his fiction areas in which suffering and injustice were particularly palpable and despicable because of the highly visible exploitation of the earth's poor and wretched (through the agency of their own tyrannical rulers or by colonial powers hypocritically posing as Christian and civilizing economic forces and influences).

In his fiction Greene would therefore combine (1) his own brand of Catholic faith (Waugh described him as "an Augustinian Christian, a believer of the dark ages of Mediterranean decadence when the barbarians were pressing along the frontiers and the City of God seemed yearly more remote and unattainable")[23] and (2) a penchant to depict the world as sordid and fallen (and in the process exposing hypocrisy of all kinds, attempting to gloss over or conceal evil). Resulting from this particular vision are a number of Catholic novels that are exemplars of the genre and that, in a larger sense, can be considered masterpieces of the modern novel.

Graham Greene's long and productive career as a novelist can for our purposes be divided into two phases that correspond with the way he perceived his relationship with the Catholic Church. The first begins with his conversion and continues up through a period of commitment and intellectual adherence to Catholicism that seems to have come to a close at about the time his novel *The Quiet American* was published in 1955. The second—extending from the mid-1950s up to his death (and during which time he described himself as having become a lapsed Catholic)—reveals a dramatic shift in tone and emphasis. No longer would he rely on the certainty of Catholic truths and teachings to give meaning to the fallen world, but he would now portray the universe as increasingly unilluminated by any divine presence or pattern and defined more realistically by such factors as the absurd. In *A Sort of Life* (1971) he describes this change in conviction—from Catholic belief in providence to troubled pessimism—as a mid-life religious crisis that forced him to abandon his allegiance "to a city in which we are no longer citizens."[24] This period of social and political turmoil (Vietnam and the East–West conflicts) and the upheaval in the Catholic Church created by the Second Vatican Council were, of course, factors in his changing attitudes. Hence the kind of novels that he wrote during his later period—*A Burnt-Out Case* (1961) and *The Comedians* (1966), for example—are possible bell-wethers explaining how the Catholic novel would change and what it would become in the later decades of the twentieth century. We must first, however, study the novels of Greene's "Catholic period."

Critics consider Greene's Catholic novels to be *Brighton Rock* (1938), *The Power and the Glory* (1940), *The Heart of the Matter* (1948), and *The End of the Affair* (1951). These are not the only works he wrote during this period, nor were they necessarily the most widely read (*The Ministry of Fear* [1943] and *The Third Man* [1950], for example, enjoyed an immense popularity, with the latter becoming an important spy film of the 1950s). Greene indicated the importance he ascribed to the four Catholic works, however, by designating them "novels," whereas the others he called "entertainments," presumably to emphasize their more dominant "thriller" or detective-story content.

Indeed, viewed superficially, *Brighton Rock* (which Greene initially designated as "entertainment/novel") could be regarded as primarily a psychological thriller, and its plot certainly contains all the genre's essential elements. Greene, however, greatly expanded the novel's scope by placing at its center a "demonic" protagonist and by making his drama of perdition the focus of the plot. Pinkie Brown, or "the Boy" as he is often called by the omniscient narrator, plays out his destiny in the cheap, tawdry Nelson Place slum area (whose seediness the author makes legendary in his "Greeneland" descriptions of locale) of the popular English seaside resort of Brighton. Crushed and humiliated by a childhood of grinding poverty yet marked by and still believing in the strict, Jansenistic Catholicism in which he was raised, Pinkie is a young punk drawn into the life of local gangs and clever enough to have risen to leadership of his own band of juvenile toughs. At the novel's beginning he engineers the death of a low-life confidence man (Hale) who has invaded the gang's turf in his role as a publicity agent for local businesses (he hides in various places—under plates or place settings in restaurants, for example—cards redeemable for price reductions). Consciously aware as he makes his rounds this time that he is being stalked by the members of the gang, Hale nervously picks up a fun-loving and sensual barmaid, Ida Arnold, to serve as a kind of shield as she accompanies him in the tacky resort restaurants and amusements where he hides his cards. When Ida leaves him momentarily for the lavatory, gang members seize the opportunity to apprehend and summarily execute him.

In order to establish an alibi for the killers, Spicer, a member of Pinkie's gang, continues to hide Hale's cards in restaurants where the latter normally would go, thus distancing the gang from the time and place of the murder. He hides one in Snow's Restaurant where Rose Wilson, a new and inexperienced waitress, sees him in the act. Pinkie then goes himself to retrieve the card (in case the waitress may have seen Spicer and thus could link him and the group with the murder). When he arrives on the scene and tries to take the card back, Rose intercepts him and also innocently discloses that she has indeed seen the person who initially hid it. Pinkie immediately realizes that Rose is a potential witness who now can link the gang to the killing; he further realizes that he cannot take the risk of leaving her alone. "I'll be seeing you. . . . You and me have things in common,"[25] he says. And forcing himself on her amorously, he eventually involves her both in his crimes and in a destiny shared through sex and marriage.

Outraged by Hale's death and still feeling affectionately linked to this would-have-been lover, Ida Arnold vows to get to the bottom of the case. A woman of boundless energy and a keen sense of fair play, she makes inquiries, talks with the police, and leads them to the restaurant and to Rose. Rose, in the meantime, has gradually become aware of

Pinkie's gang connections and of his potential involvement in the murder. Still a virgin and disgusted by sex, Pinkie reluctantly makes Rose his lover in an attempt to further control her, and though both are underage, he manages, through the agency of a crooked lawyer, to marry her in a registry office. As the ring closes around Pinkie and the police are put on his track, the pursued criminal decides to murder his new wife and thus silence her for good. Rose, in the meantime, has proved to be totally devoted to Pinkie, whose humiliated and impoverished background she shares. Yet totally isolated from others, he cannot trust her and concocts the plan of a suicide pact, which he, of course, would survive. With Ida and the police in hot pursuit, the couple drive to a cliff area ("Peacehaven") outside of the city where they will shoot themselves. Ida and the police catch up with them just as Pinkie puts a gun into Rose's hand. Rose throws the gun down, however, and misinterpreting her act as one of possible complicity with the police, Pinkie throws acid (intended for the police) at her face; however, the wind blows it back on him, and blinded, he trips and falls over cliffs to his death. .

Overwhelmed with grief, Rose must now reconcile herself with the loss of the only man who she believes has ever loved her and to whom she has given her virginity. A faithful Catholic, she goes to confession, where she talks with a sympathetic priest about Pinkie's spiritual state, and neither thinks of nor receives spiritual consolation for herself. She must endure, however, one final, terrible blow: as she leaves the confessional with only the uncertain memory of what she hopes was Pinkie's love for her as a means to counter her despair and loneliness, she has in her possession and intends to play his final "gift" to her. This is a recording of his voice, which cruelly tells her in no uncertain terms of the hatred and disgust he holds for her unconditional love for him (which, he unwittingly reveals here, has nevertheless obviously touched him by threatening his vaunted toughness and for a time filling the void of his total alienation from others).

Such are the bare bones of the plot. Yet Greene utilizes them to create a fascinating study of a character caught in a Manichean vice, whose soul is equally torn between two extremes. On the one hand, Pinkie is so consumed with self-hatred and convinced of his damnation that he naturally turns his vital energies to perverse ends. Yet the monstrous qualities he displays on the surface tell only half the story. He is at the same time the innocent child, scarred and abused by a vicious society, who still has intimations of childhood purity and a longing for innocence lost. He is easily moved by memories of his Catholic past: "'Why I was once in a choir,' the Boy confided and suddenly he began to sing softly in his polite boy's voice 'Agnus dei qui tollis peccata mundi, dona nobis pacem.' And in his voice a whole lost world . . . the smell of the incense and laundered surplices and the music" (*Brighton Rock*, 52). Yet he seems to remain almost totally imprisoned in his own dark world of guilt and resentment; nor does Greene ever suggest openly that he repents of his sins (Pinkie is too convinced that his evil nature and what he feels to be his Satanic propensity to evil have damned him forever). Rather, he is described as having departed life in pain, with feelings of hatred for self and others, and seemingly without recourse to grace and the salutary intervention of the hidden God waiting in the wings.

Yet the life of Pinkie, the absolute sinner and votary of evil, has become intertwined with that of Rose, the novel's Maria Cross and vehicle of grace, and the role that this humble, long-suffering daughter of the people plays in the drama of salvation and damnation seems to throw clear lines into confusion. She first pities Pinkie, and though a pious girl, she consents for what seem primarily maternal reasons to give up her virginity to him. Living in sin and terribly aware of her probable damnation, she nevertheless remains loyal even when she knows that the "suicide pact" she immediately agrees to will damn her soul forever. Shortly before the aborted attempt, she muses to herself, "It is said to be the worst act of all, the act of despair, the sin without forgiveness; sitting there in the smell of petrol she tried to realize despair, the mortal sin, but she couldn't. . . . [H]e was going to damn himself, but she was going to show them that they couldn't damn him without damning her too" (*Brighton Rock*, 228).

When she goes to confession after Pinkie's death, Rose tells the priest that she cannot bring herself to repent of her decision to commit suicide for her husband, and she even now regrets not having died with him. Defying the priest to condemn her love and intended sacrifice as evil, she is amazed as the mild-mannered person on the other side of the screen instead relates to her the story of a certain Frenchman, "a good man, a holy man who . . . lived in sin all through his life because he couldn't bear the idea that a soul could suffer damnation" (*Brighton Rock*, 246). The priest is, of course, referring without name to Charles Péguy and to Péguy's renunciation of the consolation of the sacraments during the many years when he lived apart from the Church out of love and respect for his wife, who herself refused to be converted. And, of course, Greene is here indirectly invoking Péguy's "sinner at the center of Christendom" theme.

By placing her soul in spiritual jeopardy (and by accepting damnation for another) Rose has made the greatest of all human offerings, and even though she emerges from the confessional without having been offered absolution, she is clearly on the high road to salvation and perhaps even sanctity. (Roger Sharrock sees her in her saving role not so much as a "holy sinner" but a "holy fool," or at least one on the way to becoming that by a life of extreme and abject service, like the poor women—Clothide and Véronique—in Bloy [Sharrock, 90].)

As for Pinkie, though Greene declines to give the slightest assurance that he may have possibly repented at the last moment, the case remains intriguingly open. Rose's anguished question of whether or not her lover can be saved, though she cannot bring herself to ask it of her confessor, is divined and energetically responded to when the elderly, mild-mannered, "wheezing" person on the other side of the grate forcefully and impatiently declares, "You can't conceive, my child, nor can I nor anyone the . . . appalling . . . strangeness of the mercy of God." And, he concludes, "we must hope and pray. . . . The Church does not demand that we believe that any soul is cut off from mercy" (*Brighton Rock*, 246).

There seems reason to believe, then, that Rose's pure and total offering of self (a classic example of reversibility) has affected Pinkie's salvation. Nor will the reader (nor anyone else) ever know for sure because no one can read the mind of God. Pinkie is, certainly, the consummate sinner, whose absolute commitment to evil prompts the reader to recognize the same tragic "postulation" to vice within all of us. But one also has the right to conclude that the abused and tormented child/man is emblematic of Péguy's sinner (and even a potentially holy one through his total obsession with salvation), whom Thompson's Divine Hunter has pursued relentlessly from the very first. Pinkie's soul, then, may have been touched by grace in the very last seconds of his existence, or even beyond the boundaries of what is after all only a human approximation of what we call time. In any case, Greene has in the novel reworked Péguy's original paradox of sinner/saint into a strikingly new and brilliant pattern with this evocation of the delinquent young criminal of the Brighton slums, whose Satanic/angelic propensities even evoke comparison with the adolescent Rimbaud.

The Power and the Glory is the first of Greene's novels to be set in one of the many exotic locations that this inveterate traveler would first visit as writer/journalist (of the other Catholic novels only *The End of the Affair* is situated in England). The site of this novel is Tobasco, a northern province of Mexico in the grip of a religious persecution (and reign of terror) conducted in the early decades of the twentieth century by the victorious Party of the Revolution. Greene had spent several months there in 1937–38 to investigate the state of the Church and, as Sharrock has observed, the author immediately found Mexico a perfect locale for his fictional tastes and imagination: "The human misery and physical squalor of the country did not need a subjective stylistic emphasis to be converted into Greeneland: Greeneland was there already, even down to the irony of squalor" (Sharrock, 103).

The environment Greene portrays is that of overabundant nature and the natural cycle of birth, copulation, death in which all living things seem submerged. The impatient buzzards perched on rooftops awaiting carrion symbolize the violence of life in this monstrously proliferating yet poverty-stricken area of the world, where grinding misery and death are for the vast majority the only certainties.

In this fallen world—symbolic of what Greene would call "the huge universal abandonment"—he relates the fate of a human failure, a "whiskey priest," unfaithful to his religious vows but who continues to practice his ministry. The priest is presented as a faceless individual (his name is not given), a kind of modern "everyman" of the Charlie Chaplin variety, without distinguishing marks of valor or excellence. And, indeed, the greater part of the novel recounts his frenetic flight from the officials of the atheistic military dictatorship, which, intent on stamping out all vestiges of religion in the new social order, have marked for death all priests who do not submit to laicization and marriage.

As he flees from the hotly pursuing soldiers through the jungles and wretched mountain villages in the Tobasco province, the priest lucidly reflects on the reasons for his deplorable fall from grace. From the poverty of his early condition as a peasant, he had embraced the priesthood to become a well-nourished, pompous, and ambitious young parish priest, who loved the honors of his office and the adulation that his poor parishioners had given him. At the outset of the revolution he had taken to drink, feeling that the sufferings of persecution allowed him this consolation. Progressively more and more dependent on this drug he had at one point under the influence fathered a daughter with a peasant woman. Now an outcast among his parishioners because of his broken vow and an enemy of the state (the last fugitive priest surviving in the province), he has become a hunted animal on the run or occasionally hidden by the faithful in the remote villages through which he passes. It is important to note that, despite his desperate attempts at flight, he has never abandoned ministering to the peasants in each hovel in which he is sheltered, and at each stop he clandestinely says mass and hears confessions. The priest has no illusions about his moral state; considering himself an abject sinner, he despairs that God would never forgive the betrayal of his priestly promises. Now an alcoholic, he is forced to balance the needs of his habit with the requirements of his ministry. He is, it should be said, never portrayed as being substantially incapacitated by his dependence, nor does drink or desire for it ever impede the administering of priestly duties. Rather, it seems to be for him the indelible sign of his fallen state and a reality that never allows him to attempt to lessen or justify his guilt or deny his sinful condition.

Yet when the priest makes his furtive rounds and tries to outwit his pursuers, he becomes more and more caught up and aware of the desperate plight of the peasants. Several of them, in fact, will be taken as hostages for him by the authorities and then executed (they all heroically refuse to reveal the priest's presence in their villages). Now forced to endure the same kind of desperate existence the peasants have always had to, the priest becomes humanized, and he freely accepts and shares their sufferings. In this sense the priest becomes one of Greene's paradoxical saints, the common man who is compelled by circumstances to become a saint by giving over his will to that of God. But this evolution is only achieved by the priest's being forced to assume the basest conditions of his wretched flock.

Greene portrays this "descent to the depths" in the masterful scene when the still unapprehended priest is imprisoned for a night in a foul, horribly overcrowded cell for having purchased black-market wine. Surrounded by the most wretched elements of society, he reveals his identity to the people pressing against him (though it obviously could mean his instant execution if they speak out) and counsels a hypocritical "good" Catholic interred with the rest (for having displayed religious cards) not to feel morally superior to the unsavory group from which she disdainfully distances herself. Contesting the woman's view that the others are ugly in their state of moral degradation, he says, "Don't believe that. It's dangerous. Because suddenly we discover that our sins have so much beauty. . . . Such a lot of beauty. Saints talk about the beauty of suffering. Well, we are not saints, you and I. Suffering to us is just ugly. . . . It needs a lot of learning to see things with a saint's eye. A saint gets a subtle taste for beauty and can look down on poor ignorant palates like theirs. But we can't afford to."[26]

From this point on the priest accepts his cross for martyrdom and takes on himself the salvation of his people, particularly the fate of his daughter, whose soul he offers for salvation in his own stead. When there seems the real possibility of escaping from Tobasco to enter a province where saying the Mass and administering the sacraments are not outlawed, he is faced with an agonizing decision. The Judas-like mestizo who has arranged with the authorities to betray the priest for a price tells him that a violent American bandit, pursued by the police and now seriously wounded, is calling for a priest. In recrossing the border to aid the fugitive, the priest would obviously have to backtrack over the most dangerous areas and would almost certainly be apprehended. Even while he is virtually sure that he is falling into a trap, the whiskey priest cannot refuse the duties of his vocation and heeds the call of someone in physical (and, he believes, spiritual) distress. When he arrives at the gangster's mountain holdout, the hardened criminal refuses to accept the sacraments and instead warns the priest of the presence of the guards, who immediately seize him.

As he awaits execution the priest is extremely afraid and has no hope of salvation. The night before he is to die before the firing squad, partially drunk with brandy and overwhelmed by guilt, he reflects on his wretchedness and what he views to have been the total failure of his life as a priest: "He caught sight of his own shadow on the cell wall; it had a look of grotesque surprise and unimportance. What a fool he had been to think that he was strong enough to stay when others fled. What an impossible fellow I am, he thought, and how useless. I have done nothing for anybody. I might as well have never lived."

He further reflects that it is not so much certain damnation that he fears but the supreme scandal of having to go to God "empty-handed, with nothing done at all." And his last regret (a direct reworking of the epithet of Bloy's holy woman Clotilde) is that "at the end there was only one thing that counted—to be a saint" (*Power*, 247).

It is, of course, his total inability to see himself in any but a fallen state that remains the strongest proof of his sanctity. For he has lived out completely the Christian paradox of losing one's life to gain it. Throughout his life he had believed that God is love and had given himself over to the service of that love, despite his fall from grace, by instinctively ministering to others. Hence as an instrument of grace through the power of the sacraments, the priest becomes a very human saint and fills the gap between what Sharrock has so astutely described as "fallen knowledge and the hidden God shrouded in our ignorance." Through the agency of the whiskey priest, the novel therefore strikes an admirable balance in its portrayal of the economy of salvation between the "dark

heart of man and the Catholic sacramental life" (Sharrock, 123). It finally provides another ecclesiastical hero for modern times, the modest
priest, the "eternal little man" who, despite his more flawed nature,
resembles very much Bernanos's humble curé d'Ambricourt and like
him becomes the medium of grace to overcome the fallen modern world.

Set in the former British colony of Sierra Leone in West Africa, *The
Heart of the Matter* is the most psychologically complex of all of Greene's
Catholic novels and the one that most clearly follows the French model
perfected by François Mauriac: its central theme is the struggle of the
protagonist to overcome an obsessive passion that threatens to lead to
eternal damnation. Greene had long admired Mauriac's work and cred-
ited him as virtually the only novelist to have continued to give to the
modern novel "a religious sense" (which, he claimed, had been lost in the
English tradition since the death of Henry James). Greene also had
praised Mauriac for being a traditional novelist (not therefore having
succumbed to modernist techniques) "for whom the visible world has
not ceased to exist, whose characters have the solidity of men with souls
to save or lose" (*Collected Essays*, 116). And, indeed, in *The Heart of Matter*
Greene clearly reveals a reliance on the literary forms and intentions of
Mauriac and other French moralists in the case study of his troubled protagonist, Major Scobie.

Scobie is a colonial police chief in a dilapidated backwater town of the
West African colony of Sierra Leone (inhabited by English functionaries,
wretched natives, corrupt merchants, and other unassimilated nationals).
The locale—a torrid, parched and cruel landscape—was well-known to
Greene (he had thoroughly investigated it in a journalistic tour in 1935)
and provided him with yet another site on which to create a Greeneland.
This time it would be the portrayal of a hopelessly abandoned colonial
society whose terminally bored inhabitants live out their seemingly useless lives in quiet desperation.

Major Scobie (or "Ticki" to his wife) is from the beginning presented
as a virtuous man. A convert to Catholicism and a sincere practitioner of
the faith, he considers each problem or conflict arising from his personal
and professional life in moral terms. He is married to Louise, a weak,
socially ambitious and pretentious woman and another of Greene's "surface Catholics" who rigidly follows the rules without interior adherence
to charity and consideration for others. The Scobies have lost their young
daughter and only child and, feeling put upon by this loss, Louise lives
as if she were a semi-invalid, constantly reproaching her husband for his
lack of professional ambition and blaming him for his slowness to climb

the bureaucratic ladder and for the resulting lack of acceptable social contacts that she feels she deserves. A childish, spoiled dependent, she is selfishly unaware of the many financial and personal sacrifices that Scobie has continually had to make to keep her reasonably content; nor does she seem to understand that her husband has ceased to love her and has instead replaced this sentiment with a pity that one reserves for a helpless, wayward child.

Scobie is a very complex character. A man with a rigorous sense of honor and duty, he has, as his relationship with his wife indicates, himself become victim of a perverse and exaggerated sense of pity for others (particularly for the seemingly helpless). This feeling, his tragic flaw, has both positive and negative ramifications in his own moral and spiritual life. Positively regarded, this sentiment—rooted in charity and linked to his religious beliefs—is translated by him into unselfish concern and action to alleviate the distress of others. In this respect his feelings for his wife and the other "pitiable" characters whom he will encounter is admirable and follows the evangelical teaching of true Christian charity. Viewed in this light, Scobie is certainly a moral exemplar—one who may even be on the road to sanctity.

Yet, as W. H. Auden pointed out in his penetrating analysis of Greene's use of the theme of pity in this and other novels, the sentiment may have other, less altruistic motivations, even becoming "the vice of pity, that corrupt parody of love and compassion which is so insidious and deadly for sensitive natures." And Auden reasons that in Scobie's case pity has indeed taken on the form of vice because it conceals darker motivations: "Behind pity for others lies self pity, and behind self pity lies cruelty."[27]

Applying this analysis of the virtue/vice to Scobie's feelings toward his wife, it is apparent that his attention and care for Louise may well conceal disdain, even strong dislike for her as a burden on him. This "tainted" pity offers him a further means of detachment from her and an excuse for not dealing with her (as one must in any love situation) as a free, responsible human being but rather as an object (here a child), hence not an equal. "Pity" of this sort also may even indicate the refusal or even inablity to love another person and the wish (conscious or unconscious) to retreat—to borrow Sartre's expression—to one's "reef of solitude" and there live solipsistically, impervious to the reality and rights of the "other." Finally, in a religious context, pity can take on the form of an egregious sin of pride. This is so because it can allow us to view others from a God-like vantage point, as if we could understand, as God alone does, the roots or reasons for human motivaton or conduct, or as if we could probe the inner workings of another human being's conscience. Pity in this sense may even set us up as rivals to God in the workings of His providence and understanding of others, and it can thus have Luciferian dimensions.

So finely drawn is Scobie's multifaceted character that the reader is never able completely or precisely to isolate and identify as dominant any one of the correlatives—positive or negative—of pity I have just described. And Greene reveals himself in this literary creation to be a keenly perceptive moralist quite on the level of La Rochefoucauld in plumbing the complicated operations of the human heart.

The story line is difficult to relay in a summary fashion because much of the plot development is constructed on psychological interdependencies between the characters. Scobie no longer loves his neurotic wife but, because he now pities her, feels he must grant her every whim. The irresponsible child that she is, Louise forces him to provide money for her to leave for an extended stay in South Africa, where she hopes to recuperate her strength and come to grips with her deep disappointment at her husband's having been passed over in the filling of a vacancy for district police chief. Turned down by the bank manager for a loan to allow his wife to travel, Scobie is led little by little into corrupt doings and connections to get the money. This route leads to the agency of Yusef, a Syrian entrepreneur, money lender, and diamond smuggler who lends him the money, at first with no strings attached. In the meantime (the period is World War II) Scobie's colony has become more and more the site for trafficking in precious gems; suspecting Scobie's possible involvement, the Home Office sends a representative, Wilson, supposedly a commercial clerk but in reality undercover intelligence, to watch Scobie. Wilson becomes infatuated with Louise, who is drawn to the young man's romantic temperament (he loves poetry) and uses his company as a diversion and escape from boredom.

The novel is essentially the relation of the fall of Scobie, a good man caught in nets of complicity through his own deep feelings for others. Remaining virtuous to the end, he is corrupted by feelings of sympathy that cause him to commit selfless acts and consequently to become responsible for others in a God-like way. Thus, when his wife leaves for South Africa, he is called to the aid of survivors of a torpedoed ship. Visiting the survivors in the hospital he sits at the bedside of a dying child (who obviously reminds him of his dead daughter). At the site of the disaster he also meets Helen Rolt, a young Englishwoman who has lost her husband on one of the rescue rafts. From the outset she appeals to him because she resembles and reminds him of these two dead children. Scobie befriends her and later becomes her lover because he believes that this relationship is essential to her happiness and well being. The affair continues during Louise's absence and becomes instrumental in placing Scobie securely under the blackmailing power of Yusef. After one of their quarrels, Scobie passes a letter under the door of Helen's cabin. The letter is taken by one of Yusif's boys, Ali, and Scobie now finds himself under the Syrian's power. Using his knowledge as means of blackmail, Yusef immediately presses Scobie to place a packet of diamonds aboard a Portuguese ship. Scobie does so because he does not want his affair with Helen known to Louise, since this disclosure will hurt her.

At this point Louise suddenly returns because she apparently no longer feels socially disgraced at Scobie's having been passed over for promotion; she also claims to have come back to assure herself that Scobie is not backsliding from his religious duties. Scobie is, of course, anguished and disgusted at his duplicity in carrying on the affair with Helen. Exerting a religious "test" for his probity (she has apparently heard or been told rumors about the affair), Louise insists that he take Communion with her. When he goes to confession before Mass, he does not receive absolution because he cannot promise the priest that he will give up his adultery. In his mind, he cannot compromise the happiness of either woman, and he goes to Communion with the certainty that he is damning himself.

Scobie's betrayal of God by receiving a sacreligous Communion occurs at the same time that he slips into corruption as a policeman. Now inextricably caught in a web of complicty with the slippery Yusef, Scobie even is drawn into and can be regarded as at least materially responsible for the murder of the innocent servant Ali, in many ways Scobie's only friend but whom he now mistakenly believes has accepted bribes to disclose the affair with Helen to Louise. After hearing Scobie's fears and believing him to want the servant out of the way, Yusef has his men kill Ali, whose body a horrified Scobie describes as "a broken piece of the rosary . . . a couple of black beads and the image of God coiled at the end of it."[28] Overwhelmed by what he now fears has been his unwitting role in the murder, aware that Wilson is on to his smuggling for Yusef, and despairing of making either Louise or Helen happy, Scobie concludes that suicide is his only way out. To the very end he wishes to protect Louise from the scandal of his action, and to make sure that she is left with financial support he plans his death to resemble an attack of angina. (He carefully records accounts of false attacks in his diary to put the insurance people and all concerned off the track and then systematically takes regular doses of the drug Evipan to establish his sickness and to create the alibi of dependency on the medication.) Before he takes the fatal overdose, he learns ironically that he will, after all, be promoted to the post of comissioner, and he now realizes in hindsight that had he waited longer, he would not have have had to become criminally involved with Yusef, since, with her social aspirations satisfied, Louise would not have been in need of the money for the costly vacation for which he sacrificed his honesty and began his moral fall. Yet he feels that it is manifestly too late to extricate himself from what has become a tragic entanglement.

Scobie's last moments in life represent the most dramatically charged part of the work. In a final visit to church before the suicide he explains before the presence in the tabernacle that he is compelled to commit suicide because he cannot otherwise cease from hurting not only Helen and Louise, but also God. "O God," he says, "I'm the only guilty one because I've known the answers all day. I've preferred to give you pain rather than pain to Helen or my wife because I can't observe your suffering. I can only imagine it. But there are limits to what I can do to you—or them. I can't go on month after month insulting you" (*Heart*, 255).

In this text we clearly see juxtaposed Scobie's unconditional concern and pity for others as well as his prideful inability to accept God's mercy as a sufficient counterweight to blot out his own sins. And in a somewhat unsettling and sudden departure from conventional realist technique, Greene here introduces God as a character in the novel and has Him plead with Scobie, in the role of a humble beggar, to persuade him to renounce the project of suicide and to trust instead in His mercy and understanding. "I am," He declares, "not Thou but simply you, when you speak to me; I'm as any other beggar. Can't you trust me as you'd trust a faithful dog? I have been faithful to you for two thousand years. All you have to do now is ring a bell, go into a box; confess—the repentance is already there straining at your heart" (*Heart*, 258–59).

Scobie cannot obey God's simple plea because he cannot trust God or shift the responsibility that he feels for others to Him. He is to God as he has seen himself in relation to the others: the policeman responsible for law, justice, and providence. Yet though this is terrible arrogance on Scobie's part and tantamount to trying to deal with other people's lives as if he were God, Scobie also resembles his creator in the totally selfless

motivations that he realizes in acts that are at the same time terribly
misdirected and disastrous for his own salvation. The very last moment
of his life sees him filled with pity for still unknown victims. When he
falls to the floor in a spasm, his last recorded impression is as if some
presence "outside the room were seeking him, calling him, and he made
a last effort to indicate that he was there." To the very end Scobie thus
responds to the call for help regardless of the source (here he seems even
to imagine that God is the suffering person calling him), and he dies
uttering the ambiguous and unfinished phrase (so similar to Mauriac's
Louis) "Dear God, I love . . ." (*Heart*, 269).

When Scobie's death is known to have been a suicide, the insensitive
and embittered Louise (who now has to deal with the fact that her husband's affair with Helen is public knowledge) describes Scobie to the
priest, Father Rock, as a bad Catholic who had damned himself and who is
now beyond the pale of prayer. The priest, in characteristically Greenean
tones, indignantly protests, "For goodness sakes, Mrs. Scobie, don't imagine that you or I know a thing about God's mercy." And, in expressing
what seems to lie at the very heart of the matter of Scobie's fate, he
declares, "The Church knows all the rules but it doesn't know a thing
about what goes on in a single human heart" (*Heart*, 272).

With these words Greene brings the reader back again to the paradox
of the virtuous sinner/possible saint that he presented for the whiskey
priest. Scobie is a man of goodwill who falls into crime and sin out of his
own needs and through circumstances in which his Creator has placed
him. As such, there is a question mark over his death. When he takes
the overdose Scobie enters a sphere where rules such as we know them
no longer apply and where God alone disposes of criteria to judge the
human heart. One can view the work as thus ending on a distinctly
Pascalian note, for as this French moralist has written, "The human heart
moves in ways of which reason knows nothing" (Pascal, 163). So, for
that matter, does God. (Péguy's strong influence on the novel was also
acknowledged by Greene in the epigraph, which quotes the opening
lines of Péguy's "sinner at the center of Christianity" text.)

The last novel of the Catholic cycle, *The End of the Affair*, is also the
one most heavily laden with and indebted to Roman Catholic dogma
and beliefs. Along with the themes explored in the preceding novels
(reversibility, the pursuit of the sinner by "the Hound of Heaven," the
power of grace and sacraments), the work employs what seems clearly to
be a form of miraculous intervention as a pivotal part of the plot, and the
Catholic belief in the Communion of Saints (and in particular the inter-

cession of the dead to effect the lives of living) also becomes an essential component in the resolution of the drama. Pascalian themes continue to resonate through this novel as well, with the famous "wager" in favor of God's existence clearly manifest in one of the protagonists' evolution from disbelief to conversion and a radical transformation of life.

The novel is also more elaborately structured and experimental than the other three. Greene uses for the first time in a major novel the authorial stance of a first-person narrator—here a jealous and far from objective lover, through whose personal feelings the reader must strain the matter of the plot. This narrator's presentation is interrupted and substantially supplemented by passages inserted by him from the intimate journal of the dead woman, his lover whom he pursued during life and eventually lost. In this way the "affair" is seen from the point of view of both parties, and the reader is also prepared for the startling intrusion of a second mysterious "lover" of a romantic ménage à trois, who, we eventually learn, is God Himself. And in its minute psychological analysis of an illicit love affair (provided by the direct commentary of each of the lovers), the novel has been identified as Greene's successful attempt to expermient with another French literary form (here the *roman d'analyse* exemplified in such works as *La Princesse de Clèves, Adolphe,* or Françoise Sagan's *Bonjour tristesse*) rather than use the less personal and more socially oriented English form of the love novel (Sharrock, 59).

The novel is set in London in the last years of World War II, and this time, the author's Greeneland evokes and recalls the terror of the blitz air raids, the destruction wreaked by the German V2 rockets, the descent by Londoners into the subway during the attacks, and the general bleakness and precariousness of life. The first-person narrator, Maurice Bendrix, is a successful and well-known novelist whom we first meet in his function as air raid warden during a German bombardment of the city. In the course of the attack he meets Henry Miles, a mousey civil servant who, it turns out, is a neighbor living just across the common. Struck by Henry's submissive way, Bendrix decides on the spot to study and use him as model for a bureaucratic type he intends to feature in a projected novel. When he comes to have a drink in Henry's house, he meets the latter's manifestly bored and attractive wife, Sarah, whom he almost immediately seduces. This romantic liaison, it turns out, is not the first for Sarah—she has had several affairs, presumably to endure her mildly desperate life as the wife of a dull and gentle husband who cannot satisfy her strong emotional needs. Bendrix at first describes his affection for Sarah as nothing more than a kind of respite from the tedium of his day-to-day labors as novelist. She, on the other hand, seems to be seeking in her affair with him the satisfaction of love that will allow her to fill a troubling void in her existence.

At the core of the plot is what seems to be a kind of "miraculous intervention" that, for both of them, spells the end to their affair. During a bombing raid when both are together in Bendrix's apartment (they have imprudently refused to seek shelter because they did not want to interrupt their love-making), a flying rocket makes a direct hit and buries Bendrix under the front door. Only slightly bruised herself but believing Bendrix to be dead, Sarah in panic makes the following vow with God: If her lover lives, she promises forthwith that she will believe and will give him up forever: "Do this, and I'll believe. . . . I love him and I'll do anything if you'll make him alive. . . . I'll give him up for ever, only let him be alive."[29]

Bendrix immediately regains consciousness (he later relates that he remembers himself at that particular moment "to have been completely free from anxiety, jealousy, insecurity, and hate"), and the reader is asked to believe that Bendrix was dead for several seconds and that he returned to life as the result of Sarah's prayer (*Affair*, 85).

At first with great difficulty and much bitterness, Sarah keeps her vow and avoids Bendrix. She desperately fights against belief in the God to whom she has made the sacrifice and even seeks out an atheist preacher, Smythe, whom she hears speak on London Common, to provide her with rational reasons not to believe. This old-style nonbeliever proves much below the task, however, and cannot provide the intellectual proofs that would satisfy the intelligent Sarah.

Bendrix, in the meantime, is convinced that Sarah no longer sees him because she has found another lover. Consumed with jealous rage he hires a detective (the mawkish Parkis) to follow her. Parkis informs Bendrix of Sarah's frequent visits to Smythe, and the latter assumes that the preacher is her new lover. In order to find concrete evidence of Sarah's supposed complicity in a new affair, Parkis sends his little son to her house and the boy makes off with Sarah's diary. In it she has recorded her spiritual evolution since the day of "the miracle." On reading it, Bendrix copiously uses it to draft his own narration and commentary of the affair, and in this way the reader becomes informed of the dimensions of the ferocious struggle in which Sarah has been involved against the unwanted faith that seems to be relentlessly taking possession of her life.

As her journal unfolds, Sarah makes it clear that she is passing from a stage of defiance to one of mystical love of God. Bendrix is especially enraged by the emotionally charged entries in which Sarah disparages human love (which she finds exemplified in her affair with him) in comparison with the peace and fulfillment she has experienced by giving herself totally to God. In one passage she even suggests that Bendrix, in his pursuit of her, has been in reality only seeking a higher being, and that the two of them would eventually turn to God because both would have reached the insurmountable limitations of a purely human love: "For he gave me," she says, referring to Bendrix, "so much love, and I gave him so much that soon there wasn't anything left when we'd finished . . . but You were teaching us to squander, like you taught the rich man, so that one day we might have nothing left except this love of you. But you are too good to me. When I ask You for pain you give me your peace. Give it to him, too. . . . Give him my peace . . . he needs it more" (*Affair*, 151).

At first after reading the diary, Bendrix takes what relief he can in the knowledge that Sarah is at least not in love with another human being, and he is sure that he has the strength and will to overcome this divine "rival" in whom he does not believe. He now tracks down Sarah and follows her whenever she leaves her house. On a cold rainy evening he finally confronts her in a church. Haggard and sick, she begs him not to see her again and he is forced to relent. She dies a few days later of pneumonia, and then begins the final phase of the novel's thematic use of the "Hound of Heaven" metaphor. With Sarah dead, Bendrix is left alone and must face his hated rival.

With blinding rapidity, God seems to reveal the reality of His presence to Bendrix through what can only be interpreted as the intercession of the dead Sarah. At her funeral, her mother informs Bendrix (who had virtually compelled the weak Henry to have his wife cremated) that Sarah has all along been a Catholic without knowing it (her mother had her baptized out of spite to protest against the ill treatment of her husband). Then Sarah seems the agent in the cure of the detective Parkis's young son. Suffering from a severe stomach disorder and in danger of death, the boy is given one of the reading books Sarah used as a child (in which there is a touching inscription, written in her own hand, attesting to her childish belief in God). The boy is immediately cured and relates how, when waking from a dream-like state, he saw Sarah beckoning to him. Smythe the atheist, whose handsome face has long been disfigured by a hideous birth mark, declares that he no longer has the blemish: he further relates that it disappeared after Sarah affectionately kissed him on this spot shortly before her death.

The final part of the novel focuses on the changing state of Bendrix's feelings toward his avenging rival. Brought unwillingly to the very border of belief by these mysterious circumstances and by the intimations of his own heart, Bendrix cannot help but believe in the existence of God. And as his inner disposition seems to have shifted from hatred of a rival to fear that if God exists, he is now forced to confront another reality that opens before him—the Pascalian abyss. Yet he vainly struggles against what he now knows to be the necessity to respond to the wager of belief. He still, however, does not want to go the full route of belief, conversion, selfless love, and even sanctity that his mistress had completed before him.

After Sarah's death Bendrix does, however, change his life for the better. He becomes more compassionate and accepts Henry's offer (even though the cuckolded husband now knows all about the affair) to share his house, and he subsequently becomes committed to Henry's welfare and happiness. And though he adamantly resists admitting to Henry or anyone else the possibility of his conversion, he seems, as the novel ends, to be on the brink of the "leap to faith." What still stands in the way is his inability to accept the loss of a lifetime of human love with Sarah: "I sat on my bed and said to God, You've taken her but You haven't got me yet. I know Your cunning. It's You who takes us up to a high place and offers us the whole universe. You're a devil, . . . I hate You, God, I hate You as though You existed" (*Affair*, 239).

The reader wonders how long the atheist/turning believer can hold out against that love which alone could take Sarah from him. Bendrix acknowledges, in fact, that his journalistic account (in reality the novel) which he first intended to be "a record of hate" has been totally and dramatically altered. And he is now left with "one prayer to serve the winter mood. . . . Leave me alone forever" (*Affair*, 239). With his defenses down it is only inevitable that his strong hatred will be transformed to its equally passionate opposite. And another Pascalian theme seems to provide the key for the resolution of the drama: "You would not seek," Pascal's hidden God is made to say, "unless you had not already found me."

With *The End of the Affair* Greene wrote his most audaciously Catholic novel. It would appear, in fact, that in writing it Greene had reached a kind of impasse beyond which his artistic and creative efforts as a believing Catholic could go no further. His writing from the 1950s onward took him down a very different path and inspired him to record a different vision of reality than that contained in the Catholic cycle. In a 1974 introduction to the novel *A Burnt-Out Case* (1961) he described this fundamental change as follows: "The vision of faith as an untroubled sea was lost forever; it was more like a tempest in which the lucky were engulfed and lost, and the unfortunate survived to be flung battered and bleeding on the shore" (quoted in Sharrock, 177). Greene's change of emphasis was a bellwether for subsequent changes in the genre of the Catholic novel, and his enduring influence and importance will be examined later on in this study.

Chapter Four

Scandinavia and Germany: Sigrid Undset, Gertrud von Le Fort, Elisabeth Langgässer

Sigrid Undset

A world-renowned novelist who, during the 1930s and 1940s, was critically acclaimed as the greatest realist writer of her time, the Norwegian author Sigrid Undset received the Nobel Prize for Literature in 1928, four years after completion of her much praised medieval novel/trilogy, *Kristin Lavransdatter*. She is also regarded today as a major Catholic novelist, particularly remarkable for her genius in making the Christian society of the Middle Ages live again in her fiction. Another of the century's illustrious novelist converts to Catholicism, she was the first of six children born of prominent parents in the small town of Kalunborg, Denmark. Her father, a Norwegian from the Tronheim area, was a famous archaeologist and well-published scholar who, though an agnostic, had a strong intellectual appreciation for the role of Christianity in the history and evolution of Western civilization. Her mother, Anna Charlotte Gyth, was the daughter of a prominent chancery officer of the town. She died when Sigrid was only 11, and the family of three girls and three boys was brought up by a doting aunt on her mother's side.

A somewhat sickly child educated at home throughout most of her youth, Sigrid early turned to literature and voraciously read the Scandinavians Henrik Ibsen, August Strindberg, and Knut Hamsun, as well as Chaucer, Keats, Scott, Dickens, Balzac, Flaubert, and Zola (with whom she has frequently been compared for her minute and poetic descriptions of background and milieu). Particularly influential during her adolescent years was the ancient Icelandic family saga, *Njals Saga*, that she would later describe as a book that was a turning point in her life.[1]

Her father's death when she was only 13 placed the family in very difficult circumstances, and Sigrid soon after attended a commercial college to prepare for a career as secretary. After receiving her certificate she was employed in an office for 10 years. Though she disliked the work she was very successful because of her calm and unflustered temperament and her remarkable power of memory. (She humorously recalls always being able on demand to draw essential business details from her "mental file.") It was while employed in this position that she gradually began to realize her vocation as novelist, and she used the business milieu as material for her earliest writings. In the style of the realists she much admired, she wrote sketches of her fellow women office workers who were attempting to come to grips with their femininity and affirm their self worth in the male-dominated society that Norway was at this time. Her first novel, *Mrs. Marta Oulie* (1907), is written in the form of a diary and concerns the fall of an idealistic young married woman (for whom love means everything) into an adulterous affair and her subsequent attempts to reconcile her infidelity with her conscience. A nonbeliever, she nevertheless wishes constantly that there could be a moral reference like God that would allow her to find peace of mind and an adequate degree of moral certitude (Winsnes, 38–40).

After the warm reception given to this novel, Sigrid Undset was awarded a government grant in 1909 to allow her to devote an entire year to her writings while residing in Rome. She achieved full recognition and considerable notoriety in Norwegian intellectual/literary circles when she published in 1911 her novel *Jenny*. The protagonist Jenny's story is that of an intensely moral and religious young woman who does not have an outlet for her beliefs. She wants, nevertheless, to serve a higher power than herself but is frustrated at every turn. Jenny depends on her own natural goodness and what she hopes to find of this in others for a foundation on which to establish her relationships. Her highest priority is to meet a man whom she can respect and love—one with whom she will not waste her affections and ideals—and she especially wants to avoid falling into one of the casual sexual liaisons she sees all about as the prevailing social mode. Finally succumbing through disappointments and tedium to experimentation, she becomes involved in two devastating love affairs. The first is a degrading experience that breaks her life force and renders her unable to respond to the second, this with a hopelessly sentimental and gentle artist who, nevertheless, genuinely loves her. Burned out by her earlier affair and unable to respond even to authentic love, Jenny finds suicide as the only way out.

Unlike Nora of Ibsen's *A Doll's House* who survives in a loveless state, Jenny cannot remain alone nor can she find solace in social emancipation or sexual freedom. Her demands for love stem from a more highly developed spiritual consciousness and include needs that transcend purely physical and social considerations. No doubt for this reason the novel elicited tirades of protest against Undset from Norwegian suffragettes who felt that the women were depicted in the novel as more dependent on their sexual nature than men were on theirs, hence there was the implication that they had less need (or even right) to develop their individuality than their male counterparts. In responding to these criticisms, Undset declared that she was not a feminist if judged in the context of the views of the women's movement of that period. Yet she denied being antifeminist and expressed as her own essential beliefs on this issue that women have distinct differences from men, that the role of mother of a family is a uniquely sacred one, and that the state of marriage constitutes an indissoluble bond between a man and a woman (Winsnes, 57–60). From the publication of *Jenny* to 1920, Undset in fact wrote a series of articles concerning her views on women's rights and the role of motherhood in contemporary society. These were combined in the publication *A Woman's Point of View* (1919). (She had married the artist Anders Svarstad in 1912, and a son, Anders, was born a year later. It was not a happy marriage, however, and on her conversion in 1924 the union was annulled.)

Undset's conversion seems to have been a gradual, rational evolution to belief much similar to that of Chesterton or Waugh and not the wrenching kind of epiphany such as experienced by Péguy, Bloy, and Claudel. From her father she inherited a rationalist belief in the power of the intellect, and—an agnostic up through adolescence—she believed (à la Giovanni Battista Vico) that the concept of God was a necessary invention by humanity to support the values that society should foster. She had, however, always been opposed to a naturalist view of what constitutes a person. For her, nature was never the only or the major source of knowledge, and even before her conversion she believed that human beings had a unique position in the universe, that they had to a great extent the power to choose their destiny, and that this ability constituted a dimension by which the human spirit could transcend the purely visible and material world. She also had a tragic view of the inability of human beings to do what they should morally, which essentially approximated the Christian view of Original Sin and the Fall, and she was early on put off by the strong Darwinian currents in Scandinavian literature (particularly Strindberg's), by the Nietzschean "life worshipers" of Hamsun's novels, and by the materialism of Freudian and Marxist humanists.

Explaining her conversion in the autobiographical essay *They Sought the Ancient Ways* (1926), Undset states that her route to Rome had, ironically, been facilitated from early youth by the absence of any specific religious upbringing in her household. Hence she had first regarded the Church as "an extremely picturesque ruin" existing somewhere outside of the mainstream of real time. When she began to read Catholic authors (Johannes Jøgensen, Bloy, Newman, Chesterton, and Maritain) she was struck by the lack of theological discord in their works when compared with the works of Scandinavia's Protestant writers. The latter, she felt, seemed to have lost any sense of common teachings or accepted authority and therefore presented a welter of diverging views. The reason for this she saw as the continuing result of the Reformation: "Once poured out of the form of the Roman Church, the whole of Christianity has the effect on me of an unsuccessful, burned omelette" (quoted in Winsnes, 79). And her essential criterion for belief—"that one truth should really exist, one and one only"—had, she said, brought her "to the church steps" (quoted in Winsnes, 88). Refusing to remain outside any longer, she entered to find that "all the pieces fell into place" and that "human solidarity lays . . . in [the fact] that we are all inheritors together of the insolvent estate after the bankruptcy of the Fall" (quoted in Winsnes, 89).

Four years before her conversion Undset had completed her massive medieval trilogy, *Kristin Lavransdatter*. For many years prior to this she had done exhaustive historical research on Scandinavian (particularly Norwegian) society of the Middle Ages and had long wanted to write a novel depicting a total view of life in this historical framework. She was very much stimulated by a hotly contested scholarly battle waging from the beginning of the century between two opposing intellectual factions in Norway. The first, a group emanating from the National Romantic School and consisting mostly of historians and literary critics, regarded the Scandinavian countries as having developed a common civilization outside the mainstream of European civilization—a phenomenon scholars such as Hans Kinck and A. D. Jørgensen described as a sort of "Aryan" society that, they claimed, had existed relatively free of contact with Christian values and teachings. As such, this "Aryan" heritage had embodied the sturdy ethos of honor in combat, or the heroic spirit of the North, exemplified at its apogee by the strength and valor of the

Viking invaders. According to this school of thought, the initial contact with and eventual conversion of the rest of Europe to Christianity had had only a superficial impact on these stalwart pagans from Scandinavia, who would never really relinquish their warrior ethic. Hence, as the theory had it, the early missionary priests were not able to convince the proud Danish, Norwegian, and Swedish warriors of their sinful nature, the concept of redemption, and, of course, of the excellence of Christian humility.

The other school of thought—of which the art historian Harry Fett and the literary critic Fredrik Paasche were principal spokesmen—held that from the start Catholicism had been a vital force motivating the minds and hearts of the early Norwegian people. In studies dedicated to Old Norse Christian literature, Paasche in particular had found what he believed to be convincing evidence of the presence and major importance of Christian themes and influences on these early literary texts. And contrasting the ethos of the Old Norse texts with the earlier pagan Icelandic Sagas, he concluded that the former did not ultimately exalt the combative ethos of Viking raiders but rather emphasized the Christian ideas of justice, humility, and loyalty—virtues inherent in the moral teachings of medieval Christianity (Winsnes, 92–109).

Paasche was himself a close friend of Undset and had a strong influence on her preparations for writing her medieval saga. He was, in fact, the first to direct her attention to the documents in the collection *Diplomatarium Norvegicum*, which—with its letters, documents, lawsuits, wills, and inventories—constituted a rich mine of information concerning life and social conditions in medieval Norway. Undset had by this time become well-known as a historian in her own right, through the publication of a seminal work on early Norwegian ballads. Through her research in this early folk literature and the precious documentation of the *Diplomatarium*, she had become very well versed in the period and skillfully drew from these primary-source materials to be used in her brilliant and painstaking literary re-creation of life in the Middle Ages.

She combined in the work the technique of a realist writer with the focus of a Christian moralist, therefore depicting her characters as essentially engaged in an unchanging spiritual drama in an eternal frame of reference. This drama would take the form of a struggle pitting the individual ego and combined forces of evil against the divine call ingrained in every human heart to follow and conform to the will of God in each individual life. And though her characters were to be of another age, they would include a timeless cast of psychological types who would run the full gamut of emotions. As a historian and realist, however, Undset would differentiate her characters from the modern-day types in one essential respect: having lived out their destinies before the Renaissance and Reformation, these medieval men and women would not be consumed by the cult of individualism but instead believed themselves to be inextricably bound to society and the social weal. They also would not have lost a recognition of the evil and the necessity for each individual to take responsibility for sinful acts—moral dispositions that Undset saw as tragically eradicated from the minds of modern Europeans. Rather, her medieval characters would know what evil was and when they were sinning, and it would never occur to them to deny their guilt or fall from grace. They would, finally, never be deceived into accepting the here and now and the base pleasures of life as their ultimate reality but would instinctively know, on the contrary, that they had been called to a higher life.

Kristin Lavransdatter consists of three volumes: *Kransen* (1920; *The Bridal Wreath*), *Husfrue* (1921; *The Mistress of Husaby*), and *Korset* (1922; *The Cross*). The work recounts the spiritual life journey of Kristin Lavransdatter, dramatizing the lifelong, stormy, and passionate love relationship between Kristin and her husband, Erlend Nikulausson. It is also a realist saga that mirrors in intimate detail family life in fourteenth-century Norway.

Kristin's family tree is given concrete dimensions: her father, Lavrans Björgulfssön, is a member of the old landed nobility and as a youth served in the king's bodyguard. His wife, Ragnfrid, is also descended from a noble family. Though of the aristocracy, neither family has played a major role in the politics of the court life of Oslo. Rather, they are essentially landowners who, under the peaceful reign of King Haakon V, have prospered while living on their extensive farm, Jörundgaard, in the "Dale" area of Norway and far from the social attractions and intrigues of the capital. Lavrans and his wife are pious, God-fearing people who are known throughout their area for the charity that they bestow on wayfarers and beggars who pass through their lands. Lavrans in particular is a saintly person who, as a youth, had felt the attraction of a monastic vocation. Throughout the novel he is depicted as the consummate Christian gentleman—thoughtful, compassionate, and willing to accept the suffering imposed on him by the erring ways of members of his family in atonement for his faults.

The Bridal Wreath is a bildungsroman dealing with the educational and moral development from childhood to marriage of the couple's eldest daughter, Kristin. From her earliest years she is portrayed as strong-willed, torn between her personal desires for happiness and the laws of God against which her passions increasingly lead her. The symbol and leitmotiv Undset employs for this struggle is a wreath of golden flowers. The first time this garland appears, Kristin, a child of seven, sees also for the first time the reflection of her face, here in a crystal mountain pool. As she gazes in pleasure at what she thinks to be a comely countenance, another image—that of a "pale and fair-haired elf maiden"—appears in the water and blocks out her own.[2] The apparition, manifestly a symbol of the beauty and sensual enticements of the world, then beckons to Kristin and extends a wreath of gold flowers. Shrieking with fear at the vision, Kristin seems to grasp instinctively its significance as a representation and foreshadowing of what would become the moral drama of her own life: the struggle to suppress her strong propensities to gratify her senses and to follow her own will in place of God's.

Kristin's attachment to Christianity as a child is, nevertheless, very strong. She has from birth been immersed in the sacramental and aesthetic signs of medieval Catholicism, and these have taken deep root in her psyche. She has also been made well aware of the concept of life on earth as a battle for salvation. When she accompanies her father on a visit to the magnificent Gothic cathedral in Hamar, the splendid architecture, the stained-glass windows, and the cathedral's spirit of prayer fill her with reverence and wonder. She meets on this occasion Brother Edvin, a humble Franciscan friar, who will become for her a major spiritual mentor and (after his death) a kind of guardian angel. In the church he explains to the young girl the meaning of the biblical images in the windows and statuary and speaks to her of what she only vaguely understands but of what will become the issue of her spiritual life. As if aware of her impending struggle, he says, "There is no man, Kristin, who does not love and fear God, but it is because our hearts are divided between love for God and fear of the devil and love of the world and the flesh, that we are wretched both in life and death" (*Bridal Wreath*, 38). The power of the world has, however, already gained ascendency in the girl's mind. Deeply impressed by Brother Edvin's vibrant belief that all things are possible in God's name, she admits that "she did not want to have such a faith herself. She did not love the Lord and his Mother and the Saints so much. . . . She loved the world and longed for the world" (*Bridal Wreath*, 74).

When Kristin is 15 her father arranges for her marriage to Simon Darre, heir of the nobleman whose farm neighbors that of the Lavrans. Though handsome, the modest and retiring Simon does not compare to the romantic image of a husband that Kristin has conjured up. She nevertheless accepts the arrangement, and it is only under the meddling influence of Lady Aashild, a kind of witch whom the community tolerates because of her noble parentage, that Kristin is later persuaded to resist the arrangement. Lady Aashild constantly disparages Simon as having the narrow, rustic mentality of the Dale farmers. She further suggests that the comely Kristin should seek after a chivalrous form of love and marry a man of the court, schooled in "courtoisie," and tells her about Erlend Nikulausson, the handsome and dissolute son of her own sister.

Kristin is not too young to already know something about the power of passionate love (earlier she had had to resist the brutal sexual advances of a young male childhood friend). Listening to Lady Aashild's suggestions, she explicit understands that "she herself and all mankind had a sinful carnal body which enmeshed the soul and ate into it with hard bonds" (*Bridal Wreath*, 161). Alarmed by the passionate desires aroused within her, she begs her father to send her to a convent (she has earlier experienced on several occasions an attraction to the religious life). Believing this to be a good idea as preparation for marriage, her father sends her to Oslo.

It is at the end of the year spent there that she meets Erlend at a city fair and experiences the coup de foudre for him that will profoundly change her and affect her moral/spiritual state until the day she dies. Erlend is passionately drawn to her as well, and they both abandon decency and restraint in consummating their love. They meet clandestinely in tawdry hostels in Oslo, and in one of their trysts they encounter her fiancé. Shattered by Kristin's effrontery and infidelity, Simon nevertheless gallantly takes on himself the responsibility for breaking the engagement and wishes at all cost to protect Lavrans from the shame that his daughter's actions would surely cause him. Kristin and Erlend are even more entangled in evil when they become morally responsible (through their abusive threats) for the death by suicide of Erlend's mistress, Eline, who is also the mother of two illegitimate children by him.

After Simon Darre reluctantly renounces his betrothal of her, Erlend makes his formal suit for Kristin's hand. Even without knowing at this time the shame of Kristen's sexual involvement with the suitor, Lavrans is strongly opposed to giving his daughter to him because of the latter's dubious reputation as wastral and womanizer. Refusing to accept her father's judgment, Kristin conducts a long campaign of defiance against her family and refuses to be consoled in the matter. She is at the same time sadly aware that her attitude is sinful and that her stubborness is literally killing her father with sadness; yet not being able to renounce her passion even at the cost of grievously hurting him, she now clearly understands the enslaving nature of sin. "I didn't see," she says,"what sin brings with it . . . that one must tread others underfoot. Now I know that I can never give up Erlend, even though I should tread my own father underfoot" (*Bridal Wreath*, 259).

Kristin eventually wins out against Lavrans by wearing down his will. He very reluctantly accepts Erlend's suit, and the two young people are married in grand festivity. Already heavy with child, Kristin presents a sad countenance at the wedding ceremony, where she hypocritically accepts the bridal wreath symbolizing her passage from the chastity of maiden state to that of a married woman. At this very moment—the nadir of her disgrace—her spiritual regeneration begins. Kneeling at the nupital Mass next to Erlend, she prays to Norway's patron saint, Olav, to protect the innocent child in her womb from God's righteous wrath and solemnly swears to one day take her child in her arms and journey as a barefoot pilgrim to the Cathedral of Nidaros, where she will place her golden bridal wreath at Saint Olav's altar.

Lavrans was aware before the wedding of Kristin's sin with Erlend, and during the marriage feast he also learns from Ragnfrid that he may not have been the father of their first-born son who died in infancy. Wracked with sadness at the double betrayal, the good man still seems able to forgive and console his wife for her infidelity and to continue to love his wayward daughter.

The Mistress of Husaby describes the married life of Kristin and Erlend, much of which is spent away from Kristin's family farm, at Erlend's run-down manor house of Husaby. In this volume Undset touches on all the aspects of the life of married people: their intimate relations, how they discharge family and household duties, the birthing and bringing up of children, the rhythm and kind of social life, and the far-reaching impact that religious and political issues play in their lives. Yet her realist approach places these mutable aspects of a couple's journey through life always in an eternal perspective as both Kristin and Erlend come to grips with their spiritual identity and destiny as creatures of God.

Erlend is gradually revealed here as the more sympathetic of the two. Not the selfish hedonist he first seemed, he epitomizes more and more the chivalrous, warring knight little touched by Christian spirituality; he is a good man who genuinely loves his wife and family. He also grows through his futile attempts to understand the nature of his far more complex partner. Through these efforts he becomes a foil allowing the reader to see the degree to which Kristin, throughout most of the novel, lacks compassion and tolerance in all matters concerning her husband. Certainly a dedicated wife who scrupulously discharges her duties to her husband and seven sons, she nevertheless remains obstinate and intent on running things. She has little sympathy for the lax, wasteful manner in which Erlend's more aristocratic household was run before his marriage, and she makes every effort to manage it so as to conform with the more conservative and family-oriented ways she learned at her father's farm. She is charitable to the poor and to pilgrims who come to her door, and she is just to the tenant farmers. To her often difficult and rambunctious sons she proves to be a loving but strict mother. But she seems to have hardened her heart to her husband's casual ways and seldom allows him to forget his role and the guilt he should feel in their moral transgression. (In fact, she seems at times to hold him as primarily responsible for her fall and does not sufficiently admit her willing complicity.) Though she still clearly loves Erlend, she is driving him from their home.

In all respects but this one, Kristin does make progress in virtue and understanding. She takes into her home Erlend's bastard sons and treats them as if they were her own; she showers her father and mother with love before they die in an attempt to undo some of the sadness she has caused them; and she is happy to observe the growth of a close relationship between Erlend and Lavrans as the pious and generous older man discovers the natural goodness and helpfulness of his son-in-law.

After bringing to life her first child, Kristin keeps her promise to reconcile herself formally with God and the Church. She is required by her confessor, because of the gravity of her sins (especially her culpability in the death of Eline), to complete her penance by journeying barefoot as a pilgrim to the Cathedral of Nidaros, carrying her son on her back. Descending the fjords, she arrives in the valley where the cathedral and the shrine of Saint Olav are located. As she approaches the portals of the massive Gothic structure she experiences a deep remorse for her sins, a profound sense of her insignificance, and a renewed aspiration for eternal life that the church aesthetically portrays. When she kneels before the altar she prays the Fiftieth Psalm, "A pure heart create in me, O Lord."

The final volume, *The Cross*, begins with Erlend's imprisonment for treason: he has been one of the leading conspirators in attempting to liberate Norway from the control of the Swedish king and to bring back to the throne Haakon Knutsson. Kristin now sees her husband in a far more favorable light as a courageous and generous knight who has sacrificed his own life to liberate Norwegians from the restrictive and unjust controls of the Swedish kingship. When he is released from prison, she has acknowledged her petty meanness toward him, realizes her deep love, and resolves to be more understanding. Yet despite herself she does not succeed substantially in bringing her resolutions to actions and remains resentful. In exchange for release from prison Erlend must forfeit all rights to his manor at Husaby and is forced to live at Jörundgaard, now in Kristin's possession after her parents' death. Here Erlend lives the carefree life-style of a knight warrior on vacation, and more a permanent guest than the master of the household, he spends his time hunting and inculcating in his lusty sons the valor and skills of the warrior life. Kristen deeply resents his sway over the young men. Regarding this as sign of a diminution in their affection for her, she casts herself more and more in the role of a victim who, without any aid from her ineffectual husband, must manage the affairs of the house and farm, save her patrimony, and be the moral force in raising her children. She finally drives Erlend away by her fits of pique and anger, and he repairs to tiny cottage in the mountains, which is all that remains of his personal property. Despite everything, he is, however, not embittered, and during one of Kristin's visits to his property, he tells her that she is always welcomed, "as though you were the Queen of Heaven come down to my croft from the skies."[3]

Kristin gives birth to her eighth son and has him christened with her dead father's name. In a tragic sequence of events his legitimacy is publicly questioned by a malicious servant of the household. (The charge stems from the fact that since Erlend had long been absent from the property. A house servant would therefore seem to have been the father.) In returning to defend his wife's honor, Erlend meets a violent death as he singlehandedly battles against a hostile group of spectators. In death he resembles more a valiant pagan warrior than a Christian (he refuses to accept the last sacraments from the hands of priest who has taken part in accusing Kristin of infidelity). His last words portray him as another Tristram, thoroughly aware of the depth of the passionate and troubled love that each bore for the other (while taking on himself the brunt of the blame for the difficulties encountered in their marriage). In fact at least one critic has observed that the novel could very well have ended here with Undset having successfully written another great adaptation of the Tristram-Isolde legend of a fated love, stronger than reason and morality, and stronger even than death.[4]

Erlend's demise, however, is treated in the novel as only a necessary part of a larger ongoing drama of supernatural dimensions. And only afterward can Kristin be released from earthly ties of the flesh and proceed to complete what is God's will for her in what remains of her life. For a long time she has not followed "the roving paths" of her youth, yet her observance of the faith throughout the years, though admirable in exterior devotion and almsgiving, could be viewed as largely formalistic. In order to renounce her strong will, which, since the day the elf maiden appeared, had always blocked her path to holiness, Kristin realizes that she must accept "a will other than her own to be her guide." In order to accomplish this she must cease to be attached to material possessions or concerns of any kind. Now an old woman, she leaves her property in the hands of her youngest son and his wife, who had gradually assumed the responsibilities of managing the house. Rejoicing in her new poverty, she becomes once again a pilgrim on the road to Nidaros and journeys there to follow what she recognizes as a calling to the religious life that she had resisted from early youth. She arrives at the cathedral on Saint Olav's feast day and takes the veil as a novice.

As a nun Kristin finds that she can now bridle her strong will and live totally for the service of others. Professed during the early days of the resurgent Black Death that ravaged fourteenth-century Europe, she dies while heroically nursing the sick outside the convent walls. Her last meditation in those plague-stricken days is the hope that, despite her sinful ways and only through God's love, she might finally accomplish His will for her: "God had kept fast to a convenant made for her without her knowledge by a love poured out upon her richly—and in despite of her self-will, in despite of her heavy, earthbound spirit, somewhat of this love had become part of her, had wrought in her like sunlight in the earth, had brought forth increase which not even the hottest flames of fleshly love nor its wildest bursts of wrath could lay waste wholly" (*The Cross*, 419).

Kristin Lavransdatter has been universally praised as an astoundingly realistic portrayal of the life of men and women of all classes in the late Middle Ages. The novel leaves no area of life untouched in its powerful and realistic description of people and places (ranging from the most elaborate religious ceremonies and social festivities to the simplest details of housekeeping or laboring in the fields). The work describes the characters' lives from birth to death in an interesting and sympathetic way, and these people of centuries ago seem very contemporary in regard to their needs and aspirations.

As remarkable as this literary tour de force is in re-creating the spirit of the the Middle Ages, Undset has done far more than provide simply a realistic/historical account of the lives of her characters. As a Christian realist, she has endowed them with a spiritual inner life, and to the well-described and -defined symbiotic relationship between them and their world, she has insisted on drawing a third dimension—the timeless drama of human beings, creatures of God called to an eternal destiny, but also individuals of flesh and blood whose wills often conflict with the will of God. The story of Kristin and Erlend is, therefore, emblematic of all human beings who struggle to understand God's plan for them and who, if they are to live by this plan, must overcome their own fallen nature.

Finally, with this novel set in the age of belief, Undset hoped to make Christianity and its message visible to her contemporaries in a modern world that had lost faith in its divine origins and destiny; she therefore sought to offer, as she put it, "Something to shore up human beings from the chaotic destruction of modern relativism and of ideologies" (quoted in Winsnes, 157). The only novelists who have equalled her in the creation of such panoramic works linking people's temporal and spiritual destinies are, of course, the great Christian realists of nineteenth-century Russian literature—Dostoyevski and Tolstoy. And of the two, Tolstoy, whose Christian epic *War and Peace* bears uncanny resemblance in content and intention to Undset's great trilogy, would seem to share the closer spiritual affinity.

The German Novel and Gertrud von Le Fort

Germanic literature in the latter part of the nineteenth century was dominated by naturalism. Fiction and drama, for the most part, reflected the theories of Darwin, Marx, Zola, Ibsen, Strindberg. Exemplifying this kind of literature are the works of the German playwright Gerhart Hauptmann. In Hauptmann's best-known play, *Die Weber* (1892; *The Weavers*), a masterful example of naturalistic technique and theories, Silesian workers revolt against the introduction of machinery in the marketplace. Hauptmann portrays the weavers as subject to an insurmountable fate caused by economic and social changes that they cannot control or understand. In this late-nineteenth- and early-twentieth-century period in Germany there were no writers who identified themselves as Catholic or who dealt with the specifically Catholic themes presented by the French authors Huysmans, Bloy, and Péguy.

It was also during this period that a group of neo-romantic poets and writers—Rainer Maria Rilke, Stefan George, and Hugo von Hofmannsthals among them—became very influential for introducing expressionistic/ spiritual themes in German literature. Rilke in particular developed in his poetry art-for-art's-sake themes of beauty, youth, and regret of talent snuffed out by the evils of war. His later poetry deals with the transformation of life through love, with immortality, and with other themes that go far beyond naturalism, and his most important prose work, *The Notebooks of Malte Laurids Brigge* (1910)—the spiritual journal of a young Dane living a dreamlike existence in Paris and haunted by the past—is considered to be one of the first existential studies of the self in anguished quest for authentic existence.

The German novel in at least the first 40 years of this century is dominated by the brooding genius of Thomas Mann, who continued in the neo-romantic tradition with his novels and novellas, the first of which, *Tonio Kröger* (1903), deals with the struggle of a self-conscious young man who fits into neither the world of artists nor that of the merchant class into which he was born. Mann provided brilliant continuations of the bildungsroman in *Buddenbrooks* (1900) and *The Magic Mountain* (1924), which he further invested with philosophical disquisition and symbolism evocative of Arthur Schopenhauer's pessimism about modern civilization (for Germany and Europe). In *The Magic Mountain*, for example, Europe is metaphorically presented as an elegant tuberculosis sanatorium where Europeans from every part of the Continent are viewed as patients infected with various forms of moral sickness and unrest. An agnostic, Mann provides no reference to a spiritual order or presence in a universe that he viewed as torn by eros, violence, and contesting ideologies that would eventually engulf the world in war.

Several Catholic writers of note began to write in German in the early decades of the century. The most important of these are Werner Bergengruen, Reinhold Schneider, Gertrud von Le Fort, Elisabeth Langgässer, and Franz Werfel, an Austrian Jew who, though he never converted to Catholicism, wrote several novels with religious themes. (His novel *The Song of Bernadette* was a best-seller in the United States in the late 1940s and was made into a very popular Hollywood film.) None of these writers, with the possible exception of Werfel, are considered today as having been in the first rank of German novelists writing from the beginning of the century through the period of National Socialism and up to the end of World War II. It is only with Heinrich Böll, born a generation later and whose writings do not appear until the late 1940s, that a German novelist with an acknowledged Catholic commitment would also become an internationally acclaimed writer (Böll received the

Nobel Prize for Literature in 1971). The aforementioned Catholic authors from the earlier period are important, however, as respected authors in their own right and also as engaged writers who from the very outset opposed the Nazi regime and—to varying degrees and in different forms—protested in their fiction against the ideology and policies of the Nazi government. Le Fort, Bergengruen, and Langgässer remained in Germany during the war and somehow managed to continue to write; as a Jew, Werfel had to emigrate to the United States; and Schneider became a resident of Switzerland shortly before the war's outbreak.

Primarily writers of the historical novel and novella, Schneider and Bergengruen invested their works with veiled (and not so subtle) attacks on the Nazi philosophy and rise to power. Schneider's novels were by and large not translated into English, and he is today not well-known outside of Germany. His one novel widely read abroad, *Die Hohenzollern* (1933; *The Hohenzollerns*), investigates in a medieval setting the problems of sin motivating worldly leaders and powers and advocates the need for rulers to repent for unjust and repressive rule. Bergengruen achieved a wider international audience, and one of his novels, *Der Grosstyrann und das Gericht* (1935; *The Great Tyrant and Judgment*), received substantial notice in the United States as well under the title *A Matter of Conscience*. In the novel Bergengruen presents as protagonist the selfish and arrogant ruler of a small Renaissance state who forces his people to bear his guilt for the murder of one of his subjects that he himself has secretly arranged. After a prominent citizen of the grand prince's state accepts the role of scapegoat (to exculpate the people) and admits to a murder he has not committed, the prince is gradually shamed into accepting his own responsibility. The citizens are therefore rescued by the moral courage and sacrifice of one good individual, and the ruler is put in his place and castigated by the grand priest for having exceeded the bounds of rightful human power: "You are," he says to the tyrant, "the only one who has sinned, in that you strove to raise youself above the human and be like unto God."[5] The novel can be seen, then, as a powerful allegory opposing the cruelty and injustice inflicted on Germans by their Nazi leaders who, by implication, are also seen as tyrants having exceeded all moral and religious bounds of authority. Like the grand prince of the novel, they too, Bergengruen suggests, should repent of their sinful use of power and accept the laws of God.

Of this grouping the Baronness Gertrud von Le Fort—a convert to Catholicism—is by far the best known, and her works merit more extensive attention here because of the importance they enjoyed outside of

Germany (and most notably in France, where she was highly regarded by Bernanos and Mauriac). It should also be mentioned that she was a much respected poet of her time. Her collections *Hymen an die Kirche* (1924; *Hymns to the Church*) and *Hymen an Deutschland* (1932; *Hymns to Germany*) constitute an impassioned appeal to her fellow Germans to turn away from the violence and pride of a resurgent nationalism, to renounce the use of force and violence in the world order, and to nurture instead spiritual regeneration through the imitation of Christ and the following of Christian virtues.[6]

Le Fort's Huguenot ancestors had fled from Savoy to Geneva after the revocation of the Edict of Nantes. Migrating then from Switzerland to Prussia in the eighteenth century, they were made barons of the empire. Her army-officer father was much influenced by Enlightenment thought. Though a Deist and not practicing any formal religion, he strongly believed that people have a moral obligation to live according to a strict ethical code. He thus schooled his daughter in the Kantian ethic of respect and sympathy for all human beings and instilled in her a strong sense of tolerance and justice. Such qualities, he often pointed out, especially befitted former émigrés such as themselves, who had had to endure intolerance and religious persecution.[7] Le Fort's mother, a deeply religious Lutheran, passed on to her daughter a strong belief in Christ and respect for the Bible.

Le Fort's interest in religion crystalized while she was a student (in itself a remarkable feat for a woman in the late nineteenth century) at Heidelberg University, where she concentrated her study in history and theology. There her mentor was Ernst Troeltsch, the eminent theologian and pioneer in the sociology of religion (and in how religious belief influenced society). Troeltsch did not believe in the divinity of Christ but was intensely interested in all spiritual concerns and questions. Le Fort would later credit him with having opened up for her "the world of theological thought, the world of Christian mysticism, and the world of religious problems."[8] Her first intellectual contacts with Catholicism came at the end of World War I through reading issues of the journal *Hochland*. This cosmopolitan and scholarly Catholic periodical (edited by the very influential Jesuit priest Karl Muth) was itself at the heart of a Catholic cultural revival in Germany. It stimulated German Catholics to go beyond the narrow and reactionary boundaries of belief imposed by the parochial mentality of the Kulturkampf. The journal's focus was the study of Catholic/Christian themes and problems shared by all believers as well as the exploration

through ecumenical discourse (and without the usual doctrinal wran-
glings   so   prevalent   in   Catholic   and   Protestant   relations
of the time) of other possible forms of commitment in the larger world.
Through her encounter with the periodical Le Fort saw suddenly affirmed,
as she later expressed it, "everything that I had inherited from my pious
Protestant home. . . . For the first time in my life I became fully and con-
ciously aware that there exists a common heritage of Christian culture. . . .
[I]n other words, I came into contact with the real essence of Catholicism"
(*Aufzeichnungen*, 78).

Further investigations into the doctrines of Catholicism reinforced her
first impressions of the Church's universality and comprehensiveness.
When two years later (in 1924) she decided to convert, she was not, she
said, rejecting her past religious beliefs and traditions (to which she still
had very strong adherence) but placing them in the larger context of the
universal church of Christendom. Her conversion, then, was a natural
step toward an intellectual and spiritual affirmation of the essential unity
of all Christian faiths and the convergence of all belief in the Catholic
Communion. These strong ecumenical convictions would remain essential
to her thought and would repeatedly find expression in her writings.

Le Fort's career as a writer began only after her conversion, when she
was well into her fifties. It is therefore not surprising that her initial writings bear the mark of the deep and profound spiritual evolution she had
undergone. Her works in general do not only reflect, however, her personal religious odyssey but also serve as a springboard to allow her to
comment in her fiction on universal problems or matters of concern that
she had always nurtured (and that she felt went to the very heart of the
sufferings experienced by human beings in the modern age). These
included the problem of evil and its modern manifestation, particularly
the rise of Nazism in her country; the insecurity of "the moderns" bereft
of religious anchorage who become the victims of inhuman ideologies;
and remedies that her newfound faith allowed her to propose in con-
fronting and overcoming the problems of the human predicament.

Le Fort's first novel, *Das Schweisstuch der Veronika* (*The Veil of Veronica*),
appeared in 1928, and its sequel, *Der Kranz der Engel* (*The Wreath of
Angels*), was written several years later but could not be published in
Germany during the war because of its strong attack on the Nazi mystique.[9] Though no longer in circulation, both of these novels are deserv-
ing of analysis in any study of Le Fort because of the autobiographical
details they indirectly present (especially as concerns her religious experience), as well as their stance against the evils of the day.

Through its reflection of her life and particularly her conversion, *The Veil of Veronica* is the most autobiographical of Le Fort's novels. The work is essentially the story of the spirtual journey of the heroine, Veronica, from agnosticism to baptism. Le Fort uses as her primary theme here the mysterious workings of grace in a human soul and how in the process it makes use of disparate elements of an individual's life—family relationships, sentimental attachments, and cultural and aesthetic interests. The novel is another example of the bildungsroman; in it a young woman who, like so many of her contemporaries, has no spiritual faith yet quests after a meaning in life eventually finds anchorage in the Catholic faith.

Veronica is a 16-year-old orphan who comes to live in the spacious Roman villa of her grandmother. Here she is exposed to and for a time accepts the moral code of values and cultural vision of this powerful old woman who cares very much for her. She then submits to the strong influence of a young German to whom she becomes sentimentally attracted, and finally she succumbs to the considerable cultural influence on her by the majesty of Rome. In fact, the city itself must be regarded as a protagonist given its preponderant role in the minds and lives of the three principal characters. Through its history—which resumes Europe's past and its multifaceted architecture, which is a compendium of all artistic styles and periods—it offers the particular emblem or foundation on which to build the philosophy—and by extension the value structure—by which each of the major characters chooses to live.

The grandmother has long ago left her native Germany to reside in the city that, she believes, most personifies her ideals. She is depicted as a woman impressive in her serenity of mind. A neo-pagan, she is firmly convinced that Greco-Roman humanism (resumed in the dictum "man is the measure of all things") is the ultimate truth, and she sees this belief affirmed in the grandeur that was Augustan Rome (symbolized in such artifacts as the Forum). Rome thus represents to her both as a city and as a symbol the highest achievement of human genius and the ultimate model to which all subsequent civilizations aspire. In the first part of her spiritual awakening, Veronica, whose mind when she first arrives on the scene is virtually a tabula rasa, falls firmly under the tutelage of her grandmother and accepts the old woman's moral system and vision of reality.

The grandmother's ascendency in Veronica'a education is seriously challenged by the arrival of Enzio, who also comes to live in the villa. The son of the only man for whom the proud old woman admits to having ever loved, he is taken in and provided for as if he were her grandson because of her fond memories of his father. Several years older than Veronica and a university student, Enzio is the prototype of the agnostic young German of the generation between the two wars who has been strongly influenced in his disbelief by the philosophy of Nietzsche and other atheistic thinkers. In opposition to the grandmother's Apollonian view of the timeless grandeur and lucidity of the city, Enzio sees Rome through a Dionysian lense, as a surging, barbarous, and decaying composite of humanity. To him the "noble columns" of the Forum, which the grandmother regards as examples of "serene majesty" seem impotent and insignificant compared with the fascination he experiences at the spectacle of the stark, moonlit outline of the Coliseum—for him, the living symbol of bestial, inhuman life. And just as the grandmother finds comfort in life and solace for her approaching death in the serene contemplation of the "classical" order of the city, Enzio achieves emotional fulfillment through the chaotic vision he conjures up of Rome, symbol of the utter desolation of wild decomposing life (the flotsam and jetsam of the Nietzschean "eternal return").[10]

Torn between the two worldviews, Veronica must find her own meaning. During a chance visit to Saint Peter's where she views the Tenebrae service of Good Friday, she is introduced to Rome as the Eternal City of Christendom and thereafter is mysteriously but irresistibly drawn to belief through the power and mystery of Catholic art and liturgy, which for her Rome now comes to exemplify. As Veronica follows the path of conversion, her grandmother is greatly chagrined (though she tries not to disclose her feelings) by the young woman's abandonment of the humanist ideal that the old woman had hoped to bequeath through her own example. She also becomes horrified by the despairing and violent evocation of reality that she finds expressed in the poetry of Enzio, who seems as well to have betrayed her values through his increasingly nihilistic philosophy. She almost seems to welcome death when it comes as the way out of a cul de sac, and she dies a somewehat pathetic but also heroic figure, stoically accepting her fate and, to the very end, "full of reverence, incomplete silence, solitary, and alone" (*Veronica*, 253).

As a first novel, *The Veil of Veronica* lacks focus and is somewhat wooden in its too geometrical use of philosophical constructs (such as Nietzsche's polarities) in formulating the value systems of the two nonbelievers, Enzio and the grandmother. And though the principal concern of the plot is Veronica's response to grace and conversion (of which she herself is first-person narrator), she seems curiously underdrawn and lacking in authentically human qualities and characteristics. In fact, though they are foils to her conversion, Veronica is eclipsed throughout the novel by the two more interesting and psychologically compelling characters—the "tranquil pagan" and the decadent young poet—who accompany her along the way but cannot follow her on the road to belief.

Written during the early 1940s but not published until 1946, *The Wreath of Angels* is technically a more successful novel with a far more universal focus: the Nazi mentality that threatened the peace and well being of Germany and the world. The major conflict presented in the novel is vast and (in cosmic terms) nothing less than the eternal struggle between good and evil, crystalized here by the Nazi menace to European civilization. The heroine is again Veronica, now a committed Catholic, who arrives at Heidelberg to pursue her studies at this idyllic site. While there she lives at the home of a university professor who has been appointed her guardian after her grandmother's death. Given no name, this kind and affable scholar is obviously representative of German intellectuals of the period who are seen by Le Fort as being powerless before the onslaught of Nazi propaganda and the eventual takeover of the universities by Nazi youth groups. He is depicted as living a mildly despairing life, convinced that Western civilization has entered the twilight period before an enormous cataclysm. Yet he has no faith of any kind, nor does he take any active commitment against the evil that he sees and recognizes for what it is.

Veronica again meets Enzio, himself a student at the university, whose mind has already been poisoned by Nazi doctrines. In Enzio, Le Fort again attempts to portray the attitudes of the younger generation of Germans born between the two wars. Feeling deeply humiliated by Germany's defeat in 1918 and the harsh treatment accorded their country by the victorious allies at Versailles, Enzio and his youthful cohorts are described as eager to subscribe to any power or ideology that will overcome the weaknesses of the past and restore German grandeur and power.

From the pagan poet celebrating the ruins and decadence of Rome, Enzio has become a man of action for whom the Nazi slogan, "power of will" is the guiding principle. For him, religion of any sort is the primary enemy of the new political ideal of German might because, as he declares at one point, "as long as man feels dependent on a higher power, he does not stake his all." Enzio will now work unceasingly for a new secular order that will have broken all ties to the spiritual and religious past of Germany and Europe. "In my kingdom," he explains to Veronica, "there will be no sacraments. . . . There will only be victor and vanquished. There can never be any question of reconciliation between the nations."[11]

Enzio is presented, then, as a sick person infected by a virulent disease, the Nazi will to power, which threatens ultimately to destroy him completely as a human being. Veronica becomes a modern-day saint by taking on herself full responsibility for the spiritual salvation of the young man whom she loves but whose philosophy of life horrifies her. As much mother as lover in the role she plays, she refuses the adamant advice of one of her spiritual directors to disassociate herself from the spiritual contamination of this "enemy" of Christianity. A more spiritually understanding advisor, Father Angelo, who guided her through her conversion in Rome, sees the potential for heroism and sanctity in her desire to rescue Enzio through the sacrifice of self. "There is," he tells her, "a natural and a supernatural approach to those who have become the enemies of God. The former is to sever all connections with the sinner, in order to safeguard one's own salvation, the supernatural way is to cleave to the sinner" (Der Kranz der Engel, 623).

Mirroring Péguy's sacrifice of his own salvation for his wife and family, Veronica takes the "supernatural" path, marries Enzio, and has to suffer the loss of the sacraments, which are closed to her because of her husband's refusal to be married in the Church. There then ensues a fierce struggle for Enzio's soul. In this unequal battle Veronica must act alone and without the moral and civilizing support of traditional German culture, of which only tattered remains still exist at Heidelberg. Her guardian-professor who should act as a moral force for the good is presented as a weak intellectual foil to Enzio's virulent Nazism. A cultured humanist who believes in nothing but "the beautiful ideas of European civilization," he is rightfully regarded by Enzio and the young men who sit scornfully in his classes as a shallow dilettante, devoid of belief and convictions of any kind, and unable to commit himself to action.

Through her unswerving love and complete fidelity to her husband, Veronica ultimately makes Enzio aware of the evils of his ideology; the victory seems a pyrrhic one, however, since it occurs only after she has been verbally brutalized to the end of her endurance by her embittered husband, who emerges from his sickness only the shell of his former self. Le Fort makes the point that Veronica's living faith and total gift of self were the sole expedients capable of overcoming the harsh "power of will" theory that had reduced Enzio to a robotized vessel of hatred and force.

Le Fort reveals herself more directly in this novel than in any of her other works as being a Catholic novelist engagée intent on taking a stand against the evils of her age. And in particular, she answers affirmatively here the question "Am I my brother's keeper?" as it relates to the responsibility that the Christian bears to the nonbeliever, even if these be the bitter enemies of Christianity in the modern world. Le Fort also uses themes often employed by other Catholic novelists. By the total sacrifice that, for example, Veronica makes of herself as a pure offering for her husband's salvation, she exemplifies again the the theme of reversibility which, as we have seen, lies thematically at the heart of the works of Bloy, Bernanos, Mauriac, Greene, and others.

Le Fort's historical novels—such as *The Pope from the Ghetto* (1930) and *The Magdeburg Wedding* (1938)—continue to deal with the theme of the individual's responsibility in the face of his/her community's moral crisis. *The Pope from the Ghetto* is set in twelfth-century Rome and describes the career and fate of the anti-pope Anacletus II, a Catholic convert of Jewish origin who for a time lived a hedonist role as political power-broker in the Vatican during the period of the great Schism. He eventually leaves his privileged position when he becomes overwhelmed with grief and guilt at the spectacle of the sufferings of his persecuted Jewish people in the Roman Ghetto. Here again Le Fort explores the idea that suffering on the side of the innocent is the role the Christian must take in the world, and her use of the Jewish pope as emblematic of this offering of self is, of course, an obvious allusion to the persecution of Jews in her own time. Set in the seventeenth century, *The Magdeburg Wedding* is Le Fort's most ambitious historical work. In it she uses the politics and climate of the Thirty Years' War and the resulting disintegration of the Holy Roman Empire as a historical analogue of the dissolution of the modern German state into a political dictatorship, and she sees the Nazi leaders of the 1930s foreshadowed by this earlier period's military mercenaries, who fanatically serve one master for whom they are willing to sacrifice their integrity and their very salvation.

Critics generally believe that Le Fort's fame as a German writer does not reside in novels that now seem to have limited attraction (O'Boyle, 103–104; Moore, 92–94). She has, however, won a permanent place in posterity as a writer of the German novella. Her best-known piece of this genre, *The Song at the Scaffold* (1931), became a classic in German literature and also had much influence abroad. In addition to Bernanos's dramatic adaption of Le Fort's story, Francis Poulenc used Bernanos's work to construct his opera *Dialogues des Carmélites* (1957).

The Song at the Scaffold continues the themes and concerns of Le Fort's earlier novels, and it also presents as protagonist a victim/savior of a society gone mad through its renunciation of Christian ideals. The novella's more restrictive length, moreover, allowed the author to construct her best drawn and most successful literary personage, the unheroic saint and martyr, Blanche de la Force. In the novella she also provides a most convincing historical (even prophetic) analogue for the Nazi repression by her choice of the period of the Reign of Terror during the French Revolution. (Indeed, the godless and ruthless political ideology of these revolutionaries was remarkably similar in many respects to the Nazi philosophy, and the cruel measures that they used against their own people bore an uncanny resemblance to the brutally repressive system put in place by the Nazi dictators two centuries later.)

The plot is rooted in historical fact and recounts the martyrdom of 16 nuns of the Carmelite Convent of Compiègne, all guillotined at the Place de la Concorde on 17 July 1794 during the last days of the Terror (they were beatified by the Church in 1906). In a letter to Bernanos explaining the genesis of the work, Le Fort recounts how she came by accident on an account of the event in a footnote in a work dealing with Catholic religious orders. She confessed, curiously, to not having at first been moved so much by the fate of the 16 Carmelite nuns as she was by a fictitious character, little Blanche, who, as Le Fort went on to explain, "owed the breath of her fragile existence to my own inner life. Born of the horrors of an age which in Germany was overshadowed by the presentiment of coming fateful events, this figure rose before my mind's eye as an embodiment of the death agony of an entire epoch that was nearing its end" (quoted in O'Boyle, 44–45). Blanche de la Force thus imposed herself in the author's mind even before the composition of the work as the fictional character who would personify the suffering and agony that Le Fort feared would soon be inflicted on her own society by a new and imminent period of the Terror.

The narrator of the novella is a fictitious aristocrat, Monsieur de Villeroi, who has been an eyewitness to the killing of the nuns. His account is not merely of their execution but also relates the life of the Carmelite community from 1789, when Blanche enters as novice, up through the forced secularization of the convent and the death of the nuns. He writes his narration in the form of a letter to a fashionable female aristocrat, an émigrée who had fled during the Revolution. It soon becomes clear that she is also a nonbeliever and a devotee of Rousseau's doctrine of the natural goodness of man. The events Villeroi recounts are obviously calculated to challenge this aristocrat's trust in the nobility of human nature, or in "an enlightened humanity" that does not need God's providence or grace. As a professed agnostic and free-thinker, Villeroi finds his own unbelief in a higher power challenged by the events he will describe to the woman, and he obviously is used by Le Fort as a foil to expose the false confidence of modern unbelievers in their credo that human natural goodness is enough to keep in control the "beast in man" before the constant resurgence of chaotic forces of evil (which, for the Christian, are consequences of the Fall).

Blanche de la Force was born into one of the most illustrious families of the ancien régime. From her earliest moments in life she is described as of an extremely timorous nature, a "little rabbit" for whom everything is a cause of potential fear. A kind of physiological/psychological expla-nation of the origin of her pathological state of fear is provided through a tragic set of circumstances occurring about the time of her birth. Shortly before her pregnancy came to term, her mother became trapped in her carriage on a crowded Parisian street and was then dragged out by the "screaming, despairing crowd"—an eruption of violence, foreshadowing that of the Revolution, described as a manifestation of "chaos that slum-bers in the depth of all things and breaks the the solid armor of habit and custom."[12] After being tossed about by the mob, the dazed Marquise returns to her home on foot, with "torn garments and the face of a Medusa." She dies shortly afterward while giving premature birth to her daughter.

Thrust into the world too soon through the fright of her mother, the child is thus to be the living embodiment of the latter's fear of the wrath of the enraged crowd. Despite her temperament, Blanche nevertheless refuses all of her father's attempts to marry her off and thereby provide for her a sheltered, tranquil life. Instead, at the age of 16 she formally requests entrance as novice into the Convent of Compiègne, renowned for its austere observance of the Carmelite rule. The Marquis de la Force, a freethinker "who agreed with the most brilliant intellects in France that the Church was a institution of the past," was at first opposed his daughter's call to religion. He eventually gave in, however, because he ironically thought that the convent ("where Destiny offers no unantici-pated challenge to violence") would allow his frightened daughter to escape the world's harsh realities (*Scaffold*, 17).

The last candidate to enter the novitiate before a law is proclaimed prohibiting the admission of new members into religious communities, Blanche is given, despite her perceived excessive timidity and out of deference to her powerful family, the name in religion that she has chosen for herself, Sister Mary of Jesus in the Garden of the Agony). The date of her investiture is also of great import because, with religious orders threatened, the superior of the Carmelites will allow all postulants to be admitted immediately into the order with the usual trial period suspended. In this way they will be part of the professed community and thus be expected to share in the sufferings and possibly the death of Christ in the Garden of Gethsemani—a goal explicity set forth in the Carmelite rule as the special vocation of the members of this order.

Blanche's life in the convent does not change her at all from the timorous person she has been; indeed, she even seems to derive at the beginning an illusory sense of security from being there. When the news of the Revolution's progress reaches the sisters, she exclaims, "Here we are safe from all of this" (*Scaffold*, 20). Then slowly but inexorably the chain of events comes crashing down on the religious community. At first the convent is threatened by a commission of revolutionaries who invade their cloisture and attempt to persuade the nuns to seek release from their vows and live normal lives. The heroic defiance all the other nuns here display contrasts radically with Blanche's terror. She shrieks with fear as the men enter her cell and in so doing singles herself out for attention as a potential weak link in the community's resistance to the revolutionaries' attempt to dissolve the convent.

From this point on Blanche, in fact, is seen as torn apart by opposing emotions and as a kind of living contradiction. She refuses the prioress's counsel that, because she is not up to the coming ordeals, she should leave the community, and with the other sisters she agrees to take the vow the prioress administers as soon as the intruders have left the cloister—to be willing to expiate through death the crimes committed against God by the revolutionaries. Kneeling with the others to make this promise, she seems totally overcome with fear (her face is described as "small and pinched, wet with perspiration, distorted by the terror of all France, of Eternal Love itself" [*Scaffold*, 77]).

During the mass that follows this ceremony, Blanche, at the moment of trans-substantiation, disappears from the convent chapel, and her exit would seem to indicate the renunciation of her vow out of fear. Yet the prioress alone is aware of the mystical transference that has taken place at this moment: by her flight Blanche is destined to live out to the bitter end her terrible fear, and in so doing her sufferings become mystically joined with those of Jesus in the Garden. Like Him, she accepts, despite her fearful nature, the chalice of suffering that is presented to her.

Returning to her home she witnesses the ignoble death of her father at the hands of a crazed and unruly mob, and then she is forced to drink his blood in a consecrated chalice in a blasphemous parody of the Eucharist. She then becomes the mob's chosen mascot and is a spectator in the jeering crowd as the Compiègne nuns mount the scaffold one by one, their voices joined in singing the "Veni Creator Spiritus." As the voices are snuffed out Blanche takes up the singing of the last stanza. The narrator, who is standing with the mob, describes her countenance at that moment as "completely without fear." Then, "Singing without tremor . . . as a bird," she finishes the hymn only to be torn from limb to limb by the bestialized group of women revolutionaries (*Scaffold*, 106–109). And with the martyrdom of Blanche, the narrator announces that the Revolution had reached its end, with the reign of Terror collapsing 10 days after her death.

Le Fort uses Blanche, the unheroic and frightened child, as striking proof as to the power of grace. Seeming to be the very opposite of what her name (de la force) means Blanche witnesses to the truth of what Kierkegaard had professed in *Fear and Trembling*: that God is alone capable of transforming human weakness into strength or endurance that can resist any earthly human power, provided the recipient empty the self of all but the divine will. This trembling and frightened young woman takes her place, then, with the curé d'Ambricourt, as another authentic character created by a Catholic novelist to convey the theme that God continues to confound the powerful and mighty of this world through the agency of the weak and childlike, who play a privileged role in the divine plan for salvation. In his very perceptive comments on Le Fort's theme of the continuing power of grace in the workings of human destiny throughout the ages, the theologian Kurt Reinhardt has observed, "The French Revolution is seen [in the work] theologically and eschatologically *sub specie aeternitatis*, and the threatening 'chaos of liberty' . . . is thus converted into its very opposite, the 'freedom of the children of God,' a conversion which . . . in every concrete existential situation can and should be realized and repeated by every Christian" (Reinhardt, 234).

Elisabeth Langgässer

Another German Catholic novelist, unknown until after World War II and read today, as one critic has observed, by "a happy few,"[13] is Elisabeth Langgässer. Half-Jewish by Nazi classification and a convert to

Catholicism, she managed to survive throughout the war while working as slave labor in a munitions factory near Berlin. (Her daughter, however, died in a concentration camp.) A poet as well as novelist (she dedicated her poetry collection *Fruhling 1946* [*Spring 1946*] to her daughter's memory), her novels are written in a surrealist style and record the intimate consciousness of those who suffer, die, or survive the horrors of the Nazi terror. Two of her works gained critical acclaim in the early postwar period. The first, *Das unauslöschliche Siegel* (1946; *The Indelible Seal*), records the inner struggles of the converted Jew, Lazarus Belfontaine. Becoming a Catholic at the end of World War I, he deserts his wife and child, is remarried to a Christian, and attempts to live by blocking out his Jewish roots. The murder of his second wife a decade later provides the catalyst for his reassumption of his scorned heritage, and Langgässer describes Belfontaine's road back in brilliant dream sequences, hallucinatory passages, and allegory reminiscent of Dostoyevski.

The second novel—Langgässer's last and the one most consider her masterpiece—is *Markische Argonautenfahrt* (1950), translated as *The Quest*. Considered by Peter Demetz as one of Germany's most important postwar novels, the work is not easy to understand and continually challenges the reader through its brilliant yet paradoxical fusion of Jewish and Christian mystical themes and allusions to Greek mythology. The novel is a re-creation of the Greek fable of the *Argo*, the rescuing ship of the Argonauts, "whose sails brushed every continent and which when it was wrecked by the storm, was carried home on the shoulders of the Argonauts,"[14] as applied to the fate of Germany after World War II. In it an omniscient narrator relates the story of seven modern "Argonauts"—Berliners who, in August 1945, set out from their devastated city on a pilgrimage to gain understanding and spiritual reconciliation for what they witnessed during the terrible years just past. The destination these pilgrims (hitherto unknown to one another) have chosen is the Benedictine monastery of Anastasiendorf, located in the March of Brandenburg. On their journey they pass through a countryside that Langgässer eerily depicts as "a moonscape of death," cluttered with bodies, mangled bones, and ruined machines. The air is filled with the stench of decomposing corpses, and rampant nature covers the sinister debris with new vegetation.

The monastery at Anastasiendorf, presided over by the saintly prioress, Mother Demetria, has been, throughout the war and the more recent carnage inflicted by the Soviet army, a haven of Christian values. Here the venerable Benedictine rule—with its rhythm of prayer, work in the fields, and meditation—has never been broken. As they proceed to this destination through the devastated "graveyard" that is Germany, the seven pilgrims are described to have taken as their patron a deceased Jewish girl, Sichelchen. Her story of total devotion to the welfare of her fellow Jews—particularly her martyrdom by freely offering to accompany a doomed transport of orphans to Auschwitz—constitutes, in fact, a novel within the novel. As the pilgrims pause to rest at stations along the way, this martyr-saint, from her present resting place in a translucent sky, entertains them with the narration of the events of her life as pure victim. And she, a dwarfed hunchback, creates in the minds of the pilgrims a strange form of beauty (described as manifesting itself amidst this devastated landscape, at an "Omega point" where the human and divine converge in the person of Christ).

Like Bernanos, to whom she has been compared, Langgässer thus creates a time frame that is explicit Christian, hence eternal, where human history is presented as a series of cyclical recurrences acted out in God's presence. The tragedy of German aggression is ultimately viewed by the pilgrims as yet another manifestation in an unending succession of the periodic series of human cruelty and violence, like the burning of Troy as recounted in the *Aeneid*, the destruction of Jerusalem, or the pillage of Rome by the Goths. And perhaps, Langgässer suggests, the capture of Troy, if seen in an eternal perspective, may have been no less horrible and its scenes of naked terror no less gruesome in the minds of the vanquished Trojans than was the battle of Stalingrad to the conquered remnants of the German Sixth Army.

The question of why such evils constantly recur Langgässer believes to be at least partially explained by the stiff-necked pride of individuals and nations that become tragically intertwined. In fact there are, she states, whole nations that seem predestined to sin and disaster. Germany's guilt in all of this is inexplicable, and she refers to it as the manifestation of a kind of mental disease. She further suggests that the Germans have reenacted in modern times the role of Genghis Khan, the supreme violator of human dignity of the past. As such, her compatriots must once again repent and become reconciled, to use Dostoyevki's terms, with God and the living earth that they have violated.

As part of its ambitious agenda, the novel also explores and wrestles with problems of theodicy: Why does God permit the innocent to suffer? Why did He allow the genocide of the Jewish people? Langgässer's response seems to be a restatement of the Job parable: God remains inexplicable; He is in fact "at his most inexplicable where He loves, not

where He administers justice." She explains, moreover, that the suffering
bear a sign of God's predilection: "Whatever God looks upon with love,
that He marks with the cross. Two beams, love and freedom, this inter-
section remains God's secret to the end of the world" (*Quest*, 353).

As the novel unfolds, the pilgrims are seen as having symbolically
boarded a new *Argo*, the Ark of the Covenant, "timbered with hope and
pitched with the obstinate longing for joy that holds the planks together." Their human bonding now creates "a moment between Heaven and
Hell . . . a stillness in the waters from Lisbon to Kiev, a new beginning"
(*Quest*, 213). Europe's melancholy and its appearance as a sort of spectral
hell is to be transformed by the voyage of these modern Argonauts into a
new spirit of joy and love symbolized by the monastery of Anastasiendorf
(which itself suggests an Edenic form of human love and community).
The horrible dream of death and destruction of the Nazi era can thus be
followed by a national and communal "resurrection" as the Argonauts,
reborn to the life of the spirit, renounce the sterile death cult of the
vicious Nazi ideology.

When they arrive at Anastasiendorf the pilgrims are welcomed but
not given right of entry. Symbolically this would seem to indicate that,
as a result of their pilgrimage, they have, on arrival, ceased to be name-
less, faceless pilgrims, and they must now revitalize themselves individ-
ually using the spiritual experiences they gained en route. Each of the
characters therefore receives the gift of his new self along with the con-
comitant responsibility of building meaningful relationships with others—from now on not merely with like-minded pilgrims but with all of
humanity, to whom they are inextricably bound. The novel ends, in
short, with an existential call to action for all men and women of goodwill to bend their efforts in creating a new Covenant and a new society
based not on death and destruction but on love and concern for others.

Chapter Five

The 1950s and 1960s: From Conflict to Convergence with the Modern World

One of the dominant forms of European fiction in the 1950s and 1960s was the existential novel of commitment. Agnostic or frankly atheist in religious reference and inspired by humanistic concerns in the face of the terrible injustice, oppression, and disaster that seemed to afflict the individual at every turn during the dangerous and violent cold war period, novels by authors such as Jean-Paul Sartre, Albert Camus, Günter Grass, Alberto Moravia, Max Frisch, Simone de Beauvoir, Camillo José Cela, and Elie Wiesel described a universe where God and divine providence were conspicuously absent or nonexistent in the affairs or destinies of human beings. Rather, these authors placed at the center of their works the beleaguered individual who, in extreme situations, is forced to confront the absurd nature of things and formulate his own value system through the crucible of experience. Antagonistic to the way things are in a universe seen as impervious to the reasonable expectations of human beings for happiness, love, and security, these authors eventually developed stances of resistance, even defiance, as the individual holds out against forces (natural or man-made) that threaten to annihilate the human and to mock the legitimate quest for fulfillment and happiness in a human life.[1]

The central figure in this movement of secular humanism and the most influential European novelist in the 1950s was Albert Camus. By the time that he was awarded the Nobel Prize for Literature in 1957, he had become the moral spokesman for millions of Europeans and Americans through his philosophy of the absurd, a concept he had earlier developed and refined in essays and works of fiction such as *L'Etranger* (1941; *The Stranger*) and *Le Mythe de Sisyphe* (1942; *The Myth of Sisyphus*). The absurd he defined as a state of tension between man's legitimate demands and expectations of life and the universe's obstinate refusal to respond to or even acknowledge these desires. His novel of

greatest moral amplitude and the one in which he would postulate and
dramatize forms of active rebellion against the absurd was *La Peste*
(1949; *The Plague*). The philosophical/religious configurations Camus
introduces here in his presentation of universal evil and possible human
responses have become virtually paradigmatic and have appeared in
many other writers' fiction addressing similar themes. It is certain, then,
that Camus's thought in general—and as expressed in *The Plague* in particular—had a strong influence on European Catholic writers living in
the same dangerous and turbulent cold war period who had to come to
grips—both in their personal belief systems and in their fiction—with
Camus's arresting dramatization of the ever-recurring presence of evil in
an absurd universe where the Christian God is judged to be absent or
irrelevant.[2]

In *The Plague* Camus uses an outbreak of bubonic plague as a symbol
of evil in the world. This pestilence—an allegory of rampant evil in a
universe gone mad—first has to be identified as such, and then, as it
reaches its most malignant proportions, it is confronted through various
stances taken by the citizens of the afflicted Algerian city of Oran. One
can understand why the novel is considered the most anti-Christian of all
Camus's works by observing the moral stance taken against the pestilence and by one of the novel's major characters, Father Paneloux. This
steely Jesuit priest and intellectual would first have his fellow citizens of
the besieged city accept the epidemic as a just punishment for their sins
and as a means of testing their faith. Saint Augustine's eternal City of
God should, he declares in a sermon given at the outbreak of the sickness, be the Oranians' homeland, and what transpires here and now
must be seen, sub specie aeternitatis, as part of the mystery of God's
interaction with His creatures. Paneloux cannot, however, rationally or
emotionally maintain this abstract idea before the senseless and useless
suffering and destruction of human life.

The protracted agony of an innocent child to whom the priest ministers and whose death rales he must endure is the last straw, and the
priest has no recourse but to live out his faith, "his back to the wall,"
before the monstrous spectacle of slaughter of the truly innocent. "We
must believe everything or nothing," he says in an agitated sermon he
gives shortly before his lonely and despairing death. "There is no middle
course. . . . We must accept the dilemma and choose either to hate God
or to love Him."[3] Classified "a doubtful case" in medical statistics, he
may or may not have been infected by the plague. But sadly true is the
fact that even as an exemplary and active resistant (he is a member of the

citizen "Sanitary Corps") to this evil, Paneloux had not been able to enter fully into the human fellowship of those committed to fight the plague with all human means. And this is because his need for transcendental/vertical reference to explain and justify the plague's existence in a universe presided over by God has always stood in the way of adopting a more authentically human form of resistance.

The novel's narrator (and moral spokesperson for Camus) is the medical doctor Rieux. An agnostic, his approach to explaining this evil eschews all reference to God or transcendence. Viewing the universe as absurd through its indifference to legitimate human expectations for happiness and justice, and regarding human beings as fundamentally innocent because of the universal death sentence imposed on them, Rieux will actively combat all forces that threaten the fragile, even illusory, hope for human happiness rooted deep in the human heart. And he resumes his rationale for committed action without reference to God: "Since the order of the world is shaped by death, mighten it be better for God if we refused to believe in Him and struggled with all our might against death without raising our eyes to the heavens where He sits in silence?" (*The Plague*, 121). Rieux's motive in the struggle becomes the ethic of common decency, and he characterizes the role he must play as being among the "healers who do not aspire to be saints, and who take . . . in every predicament, the victim's side" (*The Plague*, 237).

Tarrou, the tortured humanist/pacifist who has given up previous political commitment to struggle against evil as an activist inspired by the ideologies of the left, opts for a far more difficult role in resisting evil. Anxious to guard himself from any infection at all and hence to be in no way a plague bearer, he therefore wants to combat the plague not on a purely human or horizontal ethical plane but on something higher—he aspires to be a secular "saint without God." And though he acknowledges that this vertical reference or ideal of sanctity he has chosen is less efficacious than Rieux's ethical stance as healer, he declares that he has seen too much of human wickedness (and particularly the propensity of twentieth-century Europeans to kill others for their ideas) to trust to purely human motivations. Camus's stance against absurd evil becomes here an amalgam of the active rebellion of Rieux and the anguished reluctance on that part of Tarrou to add to human suffering by violence or by ever justifying the taking of a human life in the pursuit of justice. And Camus's ultimate reponse to evil (and one that resonates throughout his writings) will become that of committed action ever circumscribed by limits respecting the nature and intrinsic rights of the human (and with one's heart and mind always vigilantly turned against a vertical reference of belief because of God's scandalous silence).

Camus's novel and the philosophy of rebellion that it advocates had great impact on European writers and intellectuals throughout the 1950s and 1960s. His rejection of traditional theological speculation on problems relating to theodicy (God's role in the world, His relation to evil, etc.) challenged Catholics and believers in general to reexamine their concepts on this score. Even more important, it obliged them to come to grips with and analyze his implict charge that, when faced with problems of evil in the world, Christians seem to use hope in another life to divert their attention from and lessen their commitment to the plight of human beings in a fallen world.

Critics have already pointed out Camus's considerable influence on Graham Greene, and I find an especially cogent example of this in the 1961 novel *A Burnt-Out Case*, where Greene uses leprosy as his metaphor for evil and a leper colony in the wilds of Africa as his locale. With the dread disease an obvious analogue of the bubonic plague, he also introduces as one of his protagonists a doctor created in the image of Rieux. A longtime resident physician of the leper colony, Doctor Colin is another humanist hero whose clearsighted, dedicated efforts to cure contest the irrational "sickness as evil" that is leprosy. Laconic, hard-working, and totally indifferent to religious speculation, he is the most sympathetic character in the novel and is conspicuous, in this Catholic leper colony run and administerd by brothers and priests, as the only nonbeliever on the staff. Unlike previous Greene protagonists, Colin is not a troubled atheist/agnostic, nor will he be converted or even challenged by the need to believe. His humanist occupation as a faithful and totally dedicated healer is obviously enough to allay any spiritual qualms.

The other protagonist—and the foil of Doctor Colin—is the intruder who arrives on the scene, an outcast from his own society. An acclaimed architect who has built many famous churches in Europe and a man who has lost his faith, Querry has traveled to Africa to attempt to escape and live beyond his past. He is, of course, the novel's "burnt-out case" not in the medical sense in which the term is used—the condition of terminally ill lepers who are consumed by the disease—but primarily because of his spiritual emptiness. Unlike many of the native Africans of the colony who are ravaged with this disease but yet find solace in religious belief, Querry is spiritually "burnt-out" and has gone far beyond even the stage of religious doubt. No longer hoping to alleviate his condition in any way, he lives without consolation in an extreme state of spiritual listlessness.

Querry's "quest" to go beyond his former self eventually humanizes him. From the arrogant, self-centered, and cruel person he remembers himself to have been when a famous and worldly architect, he becomes a dedicated, humble, and earnest worker who comes close to finding peace and purpose for his life in total commitment to the operation of the leper colony. He could in fact become very much like Camus's Tarrou in that he no longer has any ambition to be an active participant on the world stage and is determined never again to be responsible for inflicting pain or suffering on other human beings (especially as the sexual manipulator of women that he now repents of having been).

Unlike Colin, Querry, and most of the Belgian priests and brothers of the community who, as believers or functional humanists, are primarily concerned with doing their job well, the rigidly "orthodox" Catholic believers, Father Thomas and the odious Rycker are presented in most unfavorable terms. Insensitive to the immediate needs of others, self-centered, and trapped in theoretical dungeons of dogma that pass for the substance of their religion, they become problematic to themselves and to the efficient running of the leper colony. Rycker, the manager of the local palm-oil factory, is another of Greene's spoiled priests. After having to leave the seminary, he marries a woman much younger than himself whom he gradually reduces to the level of a bond servant and virtual sexual slave (he justifies his master/slave ethic religiously by reading to his young wife the passages of Saint Paul on the submissive role that wives should fill for their husbands). Father Thomas, the only one of the Belgian priests stationed at the colony to think through catechism and dogma alone, is also the last to "see" things or people with any sort of critical objectivity. And though he has none of Rycker's cruelty and very little of his egotism, his rigidity and intolerance for what he cannot understand will make him Rycker's natural ally and foil in bringing about the destruction of Querry. Both characters are caricatures of certain approaches to observance and practices of faith associated with the "triumphal" church before the Second Vatican Council, which went into session shortly after Greene had finished writing the novel.

Because the self-righteous Rycker has his faith rooted neither in love nor service for others (and is unable to incorporate the spirit of the beatitudes into his life), he is a dangerous time bomb in the action of the plot. He finally self-destructs and kills Querry (because he cannot accept that his previous image of the famous architect-recluse as a committed

Catholic living a saintly life of self-sacrifice in the bush may indeed be less than true). Querry, in fact, has on several occasions tried to convince Rycker of his long-standing estrangement from the Church and his total disinterest and fatigue with any such concept as sanctity. Out of a Scobie-like pity he becomes innocently involved with the latter's wife when she asks him to drive her to the provincial capital and away from her unhappy situation; in the process, however, Querry provides circumstantial evidence that will be interpreted by the madly jealous husband Rycker has become as proof of some kind of romantic involvement between the two (they take contiguous rooms in the hotel and Querry reluctantly and imprudently enters her room when she calls him to comfort her in her anguish at now being completely uprooted and alone).

At this point in the novel Querry's natural helpfulness and compassion for the suffering of others bring him into violent conflict with Rycker's false and self-seeking views of religion and his totally inadequate understanding of human nature. He is especially blind in his inability to see and accept his wife's understandable revolt against his sexual domination and cruelty, and he thus feels justified in killing Querry because he believes Querry to have caused the disunion of the sacramental bond God created between himself and his suffering wife. Querry is therefore judged to be an enemy of God and hence disposable. Father Thomas's reaction to Querry's purported sin follows along similar lines. Now named the leper colony's superior, the young priest will not allow Querry to remain and work there after Rycker has aired his false charges. Because he cannot understand the ethical ambiguities in any human situation of passion and is unable to understand the human heart, he can only see things in abstract concepts. If Querry is not a saint, then, the priest reasons, he is a sinner and must be cut off from the society of "good" Christians.

The novel closes with the death of Querry, who, when shot by a delirious Rycker, seems bemused by what he regards as the tragicomic circumstances leading to his death.[5] With this ending Greene has left behind such themes as the "hidden God" waiting to save or redeem at the last moment a Pinkie or Scobie with a love inscrutable to simple human beings. The universe that would hereafter matter to Greene would not be a tragic one in which sinful human beings are torn between good and evil, God and the devil, in an eternal time frame; rather, it would be viewed as pathetic, absurd, or even comical.

Greene's somewhat radical adoption of the Camusian politics of grace—a revolt against injustice, suffering, and death that continues despite the knowledge that it will never be complete—can be viewed as perhaps an extreme case among other Catholic authors who came to maturity during the 1950s and 1960s. The humanistic concerns that would become paramount in Greene's fiction would be shared, nonetheless, by other Catholic novelists who became renowned as authentic practitioners of the genre in this later period. And this resulting convergence of attitudes would in fact prove a decisive factor in the changing form and emphasis of the Catholic novel. Among other factors are Catholics' changes in attitudes toward religious belief and practice that have occurred since the 1960s and that to a great extent reflect the emphasis given to Catholic doctrine and practice as a result of the Second Vatican Council. I offer the following as some of the most important concepts to have influenced the form the Catholic novel has taken in recent years.

First, there is the acceptance of what has been called "the perspective from below," or the commitment to confer on secular forms of human life not merely social and functional significance but also deep sacramental meaning.[6] From this concept it follows that all aspects of human life, even the most profane, are to be viewed as sacred. Hence any maintenance of the sacramental life of the Church that does not witness the full acceptance and putting into practice of the charismatic counsels of the Gospel is a pointless performance, a reductio ad absurdum quite like a sterile magic show. Implicit in this attitude is a rejection of the belief in the sacraments as causal signs of grace in their own right (or the concept ex opere operato), which held wide currency in the Church of the "triumphal" period. (One has only to review the earlier novels of Mauriac, Waugh, and Greene to assess the importance that this view of the absolute power and mystery of sacramental forms played in the Catholic imagination and to understand what a change would be effected by its loss.) Today, however, the action of the sacraments is viewed in a form of dialectics combining the profane and the sacred, and not as isolated actions stemming from intervention from on high.

A secondary but no less important corollary to be drawn from this transformed view of the workings of the sacraments is, as I have mentioned earlier, the turning away from the static dualism of body and soul to a more holistic view of human nature. As one of the most famous "progressist" theologians of the Second Vatican Council, the French Dominican Marie-Dominique Chenu, wrote of this matter, "Man is a composite of spirit and matter . . . body and soul are not merely in juxtaposition nor united by an extraneous force. They are consubstantial, one through and in the other."[7] Such a concept would, of course, have tremendously important ramifications on such matters as the dignity of the human person, the holiness of all human functions (including sex), and the sacramental nature of human work itself. If Christ has taken on Himself our human nature, then everything human is material for grace. Obviously this comprehensive view of human nature and its corollary— the inclusion of all that is human in the economy of grace and redemption—differ markedly from the concept of a warring dichotomy between flesh and spirit that Conor Cruise O'Brien and others have described as the essential dramatic component of the classical Catholic novel.

Finally, there are the changes in the way the Church regarded itself and the outside world that emerged from deliberations of the Second Vatican Council. Though the vast majority of doctrines remained firmly in place, some important elements of traditional Catholic theology and teachings were altered. One of the most significant is that of including the Church in the sacramental order. In so doing the council laid the groundwork for the whole process of future renewal and reform (therefore involving the institution in the dialectical fusion of the profane and sacred elements in life). Then there was the decoupling of the Catholic Church qua institution from the Church of Christ (they both had been regarded as "one and the same" before the council). Now the Church of Christ is said to "subsist in" but is not the Catholic Church. Even more disturbing to conservative Catholics (and in particular to Monseigneur LeFebvre and his followers) was the possible imputation of sin to the Church itself (before, sin was never attributed to the institution but only to individuals). In this momentous ruling of the council, the Church is at the same time holy and sinful, always in need of being purified and hence ever required to pursue, with its members, the path of penance and renewal. And in a change that Péguy would welcome is the declaration that the Kingdom of God and the Church are not as essentially one and the same. Henceforth the Church is to be regarded as "the initial budding forth" of the Kingdom and, like its individual members, it is a "pilgrim" institution on the road to salvation. And, of course, the council abandoned the teaching *extra ecclesiam nulla salus* to adopt that startling change that not only is salvation available outside the Church, but non-Christian religions may also serve as instruments of salvation.[8]

The four authors I have chosen to present as practitioners of Catholic novel in the contemporary period do not necessarily agree, in concept or approach, on what constitutes the Catholic novel today, and each to varying degrees resists the label of "Catholic" novelist. As is the case with most important contemporary novelists, they are highly individualistic and lend themselves far less easily to categorization than their predecessors of the genre's Golden Age. When examined to any reasonable extent, however, the works of Heinrich Böll, Muriel Spark, Jean Sulivan, and David Lodge unquestionably reflect and are seen as influenced by recent modes of thought and approaches to belief and the practice of faith that have gained wide currency among post–Vatican II Catholics. These four are, then, eminently important as writers who, by tapping new sources of spiritual and artistic inspiration, have reshaped or are reshaping the form and spirit of the Catholic novel.

Heinrich Böll

Heinrich Böll was born of a Catholic family of craftsmen whose ancestors had left England to settle in the Rhineland during the reign of Henry VIII. The Catholic identity of the family was strong, and Böll was brought up in close-knit, supportive Catholic environment of working-class people living in tenements. His family was, from the start, opposed to the Nazi philosophy and takeover. Through his parents' clever manipulation Heinrich was sheltered from formative contact with the Nazis and was one of a very few students in his high school who never enrolled in the Hitler Youth Movement. After he finished the gymnasium Böll lived an aimless existence under the certainty of war and eventual involvement as a soldier. Spending the next few years studying literature at the University of Cologne, he was then drafted into the Wehrmacht at the age of 22. His military career was spent in an extended state of despairing hope for the eventual defeat of Hitler. Serving on several fronts and a survivor of the Russian campaign, he was wounded four times and, in hope of living out the war, devised clever stratagems to avoid future combat—false permissions for leave or travel, medicines taken to stimulate sickness (Demetz, 88–90). He was taken prisoner in the final months of the war by the American army in West Germany. Returning to Cologne, he first supported himself and his family through his craft as a cabinetmaker. Gradually he devoted himself full time to his writings, and he was a founding member (along with Günter Grass, Uwe Johnson, and Hans Richter) of Gruppe 47, an organization of young German writers established in 1947 and dedicated to the renewal of German literature to be created in the rubble of defeat. Beginning with his graphic short stories and novellas in which he drew from his experiences as a wandering common soldier (he only achieved the rank of corporal), Böll gradually broadened the scope of his works to include novels of great influence and importance to postwar Germans. These deal with such themes as the continuing problems of war guilt; alienation from and protest against a society whose institutions of church, school, and state are viewed as mere appendages supporting a corrupt social class; and the greedy consumerism of postwar Germany. Juxtaposed to these themes are more personal ones that involve his protagonists in a continuing quest for ethical meaning and spiritual regeneration played out against the backdrop of the fallen world. When he was awarded the Nobel Prize for Literature in 1973, Böll had become Germany's most influential novelist (only Günter Grass rivaled him in prestige).

Böll's early works, which use the war as living metaphor of universal evil, also have deep religious themes of guilt and the need for repentance—for both individual and collective sins of aggression and cruelty. And he introduces the expedients of prayer and communal bonding as the sole means by which to transcend the terrible fallen state of the world at war. His protagonists—anonymous and sick-to-death sufferers who participate unwillingly in a hellish national venture—observe the evils that surround them through their Christian conscience, and as powerless, common soldiers they become resigned to their role of pure victim. In each of the two best-known novellas of this period—*Der Zug war pünklich* (1949; *The Train Was on Time*) and *Wo wast du, Adam?* (1950; *And Where Were You, Adam?*—Böll describes the progression to an absurd death of two infantry soliders. The first, Andreas, is seen returning from home leave to what he increasingly is certain will be his imminent death on the Russian front. As his train passes through the various Polish towns and cities, he ruminates over his fate and passes the time with other soldiers riding to the same destiny. Returned since the war to his Catholic faith, he would like to make this final journey a kind of voyage of prayer and repentance for his sins and those of all the others forced as well to take part in this insane enterprise. As the train ticks off the miles of tracks and passes through the devastated Polish countryside he reflects, "'Now I'll pray. . . . I'll say all the prayers I know by heart and a few more as well.' First he said the Credo, then a Paternoster and Ave Maria, *de Profundis* . . . then the Good Friday intercession because it was so wonderfully all-embracing, it even included the unbelieving Jews. That made him think of Cernăuţi, and he said a special prayer for the Jews of Cernăuţi and for the Jews of Lvov, and no doubt there were Jews in Stanislav too."[9]

Though he would like to make the train ride a continual memento mori of prayer and reflection, Andreas opens himself to share his own fears and frustrations with others. In so doing he illustrates Böll's most strongly held conviction that the most simple and natural modes allowing human beings to communicate (here sharing food, drinking bouts, and card games) are sacred and possess authentic sacramental dimensions. Andreas's death in Poland occurs at precisely the city that he had conjured up in his meditations. Before this occurs, he is consoled by a deeply spiritual experience gained from a night spent in a brothel with a young Polish prostitute who is also a member of the Partisans. Not wanting to engage in sex, both find peace of mind, dignity, and the beginning of love through open dialogue and the exchange of their most intimate feelings. They die together when the car taking them away from the city is blown up by other Partisans tipped off to the presence of German soldiers in the brothel.

In *And Where Were You, Adam?* the journey to death takes the opposite geographical direction as the soldier protagonist, a certain Feinhals, retreats in the final days of the war from the chaos of the Balkan front to his native German town in the West. Much of the novel is concerned with his love for a beautiful young woman, Ilona, whom he briefly encountered while billeted in a small Romanian village. Though they had hardly exchanged words, both were aware of the possibility of a sincere "I-Thou" relationship and were at the brink of opening themselves in trust and respect to the other. But tragic circumstances then intervene as the woman, a Jew, is seized as she visits relatives in the ghetto and is then shipped to a concentration camp at the very moment Feinhals's regiment receives orders for an immediate retreat. In what is surely one of the most disturbing dramatizations of the horrors of the extermination camps, an SS officer shoots Ilona as she auditions for the chorale group that the man has organized and to which he has given tender care ever since being named head of the death camp. The only possible survivors of those shipped there for extermination have always been, in fact, young women who pass the voice test. Because Ilona does not resemble the crude caricature of "Jewish type" that this man recognizes (she in fact has passed for a Christian in her own society and was educated by Catholic nuns), and because she overwhelms him during the audition by the exquisite way in which she sings the All Saints' Litany, he shoots her down in a paroxysm of despairing hatred because her beauty and talent threaten his prejudices.

Feinhals, though not knowing Ilona's fate, had instinctively sensed as she departed for the ghetto that she would never return. He nevertheless resigns himself to God's will: "He must," he thinks, "give God the chance of making everything turn out as it should, as it might have although there was no doubt in his mind that everything had already turned out differently: she wouldn't be back . . . perhaps it was asking too much to love a Jewish girl while this war was on" (*Train*, 90). Increasingly sure that the young woman is dead and motivated by her as if she were a patron saint, Feinhals prays in mystical union with her for all fellow sufferers, and even for God: "He suspected all these people of praying for something, for the fulfillment of some wish or other, but Ilona had told him, 'We have to pray to console God.'" Heretofore a reluctant churchgoer, he now will even consent, he says, to pray in church, "although he found it hard to bear the faces of most priests and their sermons, but he would do it to console God—maybe to console God for the faces and sermons of the priests" (*Train*, 128). His resolution will never be tested, for he is mortally wounded only a few steps from the door of his home, which has been draped with a white sheet of surrender, when a mortar shell exploded by remnants of the German army makes him one of the last casualties of an absurd war.

Böll's later novels are much broader in scope and more morally explicit and engaged in regard to social, political, and religious problems in postwar German society. His most complex novel, *Billard um halbzehn* (1959; *Billiards at Half-Past Nine*), is written partially in *nouveau roman* style and consists of interlocking interior monologues delivered by a sometimes confusing cast of characters, stream-of-conscience passages, and more conventional direct authorial narration. The novel involves three generations of a family of architects, the Faehmels—a period extending from the reign of Bismarck to the Adenauer government of the 1950s. A kind of modern House of Atreus, the Faehmel family is used as a microcosm of Germany's tragic history of the last century. Within the plot's time frame of only one day (the eightieth birthday of Heinrich, the grandfather and founder of the Faehmel architectural firm) Böll develops a moving study of the disastrous toll that the pernicious Prussian militarist tradition and resulting wars (culminating with Hitler, who is never mentioned) have taken on the members and fortunes of this family.

The novel is also particularly concerned with the question of German guilt and responsibility, in regard to both institutions and individuals, for World War II. In this large sweep of German history, the Faehmel family, with its long and solid Catholic tradition, is depicted as never having embraced or supported Prussian, then German, expansionism. Though a dutiful solider in World War I, Heinrich is mainly concerned about establishing a successful career as architect and caring for his growing family. (Böll suggests that it was this indifference to politics and a reluctance to contest German nationalism on the part of decent people like Heinrich that paved the way for the rise of Nazism.) Indeed, Heinrich's noninvolvement is seen as a stance no longer possible for his two sons. The elder, Otto, becomes infected with the Nazi virus and develops into a monstrous being (with only "the husk of a man" remaining).[10] As an adolescent he had reported his nonconforming mother to the Gestapo and, becoming a Storm Trooper, enthusiastically throws himself into combat and dies at Kiev. As an adolescent growing up in the 1930s, the younger brother, Robert is deeply opposed to Nazi ideology. By sheltering political dissidents during his adolescence, he barely escapes execution. He was spared, however, through his father's influence and on the condition that he immediately enter the military. As a German officer during the war, he conceals his rage so as to protect his wife and children from reprisal.

The mother of the family, Johanna, is, on the other hand, an uncompromisingly vocal opponent of the regime. Never able to overcome her grief at Otto's transformation into a Nazi thug, she transfers her concern to the other victims of the regime and is the only member of the family to protest through committed action. Especially repelled by the policy against the Jews, she at one point even attempts to board a train to share the fate of those being transported to an extermination camp. Once more the influential Heinrich is able to save a member of the family, but this time he can do so only by having his wife declared legally insane and agreeing to have her incarcerated in a rest home, where she has resided ever since.

To symbolize the patriarch's long-standing moral compromise, Böll uses the architectural accomplishment that establishes Heinrich's reputation—the Benedictine Abbey of Saint Anthony. Moreover, the abbey itself is indicted by Böll as having collaborated with the regime during the war (the monks have permitted Nazi "pagan solstice celebrations" on its premises, thus defiling the chapel). More generally, this monastery, like much of the German Catholic Church, had remained silent about Nazi atrocities and had failed to aid the victims. Robert, the architect turned demolition officer, eventually views the site as a living representation of his family's and the Church's guilty compromise with an evil regime. In the closing days of the war, and as his supreme act of opposition, he reduces it to rubble. Ironically, he receives an Iron Cross for what is mistakenly viewed as a strategic act of valor to encumber the advance of the victorious Americans. Though officially resuming his position as architect in reconstructed Germany after the war, Robert lives a marginal existence and represents the schizoid mentality of that generation forced to fight for Hitler and now unable to overcome deep-seated guilt and accompanying aversion to all forms of political commitment.

Both Heinrich and Robert must come to grips with the family's complicity in Germany's tyranny, and Böll effects this through Johanna, who is characterized as a kind of "holy fool." Released from the asylum to attend her husband's birthday celebration, she shoots but does not seriously wound a prominent cabinet member of the Adenauer government, which Böll depicts as essentially a holdover in personnel and compromising attitudes from the Nazi period. Johanna's mad act serves as the means to bring the family together in a newfound determination to live for the service of victims, be they of the past war (stateless survivors, like the former political prisoner of the Nazis, Nettlinger, who still remain unreconciled with the "new Germany") or more recent casualities of the greedy and cynical "democratic" state Böll sees as having emerged from the war's ashes. And in the book's last scene the members celebrate the patriarch's birthday by consuming an elaborate cake in the form of Saint Anthony's Abbey, thus overcoming their paralyzing complicity with their past and ready to affirm a new beginning.

The novel also presents an intricate and deeply religious pattern of symbols not immediately evident in a summary plot description. In the study of a German family as microcosm of Germany since the 1870s, Böll uses a timeless, biblical frame of reference. Using the Cain and Abel conflict, he separates the Germans of this drama into two antithetical groups: those partaking of the sacramental "host of the beast"—the powerful of the world—and the "lambs"—the victims on whom the powerful prey. From as far back as Cain and Abel, Böll then suggests, the world has seen the reenactment of this persecution of the innocent by the natural predator whose violence and arrogance are palpable "signs of the beast," and in this context the Nazis are one more extremely vicious manifestation of evil and fallen human nature.

Through the saga and example of the Faehmel family Böll affirms a third stance along with the factions of the "host of the beast" and the lambs—the role of the shepherd, who, like Christ, accepts to live and care for the persecuted. Dedicating himself solely to the interests of career and family, the grandfather Heinrich never commits himself to fight in any substantial way for the spiritual and temporal well-being of victims of oppression. A Christian with the grace and sensitivity to become a holy shepherd and never having taken to his lips the sacramental "host of the beast," he nevertheless shares the guilt of the politically noncommitted, and for this reason he bears heavy responsibility for the moral destruction of Otto and the guilt-laden conscience of Robert. As the novel ends, the Faehmel family closes rank, vows to no longer compromise itself with an enduringly corrupt political system, and will in the future place itself uncompromisingly and actively on the side of the victims against their executioners.

Böll became increasingly outspoken in his criticism of the Catholic Church in Germany in the 1960s. The crux of his problem with the institution was what he believed to be its open-and-close alliance with the dominant and powerful political factions in West Germany and the resulting dereliction of its role as spiritual teacher of the Christian message and values. He even formally withdrew as practicing member at the end of the 1960s. Part of his quarrel with the institution can be described as his repugnance for what he called the "milieu" Catholicism practiced by the German burgher class. By this he meant a value system that stressed externals and the secondary virtues of appearance, deportment, good manners, and of course, obedience. Rather than having accepted its share of guilt after the war and having attempted to change the minds and hearts of its communicants to live the Christian commitment, the postwar Church had, in his opinion, looked to its own survival and financial well-being. It had not, for example, opened its doors to refugees and sufferers of the war, and it had not tried to galvanize the social strife with openness and charity. Instead, in a continuation of its earlier policy of obedience and appeasement under the Nazi regime, the organization merely capitulated again before the new political powers after 1945.[11]

It is against this efficient and "clean" organization closed to the plight of the wretched, the poor, and the troubled and that Böll felt had truncated and reduced the sacraments to mere exercises of sterile hygenics that he would write much of his fiction after *Billiards*. His most bitter and sustained attack is contained in the novel *Ansichten eines Clowns* (1963; *The Clown*). Here Böll presents a protagonist reminiscent of Dostoyevski's "underground man," that nasty but uncannily perceptive critic of functional human beings and society. Like the Russian author's bitter anti-hero, Böll's young German, the professional clown Hans

Schneir, is able to evaluate (and castigate) the German Church and the society it supports from the privileged position of the outsider who has been made to suffer at the hands of both institutions.

Another important later novel is *Gruppenbild mit Dame* (1971; *Group Portrait with Lady*), wherein Böll presents as protagonist Leni Gruyten, the good woman of Cologne. An extremely sensuous and at the same time deeply saintly person whose life spans the period of World War II and German reconstruction, this woman of the people is a model for the kind of openness and concern for others that Böll felt Catholicism should foster in its adherents.

Despite his sharp attack against the German Church, Böll never denied being spiritually Catholic and insisted that he should receive a Church burial at his death. Like Péguy, whom he much admired, Böll was always careful to distinguish between the mystical body of the Church extending above and beyond the human institution and the essentially worldly and political corporation for the wealthy social classes that he judged the Church in West Germany to be.

Muriel Spark

During more than 30 years of a very productive career as writer, Muriel Spark has eluded easy categorization as a Catholic novelist. One critic claims, for example, that her novels "deal with religious themes in a deceptive manner."[12] Another asserts that "satire is indeed what her books seem to be concerned with."[13] Still another concludes that "the novels of Muriel Spark are written from a Roman Catholic standpoint, whether or not her religion is specifically mentioned."[14] In addressing such matters as the kind of literature she writes and the particular influences responsible for her special literary vision, Spark points to her conversion to Catholicism as the single most important factor providing a sense of meaning and direction to her life and art. In a 1961 interview with Malcolm Muggeridge she said, "I wasn't able to work or do any of my writing until I became a Catholic. . . . Nobody can deny that I speak with my very own voice as a writer now, whereas before my conversion I couldn't do it because I was never sure what I was."[15]

Born in Edinburg of a Jewish father and Presbyterian mother, she received an excellent education in one of the city's leading girls' schools but did not enter university. Instead she married and went directly after high school to live with her husband in Rhodesia. When her marriage foundered she returned in 1944 to London, where she would live with her son. There she first worked briefly in the branch of the British Intelligence Office that dealt with the preparation and writing of anti-Nazi propaganda, and she credits this stint for awakening her latent interest in creative fiction. After the war she went through a very difficult period with little financial income, turning out free-lance pieces for commercial firms while writing poetry in her spare moments. She was named editor of the official journal of the British Poetry Society, *Poetry Review*, and she became known as a writer in her own right after the 1951 publication of her well-received biographical piece on Mary Shelley, *Child of Light*. It may seem surprising to note that during this period of literary apprenticeship Spark had not as yet begun to write novels, particularly since she has subsequently become a very productive writer of the genre with just under 20 titles published. She says that she finally found her "writing voice" at the same time she converted—an event that had, in her words, "a very, very releasing effect" on her creative impulse.

As Muriel Spark describes it, the process of conversion had not been the result of intense intellectual study and reflection but rather was an "instinctive decision" to do what she recognized as only right and inevitable for her. Having had little religious faith during the years that she was brought up as a Presbyterian, she became an Anglican in 1953 (with religious views that she describes as very similar to those of T. S. Eliot, whom she much admired). She credits her discovery and reading of Cardinal Newman for giving her the impetus to go the further route to Rome, and she became a Catholic a year later. Her new faith provided her with a foundation and rationale for which to live and write, which she describes as grounded in the doctrine of the incarnation. By assuming a human form and by His death and resurrection, Christ had provided the economy of salvation for all human beings; in this process the supernatural had entered into the temporal reality of human history and fully completed it. Behind the flux of life Spark now acknowledged some grand design and saw life as a whole rather than a series of random happenings. Events, too, were "providentially ordered," and the absurdity of human behavior could now be viewed in the context of and part of the divine purpose.[16]

"Fiction to me is a kind of parable," Spark has written, "Some truth emerges from it" (quoted in Kemp, 8). And she strongly adheres to the opinion of her spiritual mentor, Newman, that "a Christian picture of the universe is almost always a poetic one" (quoted in Whitaker, 44). From this it follows for her that a poetic/metaphoric vision of the external world cannot be separate from the invisible one of the spirit but stands as a sacramental manifestation of it. This idea, absolutely central to her literary vision, she has most clearly expressed in an article dedicated to Marcel Proust, whose poetically drawn universe influenced her greatly. What one finds most valuable in Proust's work is, she says, "the idea that the visible world is an active economy of outward signs embodying each an inward grace."[17] Perhaps no better definition than this could be given of the artistic/religious motivations that have constantly guided Spark in her writing—admirably elucidating as it does her constant efforts to mark presence and convergence of the supernatural in the play and affairs of the physical/visible world. Her writing also reveals her profound belief that no matter how shapeless, muddled, or illusory life may be, this is only appearance and the result of a purely human inability to perceive, beyond faintly intuitive glimpses, the existence of a divine plan.

Muriel Spark's novels have been seen by critics as falling into discernible patterns or cycles of composition that indicate a definite evolution.[18] Certainly the earlier works—from her first novel, *The Comforters* (1957), to *The Prime of Miss Jean Brodie* (1961)—can be regarded as most similar in theme and emphasis to the traditional form of the Catholic novel. Written by a recent convert still insecure within the Church (and who even expressed aversion for the way Catholics acted), these works emphasize reliance on the Church as a refuge from the illusions and errors of a fallen world and on the drama of salvation as plot structure. Evil is seen, moreover, as a real presence incarnated in various "diabolical" characters who perform or are responsible for vile acts. The protagonist of *The Comforters*, the young woman Caroline Rose, is a convert and also a promising young novelist, and she obviously can be seen as mirroring Spark's situation in the moral difficulties she is portrayed as undergoing in adapting the demands of her new faith in the spheres of her public and private life. Against the gross forms of hypocrisy found in the abominable practicing Catholic, Georgina Hogg, the pleasant but detached cultivation of refined humanist Edwin Manders, and the relaxed hedonism of her lover, Laurence (whom she leaves after her conversion), Caroline gradually develops her own ethical system derived from her faith. And in so doing she is seen as exemplifying one of Spark's most deeply held convictions: that the practice of faith must also include a wholeness of the person that rejects a dualistic attitude to mind and spirit (sex, though troubling to Caroline, is never regarded as a taboo).

The short novel *Memento Mori* (1959) skillfully describes the intrusion of the supernatural in the everyday existence of a group of elderly English people who are, in varying degrees of debility, enduring their last days. The book was inspired, Spark has said, by memories from her childhood in Edinburgh of hospital visits to the aging sick that she had made with her mother. Greatly impressed in these occasions of the "power and persistence of the human spirit" among these suffering people, she had determined to write a work embodying "a tragic side to this situation and a comic side as well" (Kemp, 38). The supernatural element involves a mysterious phone call received by a full complement of old people in various physical, mental, and spiritual states or conditions. The caller simply utters the sentence, "Remember you must die" (in Latin "Memento mori," the phrase uttered by the priest in the distribution of ashes on Ash Wednesday, the first day of Lent). Reminded of their imminent end, all of those called are forced to abandon whatever hedge or shelter they may have constructed to mask this truth from their minds, and of course their respective responses are seen as being motivated by factors in their lives. For most of those called (and especially the manipulators or the selfish) the common reaction is to insist on a natural cause—the caller is a "maniac" or practical joker—and to refuse even to acknowledge the message. Yet for two converts to Catholicism (Charmian Colston and Jean Taylor) the caller is accepted as an agent of the supernatural world and becomes the catalyst for both to turn their minds with greater application than before to the "four last things" enumerated in the Baltimore catechism as "Death, Judgment, Hell, and Heaven."

Of all the characters, Jean Taylor's stance to death is particularly edifying, even heroic. As a former servant/companion to the wealthy Charmian, she has had to live in a public ward upon her retirement because of ill health and lack of economic security. A refined and gentle woman, she at first finds it extremely difficult to adapt to the cruder aspects of life and manners of the poor, lower-class women who are her companions, as well as to the good-natured yet patronizing attitude of the nurses for whom all the patients are "grannies." She will use this period of trial, however, as means of grace: "After the first year she resolved to make her suffering a voluntary affair. If this is God's will, then it is mine. She gained from this state of mind a decided and visible dignity, at the same time as she lost her stoical resistance to pain."[19] The full import of the message and its invitation to meditate on the reality of death is, however, not only grasped by believers. The admirable agnostic, Henry Mortimer, also responds positively to the message and comes to an evaluation of his own truth on the place that death must play in his own life: "If I had my life over again," he says, "I should form the habit of nightly composing myself to thoughts of death. I would practise, as it were, the remembrance of death. There is no other practice which so intensifies life" (*Memento Mori*, 153). The message of this pessimistic novel, as Ruth Whitaker perceptively has described it, is "that the inevitability of death should imbue everyday actions with significance: those with faith are reminded that they will be accountable to God for their earthly life; to those without faith it gives, paradoxically, an even stronger motivation to live fully . . . since they believe that they alone are responsible for their own redemption of existence from absurdity" (Whitaker, 58).

Perhaps the most important (and certainly the most successful artistic achievement) among the novels of the "cycle after conversion" is the novella-length work *The Prime of Miss Jean Brodie*. In it Spark presents, to use one critic's useful terms, another "angel/devil" character and places her in a modern morality play (Hosmer, 236). This time, however, she creates a plot situation anchored in larger historical context in which she would identify current ideological and political evils and show how these could be seen as doing violence and raising havoc in the personal lives of individuals themselves. This very popular novel became, in fact, the first of her studies in which, in the words of Peter Kemp, she attempted "to redeem the time" in which the plot is set "and rescue the transient moment by lifting it from history's flux and giving it some kind aesthetic fixity" (Kemp, 71). Here the moment is that volatile period of the rise of fascism in the 1930s, and symbolic of this malady's successful infection of the European conscience would be the motivations and influence that a charismatic but decidedly dangerous Edinburg teacher has on the minds and lives of her students.

As a teacher of young girls in the Marcia Blaine School, Miss Jean Brodie has succumbed to the temptation so threatening to all members of that profession: not only to teach but to live vicariously through the lives of her students. Each year she forms her own little coterie of young girls, to whom she gives herself unstintingly but from whom she also demands total loyalty and dedication. "Give me," she is wont to say, "a girl at an impressionable age and she is mine for life."[20] In the girls whom she selects she instills a sense of elitism and pride that they soon accept and recognize as setting them apart from the rest of their classmates ("Miss Brodie had told them at that time, 'and all my pupils are the crème de la crème'" [*Prime*, 12]), and she holds her particular role as teacher to be both that of sacrificing her "prime" for her protégés and of educating them so that in later years they too may learn to live to the full their own "prime."

On the surface such a total concern for leading each of her students to recognize and draw her own unique talents and interests in preparing for life is admirable and unfortunately often neglected in the educational process. Her motivation conceals, however, a sinister premiss: the arrogant assumption that she has the right and duty to manipulate all aspects of the lives of her students. She is essentially, then, a dangerous and deluded woman whose soul is torn by contradictory impulses of charitable concern and the most blatant refusal to allow those over whom she imposes her dictatorial ways the dignity of moral freedom to make their own decisions in the most personal matters. Moreover, the power Miss Brodie insists on exerting in her prime is analogous to that wielded by Mussolini in his own project for totalitarian control of Italy and aggrandizement of power throughout the rest of the world, and Spark makes this clear through numerous indices: laudatory remarks Miss Brodie makes in the classroom about the character and power of the Duce, touristic visits she takes during summer vacation to the new "Fascist paradise," and descriptions of Miss Brodie's elect as little groups of "fascisti," moving and speaking in disciplined patterns. And as her lust for power over others grows, she is seen to transfer her admiration for the Italian tyrant to the more "efficiently successful" German upstart, Hitler.

Obviously, Miss Brodie's totalitarian inclinations will also have the gravest consequences on her spiritual state and will profoundly affect the matter of her salvation. And though never even dimly aware of the fact, she personifies throughout the work a genuine diabolic presence and force. (Spark remarks on the "whiff of sulfur" [*Prime*, 134] that accompanies the ideas she imposes on her chosen ones.) As a result, what is more reprehensible than her penchant to live vicariously through her charges is her insistence to play the role of God and providence in their lives. As Miss Brodie puts this in action fascism as a political philosophy gives way to, or more correctly meshes with, Calvinism, the theological system justifying in spiritual terms through its doctrine of predestination Miss Brodie's passion of dictatorial elitism. As Peter Kemp has observed, Jean Brodie acts "like some justified sinner elected to grace" who claims to see what predestined roads her girls will follow (Kemp, 73). She therefore assigns to them the particular roles that she judges each must

follow as helpless victims of their temperaments that she alone can decipher: Rose will be a free-spirited even somewhat wanton woman and
a "great lover" because of her "gift of intuition"; Sandy will be a psy-
chologist because she is a keen observer of human nature; Joyce Emily
Hammond will become a political activist because of her passionate,
undisciplined nature; and so on.

As Miss Brodie becomes more and more blinded to the perversity of
her influence on and uncontrollable tampering with the girls' lives, she is
brought down by tragic circumstances for which she is primarily responsible: Joyce Hammond is killed en route to Spain, where, urged on by
her teacher, she intends to fight in the Civil War (she is confused as to
which side she is on). The person to disclose this horrendous indiscretion
is Miss Brodie's favorite, the only one she treats as an equal and, as she
adamantly believes, the one who under no circumstances would ever
betray her. Sandy Stranger, the Judas of the band, is ironically but logi-
cally the student most powerfully influenced by Miss Brodie's elitist philosophy. An alienated searcher for truth, as her name implies, she has
attained sufficient distance at her tender age to recognize the true identity of her teacher as angel-devil; hence though continuing to admire
her, Sandy is also sufficiently torn in conscience to realize the danger the
woman poses for young minds and to be outraged by her blind and all-
consuming arrogance in manipulating the lives of others. When Miss
Brodie declares at one point that she has sacrificed her own love for one
of the male teachers at school so that Rose, whom she urges to have an
affair with the same man, can through this experience begin to fulfill her
own destiny as sensual lover, Sandy "sees" into the very depths of her
teacher's problematic nature and resolves to report her to the school
authorities: "She thinks she is Providence, thought Sandy, she thinks she
is the God of Calvin, she sees the beginning and the end. And Sandy
thought too, the woman is an unconscious Lesbian" (*Prime*, 147).

Forced to retire, Miss Brodie only learns of Sandy's betrayal shortly
before her lonely, solitary death. Sandy soon abandons the God of
Calvin, is converted to Catholicism, and becomes a cloistered nun. She
then gains prominence as the author of a famous psychological study on
religious belief, *The Transformation of the Commonplace*. Yet Sandy is not at
peace (she continually "grips the bars of her cell") and continues to live a
life of extreme religious tension that distinguishes her from the other
"serene" nuns of the community. She remains throughout her life much
taken with Jean Brodie (and credits her for being the dominant influence
in her upbringing). In fact, Sandy's agitated state would seem to be a

sign that, despite conversion and acceptance of God's will for her, she still is tempted by Miss Brodie's demonic assumption of divine authority and vision in a terribly sinful but grand attempt to rival and even become God.

With *Jean Brodie* Muriel Spark ends her cycle of "Catholic novels" and took different directions and approaches. One very apparent change involves a transfer of emphasis from events of the world seen as part of God's divine pattern to the way human beings manipulate forces and events for their own ends. Although she never rejected the divine role as the ultimate source of meaning and order in the universe, Spark became more interested in the way individuals perceive or do not perceive this and act in the light and context of this ultimate reality. She also is seen to have developed a more ambiguous stance to her major characters. No longer were they viewed primarily on a religious/moral scale of what is good or bad. In fact, her sympathies sometimes seem strongest for her amoral types—those who, without much or any religious belief or sentiment but with canny good sense—seem able to make the most of their lives from the point of view of happiness, success, or pleasure.

Like Graham Greene (who gave her decisive finanical and critical support during her early impoverished years as a novelist), Spark developed a humanistic perspective in which the "hidden God" and the action of grace become obscured by the fallen nature of things, to be replaced by an absurd universe requiring existential choice on moral issues on the part of her characters. And the quest for the authentic self became the primary goal for believers and nonbelievers alike. Muriel Spark's novel that first registers and perhaps best exemplifies these shifts and changes in perspective is *The Mandelbaum Gate* (1965). It is also her longest work and the one that most successfully introduces and integrates the major Catholic themes that resonate throughout her writings. It is, finally, the richest of all her novels in autobiographical allusions and detail regarding the matter of her conversion and subsequent religious evolution.

Barbara Vaughan, the protagonist of the novel, is a woman approaching her forties and a recent convert from Judaism to Catholicism. Her conversion, a watershed in her life, has obliged her to come to grips not only with her fundamental basic beliefs but also with the most basic question, "Who am I?" At the outset of the novel she realizes that not only is she unable to answer this question but "that her self image was at variance with the image she presented to the world."[21] To her relatives and friends this English teacher in a private school for girls is simply "a settled spinster of thirty-seven, one who had embraced the Catholic church instead of a husband, one who had taken up religion instead of cats" (*Gate*, 12). Yet this surface appraisal is far from accurate. Despite her somewhat dowdy, settled appearance Barbara is actually a vital, intelligent, and sensual woman who has for some time been involved in a passionate affair with Henry Clegg, a prominent archaeologist and expert currently at work on the Dead Sea Scrolls. Indeed, Barbara's conversion has posed serious problems for their relationship. An agnostic, Henry would like to marry Barbara, but he is a divorced man, and as a Catholic Barbara now must accept the fact that continued sexual relations with Henry outside of marriage is a grave sin. Moreover, if she marries him outside the Church she will be formally severed from her newly professed creed. As she turns to a new existence as a Catholic and tries to resolve these difficulties, she realizes, however, that no matter what the outcome she must begin to live her life with, as she describes it, "the beautiful and dangerous gift of faith which, by definition of the Scriptures is the sum of things hoped for and the evidence of things unseen" (*Gate*, 20).

The binary theme of the quest for authenticity on the purely human as well as spiritual plane is acted out as Barbara visits Jerusalem to take stock of her situation as well as visit the shrines so important to her new-found faith. The historical moment of her visit is the year 1961, when the city is both an armed camp because of the Jewish-Arab conflict and also at the very center of world news because of the ongoing Eichmann trial. As a Jew with relatives living in the city, Barbara must hide her identity if she is to be able to visit Catholic shrines in the Arab zones of control. The work thus thrusts her into the maelstrom of political hostilities, and during her stay her safety and even her life are threatened as she furtively enters and exits the Arab-Jewish sectors from the checkpoint at the Mandelbaum Gate (one of the major border crossings in the city separating the Jordanian and Israeli territories). During these sorties she must literally be smuggled across borders by hired agents, and she becomes deeply involved with a colorful cast of dealers in contraband, opportunists, and political extremists—a number of whom Spark favorably presents as charming, resourceful scoundrels who, in the face of the worst circumstances, always seem to know how to survive with consummate style and cunning.

Yet the work's real drama is contained in the theme of pilgrimage in the quest for spiritual authenticity. During her difficult sojourn in this dangerous and strife-torn city, Barbara eventually undergoes profound religious experiences that allow her to reconcile the two elements that at

first seemed virtually incompatible: her sexual needs and spiritual fulfillment in her newfound faith. To bring this about, she must break down
rigid and confining absolutes defining self-identity and conduct, but she
must also effect this while remaining within the limits and according to
the guidelines of what she views as legitimate for her as a Catholic.
Barbara begins the quest by examining who she is as a human being. In
partial response she admits to herself that she has always been a deeply
sexual person, even that she was "more blessed by sex" through her
Jewishness than were her Gentile relatives and friends (*Gate*, 45).
Obviously without a deep conviction of the sinful nature of sex, Barbara
begins her quest in marked contrast to so many protagonists of Mauriac,
Julien Green, Waugh and others for whom overcoming the thorn of the
flesh provided the essence of the drama of salvation. Barbara for some
reason has never viewed body and soul as warring entities (Spark of
course implies that her heroine owes much of this holistic view to her
Jewish background). Now as a Catholic Barbara does not develop com-
plexes on such matters (which Spark implies is the case with many core-
ligionists) but rather will put them in proper perspective: "Sex," Barbara
says at one decisive point in the novel, "is child's play. Jesus Christ was
very sophisticated on the subject of sex. And didn't harp on it. Why is it
so prominent and serious for us? There are more serious things in the
world. . . . It was child's play, unself-conscious and so full of fun and
therefore of peace, that she had not bothered to analyse or define it.
And, she thought, we have invented sex guilt to take our minds off the
real thing" (*Gate*, 318–19).

Barbara's openness in this matter provides the key to the process of
authentic self-fulfillment. And in insisting on the need to rely on her
freedom of conscience, she does not fall into the trap of being defined by
abstract, legalistic absolutes in approaching and resolving moral dilemmas involving her spiritual and human needs. The reader becomes aware
that Barbara's strong and independent resolve to deal personally with
matters of conscience regarding such questions is at least partially the
result of a catalytic experience she undergoes when, out of curiosity, she
becomes a spectator during one of the court sessions of the Eichmann
trial. Viewing the common appearence of this little man in his glass
booth she seems first to be struck by a reaction similar to that of Hannah
Arendt (who saw in Eichmann's insignificance the very personification of
what she termed the "banality of evil"). And as this pathetic-looking
creature persists in his whining claim that he had exterminated Jews
only because he had followed the orders of his superiors, Barbara clearly

sees on what grounds his self-defense really rests: "The man was plainly not testifying for himself, but for his pre-written destiny. He was not answering for himself or his own life at all, but for an imperative deity named Bureau B-4, of whom he was the High Priest" (*Gate*, 212).

As Whitaker has so well indicated, the emotional experience of hearing Eichmann is epiphanic, revealing to Barbara as it does "the acute danger of shifting one's responsibilities and decisions on to an impersonal force, whether it be the Church, or a political party, or a national movement" (Whitaker, 73). And she resolves henceforth to use her own moral judgment and hopes that God will approve of her decisions. In fact, the very evening after she returns from the trial, she calls Harry and informs him that no matter what the outcome in the process of annulment for his previous marriage, she has decided to marry him. She presumably has taken here an existential stance and will act according to the inner dictates of her conscience. Yet this in no way means that she has ceased to be a believer or that her religious commitment no longer remains her ultimate concern. On the contrary, she only seems more convinced that every such dilemma has religious dimensions and that taking a decision on either side should not cut the person off from faith in or union with God.

Now a more serene and integrated person, Barbara says, "Either religious faith penetrates everything in life or it doesn't. There are some experiences that seem to make nonsense of all separations of sacred from the profane—they seem childish. Either the whole of life is unified under God or everything falls apart. . . . She was thinking of the Eichmann trial, and was aware that there were other events, too, which rolled away the stone that revealed an empty hole in the earth" (*Gate*, 344). By a fortuitous sequence of events, in which a malicious former friend's attempt to legally block Barbara's marriage in the Church actually backfires to allow the removal of canonical difficulties, Barbara then completes her pilgrimage to Jerusalem and departs a "new person." And in the end Spark has enlarged the iconography of this ancient capital of the Jews to embody for Barbara (and all other pilgrims as well) the designation given it much earlier by another Jewish convert, the apostle Paul—as "the everlasting city of faith."

In the 10 novels Spark wrote after *The Mandelbaum Gate* her vision became darker and less tied to specifically religious themes. She shifted her focus to the depiction of the absurd and observed the actions of human beings who, in opposing the absurd, act as if there was no divine pattern for life with far more detachment than in her previous novels. She also increasingly adapted the satirical mode as she investigates secular forces, ideas, or institutions that are used by many as replacements for authentic belief—trendy philosophical movements, psychoanalysis to replace moral responsibility, even dietary and physical fitness regimens. In her portrayal of the human comedy she reserves a substantial measure of criticism for the post–Vatican II Church as a very fallible institution whose members are seen as often caught up in their own power schemes or delusions of power, and where the quest for influence and crass, materialistic gain is often masked by pious motivations. Though her canvas became darker in these novels, Spark never loses faith in the divine scheme of things, nor does she accept the universe as essentially absurd. Rather, in these works she transfers her attention from God's patterning of the world to human behavior and the malevolent designs that, through their schemes and actions, human beings concoct for one another in a fallen world.

The Abbess of Crewe (1974) is a good example of Spark's novels of the past two decades. It reflects the times and corrupt ethics of the Watergate scandal (which it mimics in its use of electronic bugging devices). Yet Spark did not intend the novel to be simply a lighthearted comedy of manners: she subtitled it "A Morality Play" and has presented it as a timeless parable of power, politics, and corruption—in this instance played out in the Catholic Church. The Benedictine Abbey of Crewe is hilariously and even shockingly portrayed as a thoroughly secularized institution awash with intrigue, snobbery, and worship described as a kind of elegant "poetry" devoid of religious conviction. The intrigue revolves about Alexandra, the future abbess of Crewe, whose delicate manipulation and iron-hand control of the liturgy and life-style of the religious in her monastery obstruct the reforms in worship and the new spirit of Vatican II. An aristocrat whose lineage goes back 14 generations in English and 10 in French nobility, she is an aesthete who uses her vocation as a nun to create a "poetry of life." Yet she is also one of Spark's sinister types: she quotes Machiavelli and serves him up often for her edification and that of the other nun conspirators who support her grab for power. She is further described as that curious combination of the aesthetic hanger-on to the beauty of the traditional Benedictine liturgical forms and conservative religious life-style and at the same time an exponent of the most advanced forms of technological bugging.

Another leading character is Sister Felicity, an activist nun who sets herself up as rival to Alexandra through a campaign to "modernize" the

rule and worship of the community of Crewe. A younger woman from
the lower classes, she is described as a kind of religious hippie who strives
to win the convent over with her ideas of free love and individual freedom redolent of the "do your own thing" ethic of the cultural revolution
of the 1960s. Felicity is having an affair with a Jesuit, and in the ensuing
imbroglio of scandal and blackmail, she becomes disgraced and put out
of the running in the imminent election for abbess when letters revealing her liaison are stolen from her cell. (The theft occurs when two Jesuit
novices enter the the abbey in a Watergate-like break-in engineered by
one of Alexandra's supporters.) Elected abbess and firmly in control of
the community, Alexandra must nevertheless travel to Rome to explain
away the rumor of political turmoil at the abbey that has come to the
attention of the Vatican authorities. Although the work ends before we
know the results of the investigation, we are sure that Alexandra will be
able to defend with mendacity her honor and reputation before an ecclesiastical board of bureaucrats whose personal and collective integrity is
also apparently very far from intact.

In the work Spark seems, finally, if not to condone then at least to
find amusing the megalomaniacal propensities of the subtle and fiercely
intelligent abbess. Alexandra outclasses Nixon in every way and becomes
a survivor because, unlike him, she does not fall into paranoia or self-pity
but cleverly uses her resources to the end. (And she will not destroy her
own tapes: "We cannot," she explains, "destroy evidence the existence of
which is vital to our story and which can be orchestrated to meet the
demands of the Roman inquisitors who are trying to liquidate the convent. We need the tapes to trick, lure, lime, bamboozle, et cetera.")[22]
There is clearly something demonic about Alexandra that no doubt
explains much of Spark's obvious fascination with her, and, as Whitaker
observes, the abbess certainly is amply enough drawn to illustrate brilliantly the novel's satirical thrust against "power, its corrupting forces,
the reforms of the Catholic Church, and the farcical nature of world politics" (Whitaker, 105).

Jean Sulivan (Joseph Lemarchand)

Jean Sulivan is now recognized as one of the major continuers of the
Catholic novel in France from the 1950s up through and beyond the
years of the Second Vatican Council. He is of that generation born in the
decade before World War I which, as David O'Connell has observed in
his important study on Michel de Saint Pierre, has produced a number of

important authors forwarding the tradition (Jacques de Bourbon Busset, Pierre Emmanuel, Cesbron, and, of course Saint Pierre, to mention some of the most important) (O'Connell, 2). My choice of Sulivan to represent his generation may not initially be viewed as the most obvious, since this author has been and perhaps still is less well known and read in France than most of those in the generation O'Connell identifies. The best known of these, Michel de Saint Pierre, for example, began his career as a novelist in 1948, a decade before Sulivan's tardy entry at the age of 45. At Saint Pierre's death in 1987 his literary production was far more extensive than that of Sulivan (who had died seven years earlier), and one of his novels, *Les Nouveaux Prêtres* (1964)—which deals with the struggle for control of the French Church between the conservative *"intégristes"* and the liberal *"progressistes"* just after the Second Vatican Council—had even been a best-seller in France.

Saint Michel's novels have continuously been reprinted and are in great demand. In contrast, though all of Sulivan's novels have been published by prominent French publishing houses (with several titles appearing in Gallimard's popular "Folio" series), he has so far not been regarded in his own country as a leading writer of his time, nor, for that matter, have his works been published in translation to any major extent abroad. (In the United States, for example, the only novel to have yet appeared in English is *Il y a la mer* (translated as *The Sea Remains*, 1991).

Yet in any study of the Catholic novel Sulivan is an important and representative figure in regard to the change in form, emphasis, and themes the genre has undergone in the contemporary period, arguably as much so as the far better known Michel de Saint Pierre. From the start of his career Sulivan has been recognized as a direct literary descendant of the French giants of the Catholic novel's Golden Age—Bloy and Mauriac, but especially Bernanos, whose influence on Sulivan is both immediately obvious and commanding. The principal Bernanosian themes—the holiness of poverty, life seen as drama of salvation/damnation, the need to strip the self of materialistic attachment and so return to the spirit of childhood, the necessity to risk all in order to advance in spiritual growth, to name the most obvious—are also major thematic components in Sulivan's novels. And he further shares Bernanos's penchant for creating as protagonists very human, problematic priests whose lives on the periphery of respectable society reflect his views of what it means to be a Christian and how to confront the spiritual dessication prevalent in modern society. Sulivan, moreover, reveals his admiration for and reliance on Bernanos by often referring and alluding in his works to the latter's essays and novels. And like Bernanos, Sulivan considered a career of writing as an essentially spiritual vocation that, in his case, allowed him to live fully his role as a priest.

Second, despite Sulivan's undeniable link with the traditional Catholic novel, he nevertheless broke away early and decisively from the attitudes of the pre–Vatican II Church and the approach to the practice of faith that these supported. Unlike Michel de Saint Pierre, who resisted the changes to become regarded at least at one point in his career (and perhaps incorrectly) as a formidable spokesman against the new spirit fostered by the council, Sulivan was from the start a fervent *progressiste* and exponent of Vatican II. In fact, because of his adamant insistence that the Church divest itself of its traditional trappings of meaningless power and ritual, some conservative French Catholics have come to regard him as a radical figure, and even one gone beyond the pale of acceptable orthodoxy. A recognized advocate of the most evolved postcouncilar attitudes and doctrine and at the same time an author whose works are written with conscious knowledge of and reference to the older tradition, Sulivan therefore represents a most fortuitous point of reference.

Sulivan has also broken new stylistic ground in his novels. The kind of authorial "voice" he developed would become markedly different and innovative in comparison with the more straightforward and didactic narrative devices used by most Catholic novelists of the past. Sulivan's narrative voice—ever emanating from "the edge of the desert" of what he judges modern society to be—insistently and humbly urges readers to divest themselves of all traces of social pose, pretense, and self-importance so as to achieve the state of "transparency"—the emptying out of all that is not of the spirit.[23] Only in this condition, he believed, can human beings take stock of their authentic nature and recognize the deeply religious, sacral dimension residing in what have hitherto been regarded as the merely profane aspects of everyday life. Sulivan's evolving narrative voice/persona thus would come to regard and to celebrate all means of human communication as authentic sacramental signs and all human beings, no matter how dispossessed or humiliated, as children of God, each unique and holy.

Sulivan's decision to become a novelist did not materialize until he was well into his priestly career. (He did not try his hand at fiction until his mid-forties, with the novella, *Le Prince et le mal*, appearing in 1958.) Prior to this he had spent most of his professional life, after his ordination in 1938, first in parish work and then as chaplain at the University of Rennes, in his native Britanny. The intellectual form that his campus ministry eventually took became closely linked to the medium of film. At the end of the 1940s he established a lecture series and a ciné-club (La Chambre Noire), both of which allowed him to use films as an integral part of his conferences and talks, and in 1948 he eventually founded the periodical *Dialogues-Ouest*, dedicated to systematic review of contemporary films. Sulivan's interest in film dated back to the earliest period of his intellectual formation. As Patrick Gormally has pointed out, Sulivan had long been an ardent moviegoer and believed that cinema had become the "seventh art." As "the son of a peasant," as he liked to call himself, he was especially taken by the immediacy of the medium and the democratic means by which it conveyed its message. As he would explain in his periodical, "Film is, in reality, totally different from pure entertainment. It is a new language and as an art form, the most popular and the most proletarian of all the languages and arts."[24]

Joseph Lemarchand had, in fact, even taken his pseudonym, Jean Sulivan, from a cinematographic source. As Gormally explains, the name originally belonged to the protagonist of the American film *Sullivan's Travels* (1941), directed by Preston Sturges. The film's hero, John L. Sullivan (a movie producer played by Joel McCrea), enters into what at first is a lighthearted publicity stunt and game: he wants to "get inside" true-to-life types living on the fringes of society and know their true feelings. To do this, he assumes the disguise of a vagabond and heads out from his Hollywood studio to meet life on the road. On the way he picks up a disengaged woman (Veronica Lake) who becomes his traveling companion and confidente as they plunge into the "lower depths" of society. The light comic tone of the film turns somber as Sullivan loses proof of his identity, is arrested as tramp, and is subjected for some time to cruel treatment in a prison work camp. All is eventually resolved, and after returning to his authentic identity Sullivan has become the wiser for the experiences and insights he has gained through his adventures.[25]

The reasons for Sulivan's enthusiastic adoption of this name for himself have, of course, much to do with the kind of character presented in the Sturges film. A caring person concerned enough to investigate the human condition of the most underprivileged and neglected members of society through personal experience, the original Sullivan opens himself in his travels to authentic contact and dialogue with those he encounters along the way. Never feeling superior and seeing the falseness of social pretensions and veneer, he finds his own more authentic self by sharing the life and sufferings of those from whom he would normally be cut off in this own bourgeois world. Lemarchand, then, drew from the film not only his pseudonym but a kind of model for the protagonist narrators of his future novels as well as an example of the tone he wanted to give to his own literary "voice."

In 1958 Sulivan received permission from ecclesiastical authorities to leave his post in Rennes and dedicate himself full time to writing. He took up residence in the tawdry Pigalle area of Paris where, with travel to India, Israel, the United States, and Eastern Europe intervening, he lived until his death in 1980, when he was struck by a car on a Paris street. During a very productive 22-year period he published 29 works consisting of essays, meditations, novels, and journalism. Sulivan gave as the principal reason for his career change from a well-known and appreciated chaplain-preacher to the solitary existence of a writer in Paris the fact that he had felt extremely stifled in a society to which he nonetheless continued to be attracted. His need to write, he says, arose from his desire to create a world in which "there is a little less oppression" and where he could communicate with friends and associates more freely and humanly.[26] And he described his goal as a writer to be that of helping others find their interior freedom and at the same time remain in the Church. He would strive to achieve these ends by writing novels that would challenge and trouble the reader, not "opium novels" that soothe or flatter the conscience (*Rencontres*, 37–38). He never relinquished his conviction that his double vocation as priest and writer was artistically and morally congenial (since for him writing represented the same kind of religious vocation as it had for Bernanos).

Viewing the Church as an institution in the most critical terms, Sulivan believed that the official Church does not express the spirit of creative liberty announced by the Gospels but is rather a sad "guardian of duty."[27] He further saw this misguided stance as largely responsible for the conflicts in the contemporary Church, and he characterized many of the present forms of institutional belief as "prison houses of abstract ideas" imposed on believers from without, thus obstructing the words of the living God and His hope-filled message of salvation (Onimus, 80). Yet he still felt that the Church was his home and the only institution in which he could purposefully and congenially fulfill his vocation as a writer. And, in the final analysis, he believed that despite its "vices, conformities, and intellectual sloth," the Church's true spirit has ever borne witness to a "spiritual beyond" by teaching the individual to renounce the self and refuse to be limited to surface reality and earthly appearances (*Rencontres*, 37–38).

Of Sulivan's 11 novels, critics have designated those he wrote during the 1960s up to *La Joie errante* (1974; *Errant Joy*) as his best and most challenging. From this period I discuss the novels *Devance tout adieu* (1964; *Anticipate Every Farewell*), *Car je t'aime, ô éternité* (1966; *Eternity, It Is Thee I Love*), *Consolation de la mort* (1968; *Death's Consolation*), and *Il y a la mer* (1972; *The Sea Remains*).

In *Devance tout adieu* Sulivan as narrator personally relates his mother's death, the circumstances surrounding it, and his own virtually inconsolable grief at her passing. His mother, *"petite maman"* as he affectionately referred to her, had during her life as a simple and God-fearing woman, incarnated for him the unshakable, immediate, and childlike belief of the peasant class from which he had come. And during the virtually unbroken skein of 20 years of Sunday visits and dinners he had taken with her during his priesthood, she had constituted for her scholarly son a kind of refuge from the sterility of the too intellectual milieu in which he labored. Then, as a reader (and often a critical one) of his early novels, she became for him something of a touchstone as to whether or not his novels were comprehensible to simpler people and whether in his literary vision he was remaining faithful to the child he had been and to those spiritual truths learned through his mother's direct counsel and example.

In what became the greatest trial of his life as priest—and one that did not leave his faith unshaken—he observed during his mother's last conscious moments that she derived little or no consolation from the last sacrament, that she did not respond or even seem to acquiesce to the prayers that were being said over her, but rather seemed to have fallen into a state of panic, even despair. Afterward, Sulivan gradually overcame the spiritual crisis caused by the scandal of his mother's tremendously sad and difficult death by regarding it as proof of the central moral teaching of Christianity: the reality of suffering and the obligation of each Christian to follow Christ on the Cross. As when, in the novel, he witnessed his mother die without apparent consolation he realizes "that she has been placed, naked, on the cross, and she now understands what it is to be abandoned."[28] And he repudiates for himself and for all times the myth that "the Christian suffers less because he believes. This is just another magical concept one has of the faith. Heaven, the beyond, impossible for me to imagine them. . . . I know no other God than the Son of Man and I don't ask other questions" (*Devance*, 77).

Car je t'aime, ô éternité begins Sulivan's "priest novels," portraying the life and ministry of Jerome Strozzi. This decidedly nonconforming yet faithful priest cannot fit in the established patterns of ministry provided by his order and becomes a latter-day worker priest acting alone and without the benefit of an authorized mission or support. When asked to leave his religious community, he goes to live in the Pigalle area of Paris where he gradually becomes, through openness and selfless caring, the recognized "chaplain/social worker" for many of the area's streetwalkers. "Tonzi," as the women call him, lives the Gospel counsel of love and commitment to one's neighbor immediately and unconditionally. He is able, moreover, to live chastely and joyfully in this sordid area and amidst the squalid circumstances of suffering that he sees on all sides. Resourcefully yet always with great humility, he is able from time to time to shield some of the women from the cruel manipulation of their pimps and clients, and he even manages to help several escape from the terrible trap into which they have fallen.

Regardless of these women's actions, he never ceases to view them as victims who, despite their promiscuous lives, are often good, and in some cases even saintly, people. And for Strozzi, the issue is not their lack of "purity." "The real struggle," he states, "is elsewhere, beyond sex, though often revealed in terms of sex. Of course a preoccupation with sex causes alienation, but a constant anxiety about purity can easily do the same. It is not purity that we must fight for directly, but for liberty and freedom."[29] And Jerome Strozzi's deepest reasons for commitment to these unfortunate women are precisely aimed at extending to them the freedom that is their birthright as social and spiritual beings. "I've met," the narrator says, "people like him everywhere— rebels, some would call them, but they're not rebels in the name of ideas or theories. It's just that one day freedom takes hold of them and turns them upside down, and suddenly they're fighting against all kinds of unquestioned social assumptions. Strozzi is, then, a kind of "spiritual cosmonaut" who through his works helps these women to "become alive and free. . . . What he represents is the leaven at work in the dough, which will take some time to ferment. People like Strozzi are opening up the spiritual space for a new renaissance" (*Eternité*, 223).

Consolation de la nuit is set in the same Pigalle milieu and deals with grace operating in the corrupt world and the reality of prostitution. This time the novel portrays the spiritual evolution of the girl, Clara, whose mother, Tamara, has been forced into the profession as the result of her father's horrendous cruelty. He had thrown Tamara and her sisters out of his house so that he could live there alone with his new wife and former mistress who, it turns out, is the wife of this man's only son (a soldier who was killed in the African campaign). Forced to move to Milan to eke out a living, Tamara was gradually drawn by necessity into prostitution and eventually moved to Paris. There she lives with her illegitimate daughter, Clara, whom she lovingly supports by continuing to work as a prostitute. The mother has managed (one wonders how) to conceal her profession from her now adolescent daughter and has brought her up as if she were from a respectable bourgeois background. Extremely bitter because of the injustice experienced at the hands of her father and, by extension, from the Church, whose Italian priests aided and justified the father's abandonment of his children, Tamara has long since left her religion and has scrupulously shielded her daughter from any contact or influence of a religious nature. When we first meet her, Clara, as a product of the totally laicized French system of education, is a young woman whose mind is a religious tabula rasa.

The novel's plot is essentially the story of Clara's conversion and her eventual decision to become a Carmelite nun. The major influence in her spiritual evolution is a defrocked priest, now living as a private tutor, whom Clara's mother engages to instruct her daughter in preparation for the dreaded baccalaureate examination. The tutor, Paul Esteban, is presented as a priest who has lost his vocation as a result of the arid and too intellectual formation received in the "hothouse" environment of the seminary. Trained to suspect and downgrade feelings and emotions, Esteban soon came to separate belief from any deep-felt human need and ended up regarding religion as mere contrivance and a vain attempt to conceal "Nietzsche's abyss" with comforting illusions. As he tutors Clara in philosophy, Esteban explains away religion as simply one of a number of attempts to give meaning to life and to rationalize the void at the very heart of human existence. After a chance entrance into a Paris church, Clara's soul opens slowly and inexplicably to the irresistible impulsions of grace. Intuitively aware of this process, Esteban indirectly but strenuously tries, through all the intellectual arguments he can introduce, to abort Clara's evident but unspoken progression to belief. In the process he seems once again to be opening old wounds and to be jousting with those former doubts and anxieties that he believed to have definitively put to rest when he left the priesthood.

The narrator describes Clara's conversion and future life as a cloistered nun to be the result of her response to the urgings not of a hidden God but of the living Christ who, even after His resurrection, refused any traditionally triumphal characterization and chose to reveal Himself under the guise of ordinary, simple creatures: "Resurrected during the night, He is mistaken for a gardener, for a fisherman cooking a fish on a fire by a lake. . . . He prefers to hide under bridges in the utter forsakenness of the homeless, among all the dangers and with the women of ill-repute. Only those who truly share in the bread and in the suffering of human beings can recognize Him, even if they do not know His name."[30]

With the publication of *The Sea Remains* in 1972, Sulivan finally received major attention and acclaim as a novelist, and he won for this work the Grand Prix Catholique de Littérature and the Prix de l'Académie de Bretagne. The novel also registered a departure from the realist/sociological context and concerns of the Pigalle novels to a more detached, timeless plot-as-parable. Hence there are considerably fewer melodramatic elements in the story itself. The narrator's voice, now less profuse and confessional than in the earlier novels, seems to draw its strength from the ever-present imagery of the sea, which ultimately serves as a powerful cleansing force for moral and spiritual conversion.

The novel recounts the transformation of a retired Spanish cardinal, Ramon Rimaz, from a seemingly pompous (even overbearing and arrogant) prince of the church to a humble and committed Christian, whose focus would eventually be that of living for and being of service to others, especially the most dispossessed and hopeless. The story line is simple: Cardinal Rimaz retires with a devoted servant to a remote fishing village in the southern part of Spain. Here, close to nature and the life of simple fishermen, the cardinal begins to see with new eyes the life he has lived and the values that have motivated him. In this respect the work is Pirandellian and Sartrean in its use of the themes of masks and role-playing. The cardinal soon becomes aware that he had never possessed an interior life but had lived solely in conformity with external motivations directed to power and career. And he has become most troubled by the image with which he now sees himself: "To have spoken all his life of an eternal life, to have ordained thousands of priests to announce it, to hold in his hands each morning the . . . and now to stand there dry as a stick. Unbelievable. Everything happened outside me. I was on exhibit."[31]

Shocked by this epiphany—which allows him to understand his true spiritual state and the ends to which he has directed his career in the Church—the cardinal then embarks on a radical path of self-renewal. He vows to dispossess himself of the vestigial attributes of his previous position—the remains of pretense, power, and the love of ceremony that habit has ingrained in him. And in a material sense he throws away the finery and fripperies of his office, adopts the simple garb of the villagers, and opens himself directly and simply to all who cross his path during his daily walks. A whole range of people he meets teach him how to live through their moral and spiritual example. And after meeting and sharing views with them, he no longer pontificates but enters humbly into dialogue with others. Adopting the persona of the Good Samaritan, he is able to initiate relationships with others based on love and understanding, thereby allowing him to overcome the barriers of ideology and prejudice that separate human beings.

In particular, the cardinal disabuses a fiery young Marxist of his rigid and doctrinaire philosophy of class hatred by his larger view of social justice based on love and respect for individual freedom. The cardinal's view of the Church also radically changes, and he no longer sees it in triumphal terms as a perfect institution but rather as a pilgrim church, fallible yet inextricably linked to the divine economy of salvation. In explaining this to the same young Marxist avid for absolute form and purity of intention in politics, he says, "The Church sticks close to the ground; she's not made for immaculate consciences that nourish themselves in their purity. For the most part, she prefers what is to a perfection that does not yet exist." Yet despite the Church's thoroughly temporizing and pragmatic approach to dealing with the powers that be (the belief "that you can spread the faith the way you run a business, setting up foreign branches, calling meetings"), the hour of truth always arrives, the cardinal concludes, "when she mounts the cross" (*Sea*, 54–55).

Becoming more and more "transparent" in his program of "dispossession" and rebirth in simplicity and openness, Rimaz's spiritual influence and effect on others increases in intensity. Jesu Gonzalez de la Riva, a wealthy Cuban exile and paragon of the colonial landowner, is presented as a foil to the cardinal. Up to now he has been able to maintain a good conscience as a practicing Catholic (despite his hard-fisted and cruel treatment of tenant farmers) by legalistic interpretation of the demands of charity. Like the cardinal, he too has lived a ceremonial and superficial life of role-playing modeled on values dictated by institutions. The sincerity of the cardinal's sermons strips him of his good conscience and, experiencing a true change of heart, he offers himself as a ceremonial victim to be "crucified" during the Holy Week observances in expiation for his sins. It is at this moment as well that the cardinal takes the most radical step in his progression to what surely now is the path of sanctity. Deliberately creating and encouraging the legend that he has retired to a monastery ("to devote himself to meditation, prepare for death, and receive the care that his advanced age required" [*Sea*, 117]), he makes a final disposition of his freedom that is, however, radically different: disguised as a local fisherman, he hands himself over to be jailed, to share the life and work of "the thieves, workers, and Communists" (as his servant refers to those imprisoned there).

David Lodge

The important literary critic and acclaimed contemporary novelist David Lodge provides a most interesting study of forms taken by the Catholic novel in recent times. Lodge, who was born in 1935, represents in his writings the generation of English Catholics—and certainly Catholics throughout Europe and the United States—who came of age in the last decade of Tridentine Church and had therefore to live through the difficult transition of *aggiornamento* in the wake of Vatican II. Lodge first distinguished himself in academic circles for his works in literary criticism—*Language and Fiction* (1966), *The Novelist at the Crossroads* (1971), and *The Modes of Modern Writing* (1972), to name a few. He has since written numerous critical essays on modern novelists, and in particular on the Catholic writers Waugh, Greene, and Spark. He published his first novel, *The Picturegoers*, in 1960, and his 1990 novel, *Nice Work*, brings his works of fiction to more than 10.

As a critic of the novel, Lodge has been from the start primarily interested not in thematic content or meaning but in language. In *The Modes of Modern Writing* he says, "All critical questions about novels must be ultimately reduced to questons about language,"[32] and in *The Novelist at the Crossroads* he writes, "I still hold unrepentantly to the primacy of language in literary matters" (Lodge 1971, ix). This preoccupation with language and form is clearly indicated in his novels by the brilliant wordplay, pastiches, and parodies of well-known writers and artfully developed word games. Lodge reveals himself to be a masterful social satirist and a continuer of the comic satire of the Restoration writers. As a Catholic novelist, he has been compared to Waugh through his creation of a fascinating gallery of characters (resembling the latter's "Bright Young Things") whose lives and destinies reflect the foibles and obsessions of the post–Vatican II society in which Lodge has grown up. A cradle Catholic, Lodge's vision of reality and his approach to ethical/moral questions have been strongly affected and marked by his Catholic history. His novels become, therefore, amusing and perceptive quests for meaning. In them ingenuous protagonists (invariably endowed with Catholic background) are cast adrift in a world without recognizable value structures and must take a stab at living in a clearly amoral and absurd world. The process most always seems to involve the deflation of impossibly idealistic or rigid moral principles to allow accommodation with "the way things are" in a fallen world in which there seems little place for heroism, let alone sanctity.

Absent, then, in Lodge's novels is the tension between the ideal and real seen as a pitched battle or drama from which the protagonist hopes to emerge victorious over the profane world, with values intact. The struggle becomes, rather, mainly one of survival and the wresting of a modicum of meaning before the presence of forces that fragile and definitely weak human beings cannot seem to surmount, let alone control. Were Lodge writing in the naturalist tradition his literary universe would no doubt have the darkly pessimistic vision of a Zola or Hardy, with characters vainly trying to emerge from under heavy weight of biological and social forms of determinism. Lodge, however, is a consummate creator of comic form, and his characters are presented in the tradition of the comic theater as human beings who, because they succumb to foibles and weaknesses that the reader recognizes as all too human, induce sympathy but also laughter at the spectacle of their problematic situations.

For Lodge, as for so many writers of satire, the most universal of foibles is the human inability to control the sex drive. And from this incapactiy there is derived that rich vein of follies and turbulations experienced by virtually all of humankind in understanding and trying to keep under control the strongest and most persistent of human passions. Lodge, of course, sees this struggle through the prism of his and his Catholic generation's experience as recipients of the Church's teaching on sex—a generation that has had to confront contradictory attitudes and practices in this area widely accepted by the secular world. Anchored in the historical moment, he recounts the universal shift in attitudes toward sexual permissiveness in society as a whole, the changing life-styles that such medical breakthroughs as the pill have had on people in general, and the problems encountered specifically by Catholics who have reached maturity imbued with the Church's Jansenist attitudes toward sex.

Although Lodge frequently introduces very explicit sexual matter in funny (even rollicking) scenes and situations, he makes it clear (for he has also the moralist's perspective) that sexual mores cannot be separated from broader ethical and spiritual concerns. And though sex in Lodge's literary universe constitutes the strongest and most profound human need for satisfaction, it is not presented as sufficient in and of itself. Rather, because of its all-consuming force, it lies at the heart of a network of relationships that people must engage in with one another. And for those touched to any degree by belief, their response to sex cannot be divorced from God but rather becomes indicative of their rapport with Him. Though it often provides the author with rich possibilities for comedy, sex therefore has tragic undertones and consequences as well. We can say, then, that as was the case with Waugh, Lodge's surface frivolity more often than not masks a darker vision replete with implicit moral concern and comment.

Among David Lodge's most obviously Catholic novels (those that present as principal plot matter the sustained portrayal or study of Catholics living out their faith in and against the backdrop of modern society) are *The British Museum Is Falling Down* (1965) and *Souls and Bodies* (1990), originally titled *How Far Can You Go?* (1980). Catholic themes and situations are not at all absent in Lodge's other novels, but the universe of Catholic belief and practice is not a central concern or component in them.[33] *The British Museum Is Falling Down* is considered by Lodge to be one of his most comic novels (he describes it as such in a direct reference to it by the narrator of *Souls and Bodies*). The work relates the hardships endured by a young, impoverished married couple when, adhering to the Church's ban on contraception, they try to use the rhythm method (which, Lodge says, "was in practice neither rhythmical or safe"). Despite their stringent observance of fertility cycles and abstention from sexual relations that such made mandatory, they have had three children in so many years and are threatened with a fourth.

Although the novel's subject matter was indeed a most serious issue for Catholics then practicing this form of birth control, Lodge's larger intention was to depict with good-natured humor the decidedly absurd spectacle resulting from an institution's attempts to regulate the most intimate relations between a married couple through a system that, as it turned out, was anything but natural and inherently faulty to boot. Leaving the matter at this point of comedy, Lodge allows the reader to draw his own moral conclusion and stops short of dealing with the dilemma of those, torn in conscience, who then decide to risk going against the Church's interdiction. The drama of acceptance or rejection of ecclesiastical authority (and how one adjusts the personal conscience after such a decisive choice) would require a larger canvas and a more concentrated approach, and this Lodge provides in *Souls and Bodies*.

The novel, a kind of pilgrim's progress, follows the fortunes through life of 10 men and women first viewed as undergraduates in London universities who have become friends, associates, and potential lovers through membership in a Catholic student organization. Of pious middle-class backgrounds, they are introduced by an omniscent narrator (whom Lodge eventually identifies to be himself) as average young people still quite untouched by the profane world existing beyond the confines of their backgrounds. With varying dispositions toward belief, they are nevertheless portrayed at the outset as faithful practicing Catholics who have been strongly indoctrinated in the attitudes and practices of the pre–Vatican II Church. To explain these young people's worldview, Lodge ingeniously uses the structure and terminology of the children's game "Snakes and Ladders." As Lodge describes the religious implications of the game, "Up there was Heaven; down there was Hell. The name of the game was Salvation, the object to get to Heaven and avoid Hell. It was like Snakes and Ladders; sin sent you plummeting down towards the Pit; the sacraments, good deeds, acts of mortification, enabled you to climb back towards the light. Everything that you did was subject to spiritual accounting."[34]

The sacramental system—viewed as a series of efficient, laundering, and even magical operations—does not, of course, provide a means of shelter for the 10 young men and women when they confront the reality of things on the outside and make adult decisions. The situation is, moreover, complicated by Vatican II and the permissive society in which they begin to launch themselves personally and professionally. Problems encountered in their sexual lives soon become paramount, and they are forced to decide whether to go along with the restrictions of their faith or, like the vast majority of their contemporaries, decide to follow their own conscience. Most of them go through courtship and early marriage trying to adhere to Church teaching and play the "How Far Can You Go?" game of the rhythm method. In the process, the fumbling attempts to learn about and enjoy sex by these woefully repressed and touchingly inexperienced young people constitute much of the humor (and pathos) of the first half of the novel. Consequently, for the four couples of the group who married in the 1950s, Lodge tells us, "the next decade was dominated by babies . . . fourteen children between them, in spite of strenuous efforts not to. That is to say, although each of these couples wanted to have children, the latter arrived more quickly and frequently than their parents had wished for or intended" (*Souls*, 73).

With the arrival of the pill, the couples, now in early middle age, all accept contraception and in so doing embark on uncharted seas—an adventure for which, Lodge declares, their antiquated belief system had not prepared them: "So they stood upon the shore of Faith and felt the old dogmas and certainties ebbing away rapidly under their feet and between their toes, sapping the foundations upon which they stood, a situation both agreeably stimulating and slightly unnerving. For we all like to believe, do we not, if only in stories?" (*Souls*, 142–43). Lodge also expresses here the opinion that the breach in their total acceptance of the old articles of faith was inevitable and would have occurred even without the crisis of birth control, and this is because as Catholics, "they had started life with too many beliefs—the penalty of a Catholic upbringing . . . [and consequently] they had to dismantle all that apparatus of superfluous belief and discard it piece by piece" (*Souls*, 143).

It is, in fact, in the necessary process of throwing away the nonessential elements of their belief system that the young people—now middle-aged—finally confront the problems of life for which their faith seems, up to now at least, not to have prepared them. How, for instance, were they to decide on issues of morality after, as Lodge explains it, they had lost the ultimate restraining principle that their religion had offered them against hedonism or sins of all kind—the fear of eternal damnation. "At some point in the nineteen-sixties," he states, "Hell disappeared. First it was there, then it wasn't. . . . On the whole, the disappearance of Hell was a great relief" (*Souls*, 112). Though it may initially have provided heady relief from the ritualistic conformity of the past, this loss of fear as motive to believe and conform forced Lodge's pilgrims to the higher ethical ground suggested by Kierkegaard. They now must confront, without benefit of easy absolutes, such questions as their own belief or lack and support thereof and the related problems of how to live in an undeniably imperfect and fallen world and deal therein with the increasingly visible and menacing prospect of death.

When one of the couples (Dennis and Angela) suffers through a late pregnancy the birth of a child with Down's syndrome and then the further tragedy a few years later of the senseless death of a daughter hit by a car, the husband is brought to the brink of despair: "Then Anne was run over and killed and Dennis gave up. He could see no sense at all in the pattern of his life. The idea of a personal God with an interest in his personal fortune become impossible, unless he was a God who took a personal interest in torturing people" (*Souls*, 146). Thrown adrift, Dennis will never regain the uplifting belief that reason exists behind a divine pattern. Yet even after subsequent trials and moral falls (in particular, a mid-life affair with his secretary) he somehow never abandons the hope of finding meaning through belief (or is it that his heavy youthful formation by Catholicism is ultimately too strong to be thrown off?— Lodge discreetly leaves the issue in doubt).

Souls and Bodies also introduces such problems as God's role in the causes of evil and suffering, especially as endured by the innocent. In this instance Lodge, for a case in point contesting belief in a just and good God, chooses the terrible tragedy that had occurred in Aberfan, South Wales, in 1965. Here the middle school with over 150 children and their teachers was buried "in a man-made mountain of mining waste become waterlogged" (*Souls*, 106). Lodge's moral approach to this tragedy immediately evokes and follows similar patterns as those used by Camus's character Father Paneloux in the stance he had developed before the death of innocent children in the plague. In Lodge's novel "the traditional response of Christians" to the tragedy is expresssed in a sermon by a progressive priest, Father Austin, as that of "regarding it as some kind of punishment for man's sinfulness, or to accept it without question as the will of God." Austin cannot accept this orthodox rationale and has precisely the same problems with it as did Father Paneloux. "For," he says, "if it was mankind's sinfulness that was being punished, it was totally unjust that the punishment should fall on these particular children and their families." Then Austin goes beyond Paneloux's stance of anguished acceptance and states, "And if it was the will of God, why should we not question it?" (*Souls*, 106). Ultimately the English priest finds consolation and offers such to his congregation through recourse to the Job parable. "God had spoken to Job," he states, "and Job eventually submitted to the superior wisdom and power." Austin wonders, however, that these words would convince "a modern Job" and concludes that such incidents "gave human beings the right to complain to God on behalf of the victims" (*Souls*, 108). In regard to the manifestation of such absurd cruelty and suffering in the world, there seems, then, to be no clear answer to the question of God's relationship to and responsibility for evil.

Still, most of Lodge's group persist in faith of some kind and hope against hope. They come to realize that the world cannot be transcended, that there are no sure signs emanating from a "vertical" point of reference, and they live preoccupied by the question of how to live decently while faced with the increasingly difficult prospect of physical decline. Yet the novel concludes on an optimistic note as Lodge makes clear his belief that this world offers the means of spiritual regeneration and hope through elevation of the commonplace to a level of sacramental significance. He ultimately posits as more important than problematic religious issues and questions an authentic commitment to live by the spirit and apply the values of faith to all aspects of day-to-day life. Despite the dark universe it describes, the novel ends in a hopeful openness as it describes the new Easter liturgy, the "Paschal Festival" prepared by an embryo group of "New Catholics" who are evolving innovative and more meaningful forms of worship to witness to the Good News. And it is not by chance that most of the original group of 10 find themselves once more reunited with one another and participating (to varying degrees of adherence and enthusiasm) in the sacramental breaking and consuming of the freshly baked bread.[35]

Notes and References

Unless the English-language edition is indicated, all translations of the works cited are my own.

Prologue

1. Richard Gilman, "Salvation, Damnation, and the Religious Novel," *New York Times Book Review*, 2 December 1984, 7, 58–60; hereafter cited in text.

2. Albert Sonnenfeld, *Crossroads: Essays on the Catholic Novel* (York, S.C.: French Literature Publications, 1982), vii; hereafter cited in text.

3. David Lodge, *The Novelist at the Crossroads and Other Essays on Fiction and Criticism* (London and New York: Ark Paperbacks, 1971); hereafter cited in text.

4. François Mauriac, in an interview with Philip Toynbee, *Observer*, 27 October, 1957.

5. François Mauriac, *The Viper's Tangle*, trans. Gerard Hopkins (New York: Carroll & Graf, 1987), 7; hereafter cited in text.

6. The Catholic philosopher Jacques Maritain engaged in a celebrated dialogue with Mauriac on the question of how sin should be presented in novels written by Catholics and viewed Mauriac's use of sinful matter in novels written up to that time as possibly establishing connivance with sin and sinful human nature. See John Dunaway's excellent treatment of this question in his chapter "Maritain and Literature," in *Jacques Maritain* (New York: Twayne Publishers, 1978); hereafter cited in text. In regard to Graham Greene and Catholic critics, one only needs to point out that Greene's novel *The Power and the Glory*, which had for its protagonist a fallen yet saintly "whiskey priest," was condemned by the Holy Office in 1940, shortly after its publication.

7. Blaise Pascal, *Pensées de M. Pascal sur la religion et sur quelques autres sujets* (1670), ed. Louis Lafuma (Paris: Delmas, 1960), 235.

8. Saint Augustine, *Confessions* (ca. 400), trans. R. S. Pine-Coffin (New York: Penguin, 1961), 80; hereafter cited in text.

9. Conor Cruise O'Brien, *Maria Cross: Imaginative Patterns in a Group of Catholic Authors* (1951: Fresno, Calif.: Academy Guild Press, 1963), 211; hereafter cited in text.

10. François Mauriac, *God and Mammon* (London: Sheed & Ward, 1936), 78; hereafter cited in text.

11. Jean-Paul Sartre, "M. François Mauriac et la liberté," *La Nouvelle Revue Française*, February 1939, 212–32.

12.   David O'Connell, *Michel de Saint Pierre* (Birmingham, Ala.: Summa Publications, 1990), 4; hereafter cited in text.

Chapter One

1.   For an excellent study on the situation of French Catholicism and the development of Catholic literary inspiration in nineteenth-century France, see Gene Kellogg, "French Catholics after 1789," in *The Vital Tradition: The Catholic Novel in a Period of Convergence* (Chicago: Loyola University Press, 1970), 7–15.

2.   Charles Baudelaire, *Oeuvres complètes*, (Paris: Gallimard/Bibliothèque de la Pléiade, 1954), 1211.

3.   "There are odors succulent as young flesh, / sweet as flutes, and green as any grass, / while others—rich, corrupt and masterful— / possess the power of such infinite things / as incense, amber, benjamin and musk, / to praise the senses' raptures and the mind's" (*Les Fleurs du Mal*, trans. Richard Howard [Boston: David Godine, 1983], 15).

4.   André Gide, *Dostoevsky* (1923; New York: New Directions, 1961), 15.

5.   Eugène de Vogüé, *The Russian Novelists*, trans. Jane Loring Edmands (1887; Freeport, N.Y.: Books for Libraries Press, 1972), 197.

6.   For further treatment of the use of theological themes and concepts in the later novels of Dostoyevski, see Kurt F. Reinhardt's "Dostoevsky the Possessed," in *The Theological Novel of Modern Europe* (New York: Frederick Ungar, 1969), 39–73; hereafter cited in text.

7.   Jules Amédée Barbey d'Aurevilly, *Une vieille maîtresse*, in *Oeuvres romanesques complètes* (Paris: Gallimard/Bibliothèque de la Pléiade, 1960), 463; hereafter cited in text.

8.   Jules Amédée Barbey d'Aurevilly, *Un prêtre marié*, in *Oeuvres romanesques complètes*, 1082; hereafter cited in text.

9.   Raïssa Maritain, *We Have Been Friends Together*, trans. Julie Kernan (New York: Longmans, Green, 1942), 119; hereafter cited in text.

10.   Léon Bloy, *Le Désespéré* (1886; Paris: Mercure de France, 1962), 290; hereafter cited in text.

11.   Léon Bloy, *La Femme pauvre* (1897; Paris: Mercure de France, 1937), 299.

12.   Joris-Karl Huysmans, 1894 Preface to *A Rebours* (1884; Paris: Garnier-Flammarion, 1978), 55; hereafter cited in text.

13.   Joris-Karl Huysmans, *Là-bas* (1891; Paris: Gallimard/Collection Folio, 1985), 78.

14.   Joris-Karl Huysmans, *En route* (1895; Paris: Plon, 1960), 278.

15.   Charles Péguy, "Un Nouveau théologien: M. Fernand Laudet," *Oeuvres de prose, 1909–1914* (Paris: Gallimard/Bibliothèque de la Pléiade, 1961), 1074–76.

Chapter Two

1. Georges Bernanos, *Les Grands Cimitières sous la lune* (Paris: Plon, 1946), ii.
2. Albert Béguin, *Bernanos par lui-même* (Paris: Editions du Seuil, 1955), 17; hereafter cited in text.
3. Georges Bernanos, *Monsieur Ouine* (1946; Paris: Plon, 1960), 94.
4. Georges Bernanos, *Oeuvres romanesques suivies de "Dialogues des Carmélites"* (Paris: Gallimard/Bibliothèque de la Pléiade, 1955), 1852.
5. Georges Bernanos, *Nouvelle Histoire de Mouchette* (1937; Paris: Plon 1960), 29.
6. Georges Bernanos, *Sous le soleil de Satan* (1926; Paris: Plon, 1957), 142; hereafter cited in text.
7. Georges Bernanos, *The Diary of a Country Priest*, trans. Pamela Morris (New York: Carroll & Graf, 1983), 247–49; hereafter cited in text.
8. Georges Bernanos, *Dialogues des Carmélites* (Neuchatel: La Baconnière; Paris: Seul, 1949), 142.
9. François Mauriac, "On Writing Today," in *Second Thoughts: Reflections on Literature and Life* (New York: World, 1961), 16.
10. François Mauriac, *Le Baiser au lépreux* (Paris: Grasset, 1922), 201.
11. Mauriac includes Gide's letter to him in the text of *God and Mammon*, 17–18.
12. François Mauriac, *Le Désert de l'amour* (Paris: Grasset, 1925), 201; hereafter cited in text.
13. François Mauriac, *Thérèse Desqueyroux* (1927), trans. Gerard Hopkins (London: Penguin Books, 1959), 10; hereafter cited in text.
14. *Julian Green Diary, 1928–1958*, trans. Anne Green (New York: Harcourt, Brace & World, 1964), 174; hereafter cited in text.
15. Glenn S. Burne, *Julian Green* (New York: Twayne Publishers, 1972), 13; hereafter cited in text.
16. Julien Green, *Le Malfaiteur* (Paris: Editions de Seuil, 1957), 11; hereafter cited in text.
17. Julien Green, *Moïra* (Paris: La Palatine, 1952), 254.
18. Julien Green, *Chaque homme dans sa nuit* (Paris: Plon, 1960), 395; hereafter cited in text.
19. Quoted in Michael Barlow, *Gilbert Cesbron: Témoin de la tendresse de Dieu* (Paris: Robert Laffont, 1965), 36–37.
20. Gilbert Cesbron, *Les Saints vont en enfer* (Paris: Robert Laffont, 1952), 192; hereafter cited in text.

Chapter Three

1. For a succinct and thorough historical treatment of the intellectual climate in England against which the Catholic writers reacted, see Gene Kellogg, "Protestant England," in *The Vital Tradition*, 79–99.

2. Graham Greene, "Frederick Rolfe: Edwardian Inferno," in *Collected Essays* (New York: Viking Press, 1969), 172–73; hereafter cited in text.

3. Frederick Rolfe, *Hadrian VII* (1904; New York: Knopf, 1925), 72–75.

4. David Lodge has thoroughly investigated their bias in "The Chesterbelloc and the Jews," in *The Novelist at the Crossroads*, 145–58.

5. Hilaire Belloc, *Mr. Clutterbuck's Election* (London: Methuen, 1908).

6. Graham Greene, "Mr. G. K. Chesterton," in *Collected Essays*, 135–38.

7. Sonnenfeld, "Don Quixote and the Romantic Reactionaries," in *Crossroads: Essays on the Catholic Novel*, 2–7.

8. G. K. Chesterton, *The Napoleon of Notting Hill* (1904: London: Bodley Head, 1968), 9; hereafter cited in text.

9. G. K. Chesterton, *Orthodoxy* (1908; New York: Image Books, 1959), 116.

10. Quoted in Calvin W. Lane, *Evelyn Waugh* (Boston: Twayne Publishers, 1981), 162; hereafter cited in text.

11. Ian Littlewood, "Religion," in *The Writings of Evelyn Waugh* (Totowa, N.J.: Barnes & Noble Books, 1983), 139–49.

12. Evelyn Waugh, "Fan-Fare," in *The Essays, Articles, and Reviews of Evelyn Waugh*, ed. Donat Gallagher (Boston: Little, Brown, 1983), 302.

13. Evelyn Waugh, *The Diaries of Evelyn Waugh*, ed. Michael Davie (London: Weidenfeld & Nicolson, 1976; Boston: Little, Brown, 1977), 566.

14. Evelyn Waugh, *Decline and Fall* (1928; Boston: Little, Brown, 1956), 24; hereafter cited in text.

15. Evelyn Waugh, *Vile Bodies* (1930; Boston: Little, Brown, 1946), 123.

16. Evelyn Waugh, *A Handful of Dust* (Boston: Little, Brown, 1934), 35–36; hereafter cited in text.

17. Jeffrey Heath, *The Picturesque Prison* (Kingston and Montreal: McGill–Queen's University Press, 1982), 166; hereafter cited in text.

18. Evelyn Waugh, *Brideshead Revisited* (Boston: Little, Brown, 1945), 45; hereafter cited in text.

19. Evelyn Waugh, *Men at Arms* (London: Chapman & Hall, 1952), 1.

20. Norman Sherry, *The Life of Graham Greene*, vol. 1, 1904–39 (New York: Viking Press, 1989), 275.

21. Graham Greene, *The Lawless Roads* (London: Heinemann, 1939), 3–6; hereafter cited in text.

22. Roger Sharrock, *Saints, Sinners, and Comedians: The Novels of Graham Greene* (Kent: Burns & Oates/University of Notre Dame Press, 1984), 177; hereafter cited in text.

23. Evelyn Waugh, "The Waste Land," in *The Essays, Articles, and Reviews of Evelyn Waugh*, 249.

24. Graham Greene, *A Sort of Life* (New York: Simon & Schuster, 1971), 169.

25. Graham Greene, *Brighton Rock* (1938; New York: Viking Press, 1956), 41; hereafter cited in text.

26. Graham Greene, *The Power and the Glory* (1940; New York: Penguin Books, 1982), 247; hereafter cited in text.

27. W. H. Auden, "The Heresy of Our Time," *Renascence* 1 (1949): 23–24.

28. Graham Greene, *The Heart of the Matter* (1948; New York: Penguin Books, 1982), 247; hereafter cited in text.

29. Graham Greene, *The End of the Affair* (1951; New York: Viking Press, 1965), 116; hereafter cited in text.

Chapter Four

1. A. H. Winsnes, *Sigrid Undset: A Study in Christian Realism*, trans. P. G. Foote (London and New York: Sheed & Ward, 1953), 9; hereafter cited in text. I am indebted to Professor Winsnes for this solid and comprehensive analysis of Sigrid Undset's major literary works, particularly his emphasis on her as a Christian realist.

2. Sigrid Undset, *Kristin Lavransdatter*, vol. 1, *The Bridal Wreath* (1923), trans. Charles Archer and J. S. Scott (New York: Bantam Books, 1981), 69; hereafter cited in text.

3. Sigrid Undset, *Kristin Lavransdatter*, vol. 3, *The Cross* (1927), trans. Charles Archer (New York: Bantam Books, 1984), 14; hereafter cited in text.

4. Carl Bayerschmidt, *Sigrid Undset* (New York: Twayne Publishers, 1970), 102.

5. Werner Bergengruen, *A Matter of Conscience*, trans. Norman Cameron (London and New York: Thames & Hudson, 1952), 302.

6. Harry T. Moore, *Twentieth-Century German Literature* (London: Heinemann, 1971), 92–94; hereafter cited in text.

7. Gertrud von Le Fort, *Aufzeichnungen und Erinnerungen* (Benziger Verlag, 1951), 21–22; hereafter cited in text.

8. Ita O'Boyle, *Gertrud von Le Fort: Introduction to Her Prose Work* (New York: Fordham University Press, 1962), xiv; hereafter cited in text. I am indebted to Professor O'Boyle for her solid and comprehensive survey of Baroness von Le Fort's major literary works, particularly the important details on her intellectual and spiritual evolution as a Catholic writer.

9. Both *The Veil of Veronica* and *The Wreath of Angels* were included under the title of *Der Römische Brunnen* in the collected works of Le Fort's prose fiction, *Erzählende Schriften*, vol. 1 (Wiesbaden: Ehrenwirth Verlag, 1956).

10. Gertrud von Le Fort, *The Veil of Veronica* (1928), trans. Conrad M. R. Bonacina (New York: Sheed & Ward, 1934), 128; hereafter cited in text.

11. Gertrud von Le Fort, *Der Kranz der Engel*, in *Erzählende Schriften*, 1: 497–98; hereafter cited in text.

12. Gertrud von Le Fort, *The Song at the Scaffold* (1931), trans. Olga Marx (New York: Sheed & Ward, 1933), 9; hereafter cited in text.

13. Peter Demetz, *After the Fires: Recent Writing in the Germanies, Austria, and Switzerland* (New York: Harcourt, Brace & Jovanovich, 1986), 23; hereafter cited in text.

14. Elisabeth Langgässer, *The Quest* (1950), trans. Jane Bannard Greene (New York: Knopf, 1953), 359; hereafter cited in text.

Chapter Five

1. See Henri Peyre, *French Novelists of Today* (New York: Oxford University Press, 1967), 337–95.

2. See John Cruikshank, *Albert Camus and the Literature of Revolt* (London and New York: Oxford University Press, 1959).

3. Albert Camus, *The Plague* (1947), trans. Stuart Gilbert (New York: Vintage, 1972), 220; hereafter cited in text.

4. See Henry F. Grubbs, "Albert Camus and Graham Greene," *Modern Language Quarterly* 10 (1949): 33–42, and Jean Duché, "Du rocher de Sisyphe au Rocher de Brighton," *La Table Ronde*, no. 2 (1948): 306–309.

5. Querry's last words are, in fact, "absurd. . . . [T]his is absurd or else . . ." The narrator then comments, "But what alternative, philosophical or psychological, he had in mind they never knew" (Graham Greene, *A Burnt-Out Case* [New York: Viking, 1961], 244).

6. I am indebted to Karl-Josef Kuschel's treatment of this change in emphasis (which he finds exemplified in the literary works of Heinrich Böll): "The Christianity of Heinrich Böll," *Cross Currents* 39, no. 1 (1989): 21–36.

7. Quoted in Oscar L. Arnal, "Theology and Commitment: Marie-Dominique Chenu," *Cross Currents* 38, no. 1 (1988): 67–68.

8. For background material on Vatican II, see Xavier Rynne, *Letters from Vatican City* (New York: Farrar, Straus, 1962), and Walter M. Abbott, S.J., *The Documents of Vatican II* (New York: America Press, 1966).

9. Heinrich Böll, *The Train Was on Time* (1949), in *The Stories of Heinrich Böll*, trans. Leila Vennewitz (New York: Alfred Knopf, 1986), 185; hereafter cited in text.

10. Heinrich Böll, *Billiards at Half-Past Nine* (1959), trans. Leila Vennewitz (New York: McGraw-Hill, 1962), 126.

11. See Böll's remarks to this effect in his epilogue to Carl Amery's *Capitulation: An Analysis of Contemporary Catholicism*, trans. Edward Quinn (London and Melbourne: Sheed & Ward, 1967), 225–31. See also Kuschel, 24–28.

12. Irving Malin, "The Deceptions of Muriel Spark," in *The Vision Obscured*, 95.

13. Peter Kemp, *Muriel Spark* (New York: Harper & Row, 1975), 13; hereafter cited in text.

14. Ruth Whitaker, *The Faith and Fiction of Muriel Spark* (London: Macmillan, 1982), 37; hereafter cited in text.

15. Malcolm Muggeridge interview with Muriel Spark, as reported in Whitaker, 26–27.

16. See Muriel Spark, "My Conversion," *Twentieth Century* 170 (Autumn 1961): 60–61.

17. Muriel Spark, "The Religion of an Agnostic: A Sacramental View of the World in the Writings of Proust," *Church of England Newspaper*, 27 November 1953, 1.

18. See Robert E. Hosmer, Jr., "Muriel Spark: Writing with Intent," *Commonweal* 16, no. 6 (1989): 233–41; hereafter cited in text.

19. Muriel Spark, *Memento Mori* (New York: Meridian Books, 1960), 17; hereafter cited in text.

20. Muriel Spark, *The Prime of Miss Jean Brodie* (1961; New York: Dell, 1980), 12; hereafter cited in text.

21. Muriel Spark, *The Mandelbaum Gate* (New York: Alfred Knopf, 1965), 40; hereafter cited in text.

22. Muriel Spark, *The Abbess of Crewe* (New York: Viking Press, 1974), 103.

23. Roger Bichelberger, "A la croisée des chemins," in *Rencontres avec Jean Sulivan*, no. 2 (Paris: Association des Amis de Jean Sulivan, 1986), 16.

24. Quoted in Patrick Gormally, "Jean Sulivan: Un pseudonyme d'origine cinématographique," in *Le Sacrement de l'instant présence de Jean Sulivan* (Paris: Albin Michel, 1990), 24.

25. Gormally, *Le Sacrement de l'instant*, 32–34, quoting the 29 January 1942 *New York Times* review of the film.

26. Jean Sulivan, "Qui êtes-vous, Sulivan?," *Rencontres avec Jean Sulivan*, 78; hereafter cited in text.

27. Jean Onimus, "Pharisien, mon semblable, mon frère," in *Rencontres avec Jean Sulivan*, 78; hereafter cited in text.

28. Jean Sulivan, *Devance tout adieu* (Paris: Gallimard, 1966), 77; hereafter cited in text.

29. Jean Sulivan, *Car je t'aime, ô éternité* (Paris: Gallimard, 1966), 163; hereafter cited in text.

30. Jean Sulivan, *Consolation de la nuit* (Paris: Gallimard, 1968), 109–10.

31. Jean Sulivan, *The Sea Remains* (1972), trans. Robert A. Donohue, Jr., and Joseph Cunneen (New York: Crossroad, 1989), 7–8; hereafter cited in text.

32. David Lodge, *The Modes of Modern Writing: Metaphor, Metonymy, and the Topology of Modern Literature* (1977; Chicago: University of Chicago Press, 1988), ix.

33. See Edward T. Wheeler, "David Lodge: The Machinery of Illusion and Effect," *Commonweal* 17, no. 16 (1990): 538–41.

34. David Lodge, *Souls and Bodies* (1980; New York: Penguin Books, 1990), 6; hereafter cited in text.

35. "The Transcript of the Elton Special: Easter with the New Catholics as Transmitted 24/4/75," in *Souls and Bodies*, 228–40.

Selected Bibliography

PRIMARY WORKS

Augustine, Saint. *Confessions*. ca. 400. Translated by R. S. Pine-Coffin. New York: Penguin Books, 1961.

Barbey d'Aurevilly, Jules Amédée. *Oeuvres romanesques complètes*. Vol. 1. Paris: Gallimard/Bibliothèque de la Pléiade, 1964.

Baudelaire, Charles. *Les Fleurs du Mal*. 1857. Translated by Richard Howard. Boston: David R. Godine, 1982.

Belloc, Hilaire. *Emmanuel Burden*. New York: Charles Scribner & Sons, 1904.

_____. *Mr. Clutterbuck's Election*. London: Methuen, 1908.

Bergengruen, Werner. *A Matter of Conscience*. Translated by Norman Cameron. London and New York: Thames & Hudson, 1952.

Bernanos, Georges. *Dialogues des Carmélites*. 1949. Neuchatel: La Baconnière; Paris: Seuil, 1949.

_____. *The Diary of a Country Priest*. 1936. Translated by Pamela Norris. New York: Carroll & Graf, 1983.

_____. *Monsieur Ouine*. 1946. Paris: Plon, 1960.

_____. *Nouvelle Histoire de Mouchette*. 1937. Paris: Plon, 1960.

_____. *Oeuvres romanesques suivies de "Dialogues des Carmélites."* Paris: Gallimard/ Bibliothèque de la Pléiade, 1961.

_____. *Sous le soleil de Satan*. 1926. Paris: Plon, 1957.

Bloy, Léon. *Le Désespéré*. 1886. Paris: Mercure de France, 1962.

_____. *La Femme pauvre*. 1887. Paris: Mercure de France, 1937.

Böll, Heinrich. *Billiards at Half-Past Nine*. 1959. Translated by Leila Vennewitz. New York: McGraw-Hill, 1962.

_____. *The Clown*. 1963. Translated by Leila Vennewitz. New York: McGraw-Hill, 1965.

_____. *The Stories of Heinrich Böll*. Translated by Leila Vennewitz. New York: Random House, 1972.

Cesbron, Gilbert. *Les Saints vont en enfer*. Paris: Editions Robert Laffont, 1952.

Chesterton, G. K. *The Napoleon of Notting Hill*. 1904. London: Bodley Head, 1968.

_____. *Orthodoxy*. 1908. Garden City, N.Y.: Image Books, 1959.

Dostoyevski, Fyodor. *Crime and Punishment*. 1866. Translated by Jessie Coulson. New York: Norton, 1964.

_____. *Notes from Underground Inquisitor and the Grand Inquisition*. Translated by E. Matlaw. New York: E. P. Dutton, 1960.

Green, Julien. *Adrienne Mesurat*. Paris: Plon, 1927.

_____. *Chaque homme dans sa nuit*. Paris: Plon, 1960.

_____. *Julian Green Diary, 1928–1958*. Translated by Anne Green. New York: Harcourt, Brace & World, 1964.

_____. *Le Malfaiteur*. Paris: Editions du Seuil, 1957.

_____. *Moïra*. Paris: La Palatine, 1950.

Greene, Graham. *Brighton Rock*. 1938. New York: Viking Press, 1956.

_____. *A Burnt-Out Case*. New York: Viking Press, 1961.

_____. *Collected Essays*. New York: Viking Press, 1966.

_____. *The End of the Affair*. 1951. New York: Viking Press, 1965.

_____. *The Heart of the Matter*. 1948. New York: Penguin Books, 1982.

_____. *The Lawless Roads*. London: Heinemann, 1939.

_____. *The Power and the Glory*. 1940. New York: Penguin Books, 1982.

_____. *A Sort of Life*. New York: Simon & Schuster, 1971.

Huysmans, Joris-Karl. *A Rebours*. 1884. Paris: Garnier-Flammarion, 1978.

_____. *En route*. 1895. Paris: Plon, 1960.

_____. *Là-bas*. 1891. Paris: Gallimard/Collection Folio, 1985.

_____. *L'Oblat*. Paris: Plon, 1917.

Langgässer, Elisabeth. *The Quest*. 1950. Translated by Jane Bannard Greene. New York: Knopf, 1953.

Le Fort, Gertrud von. *Erzählende Schriften*. Wiesbaden: Ehrenwirth Verlag, 1956.

_____. *The Pope from the Ghetto*. Translated by Conrad M. R. Bonacina. New York: Sheed & Ward, 1934.

_____. *The Song at the Scaffold*. 1931. Translated by Olga Marx. New York: Sheed & Ward, 1933.

_____. *The Veil of Veronica*. 1928. Translated by Conrad M. R. Bonacina. New York: Sheed & Ward, 1934.

Lodge, David. *The British Museum Is Falling Down*. London: MacGibbon & Kee, 1965.

_____. *Souls and Bodies*. 1980. New York: Penguin Books, 1990.

Mauriac, François. *Le Baiser au lépreux*. Paris: Bernard Grasset, 1922.

_____. *Le Désert de l'amour*. Paris: Bernard Grasset, 1925.

_____. *Destins*. Paris: Bernard Grasset, 1928.

_____. *Génitrix*. Paris: Bernard Grasset, 1923.

_____. *God and Mammon*. 1929. London: Sheed & Ward, 1936.

_____. *Thérèse Desqueyroux*. Paris: Bernard Grasset, 1927.

_____. *Viper's Tangle*. Translated by Gerard Hopkins. New York: Carroll & Graf, 1987.

Pascal, Blaise. *Pensées de M. Pascal sur la religion et sur quelques autres sujets*. Edited by Louis Lafuma. Paris: J. Delmas, 1960.

Péguy, Charles. *Oeuvres de Prose, 1909–1914*. Paris: Gallimard/Bibliothéque de la Pléiade, 1961.

Rolfe, Frederick. *Hadrian VII*. New York: Knopf, 1925.

Spark, Muriel. *The Abbess of Crewe*. New York: Viking Press, 1974.

_____. *The Comforters*. London: Macmillan, 1957.

_____. *The Mandelbaum Gate*. New York: Alfred A. Knopf, 1965.

_____. *Memento Mori*. New York: Meridian Books, 1960.

_____. "My Conversion." *Twentieth Century* 170 (Autumn 1961): 58–63.

_____. *The Prime of Miss Jean Brodie*. 1961. New York: Edition Dell, 1980.

_____. "The Religion of an Agnostic: A Sacramental View of the World in the Writing of Proust." *Church of England Newspaper*, 27 November 1953, 1.

Sulivan, Jean. *Car je t'aime, ô éternité*. Paris: Gallimard, 1966.

_____. *Consolation de la nuit*. Paris: Gallimard, 1968.

_____. *Devance tout adieu*. Paris: Gallimard, 1966.

_____. *The Sea Remains*. 1972. Translated by Robert A. Donohue, Jr., and Joseph Cunneen. New York: Crossroad, 1989.

Undset, Sigrid. *Jenny*. Translated by W. Emmë. New York: Knopf, 1921.

_____. *Kristin Lavransdatter*. Vol. 1, *The Bridal Wreath*. 1923. Translated by Charles Archer and J. S. Scott. New York: Bantam Books, 1981.

_____. *Kristin Lavransdatter*. Vol. 2, *The Mistress of Husaby*. 1925. Translated by Charles Archer. New York: Bantam Books, 1981.

_____. *Kristin Lavransdatter*. Vol. 3, *The Cross*. 1927. Translated by Charles Archer. New York: Bantam Books, 1981.

Waugh, Evelyn. *Brideshead Revisited*. Boston: Little, Brown, 1948.

_____. *Decline and Fall*. Boston: Little, Brown, 1928.

_____. *The Essays, Articles, and Reviews of Evelyn Waugh*. Edited by Donat Gallagher. Boston: Little, Brown, 1983.

_____. *A Handful of Dust*. Boston: Little, Brown, 1934.

_____. *Love among the Ruins*. London: Chapman & Hall, 1953.

_____. *The Loved One*. Boston: Little, Brown, 1948.

_____. *Men at Arms*. Boston: Little, Brown, 1952.

_____. *Officers and Gentlemen*. Boston: Little, Brown, 1955.

_____. *Unconditional Surrender*. London: Chapman & Hall, 1960. In the United States titled *The End of the Battle*. Boston: Little, Brown, 1964.

_____. *Sword of Honour*. The one volume recension of *Men at Arms, Officers and Gentlemen*, and *Unconditional Surrender*. Boston: Little, Brown, 1966.

_____. *Vile Bodies*. 1930. Boston: Little, Brown, 1946.

SECONDARY WORKS

Individual Authors

Jules Amédée Barbey d'Aurevilly

Chartier, Armand B. *Barbey d'Aurevilly*. Boston: Twayne Publishers, 1977. Best introduction to author and his works in English.

Yarrow, P. *La Pensée politique et religieuse de Barbey d'Aurevilly*. Geneva: Droz, 1961. Excellent presentation and assessment of Barbey's religious and political views.

Hilaire Belloc

Corrin, Jay P. *G. K. Chesterton and Hilaire Belloc: The Battle against Modernity*. Athens: Ohio University Press, 1943. Good study of the political and social theories advanced by Chesterton and Belloc.

Lodge, David. "The Chesterbelloc and the Jews." In *The Novelist at the Crossroads and Other Essays on Fiction and Criticism*, 145–58. London and New York: Ark Paperbacks, 1971. Studies the forms of anti-Semitism held by the two authors and reflected in their works. A helpful introduction to the two authors.

Georges Bernanos

Béguin, Albert. *Georges Bernanos: Essais et témoignages réunis par Albert Béguin*. Neuchatel: La Baconnière, 1949. An invaluable source of letters by the author, memories of friends, and an account of the evolution of Bernanos's thought and works.

Blumenthal, Gurda. *The Poetic Imagination of Georges Bernanos*. Baltimore: Johns Hopkins University Press, 1965. Excellent study of thematic structures and stylistic devices used throughout the works.

Bush, William. *Georges Bernanos*. New York: Twayne Publishers, 1969. Still one of the best introductions to the author and his works.

Molnar, Thomas. *Bernanos: His Political Thought and Prophecy*. New York: Sheed & Ward, 1960. Gives good background of Bernanos's political thought and commitment but is weak in analyzing his fiction.

Léon Bloy

Heppenstall, Rayner. *Léon Bloy*. New Haven: Yale University Press, 1954. Best general introduction to Bloy's works and thought in English.

Maritain, Raïssa. *We Have Been Friends Together*. Translated by Julie Kernan. New York: Longmans, Green, 1942. Provides valuable testimony of Bloy's example and influence on the younger generation seeking means of religious belief.

Polimeni, Emmanuela. *Léon Bloy the Pauper Prophet, 1846–1917*. Luton: Leograve Press, 1947. Brief but excellent portrait of Bloy as polemicist and prophet.

Heinrich Böll

Demeth, Peter. *After the Fires: Recent Writings in the Germanies, Austria, and Switzerland.* New York: Harcourt, Brace & Jovanovich, 1986. Contains the very informative chapter "Heinrich Böll: Citizen and Novelist."

Kuschel, Karl-Josef. "The Christianity of Heinrich Böll." *Cross Currents* 39, no. 1 (1989): 21–36.

Gilbert Cesbron

Barlow, Michel. *Gilbert Cesbron: Témoin de la tendresse de Dieu.* Paris: Robert Laffont, 1965. Excellent study of the author's religious convictions and resulting forms of commitment in his novels.

G. K. Chesterton

Boyd, Ian. *The Novels of G. K. Chesterton: A Study in Art and Propaganda.* New York: Harper & Row, 1975. Provides excellent commentary and analysis of all the major novels.

Corrin, Jay P. *G. K. Chesterton and Hilaire Belloc: The Battle against Modernity.* Athens: Ohio University Press, 1943. Good study of the political and social theories advanced by Chesterton and Belloc.

Lodge, David. "The Chesterbelloc and the Jews." In *The Novelist at the Crossroads and Other Essays on Fiction and Criticism,* 145–58. London and New York: Ark Paperbacks, 1971. Studies the forms of anti-Semitism held by the two authors and reflected in their works. A helpful introduction to the two authors.

Fyodor Dostoyevski

Gide, André. *Dostoevsky.* 1923. New York: New Directions, 1961. An insightful portrait of the Russian novelist as Christian moralist.

Reinhardt, Kurt F. "Dostoevsky the Possessed." In *The Theological Novel of Modern Europe,* 39–73. New York: Frederick Ungar, 1969. Succinct and valuable chapter giving excellent analysis of Dostoyevski's major novels from a theological perspective.

Julien Green

Burne, Glenn S. *Julian Green.* New York: Twayne Publishers, 1972. Good introduction to most of the major prose works.

Newbury, Anthony H. *Julian Green: Religion and Sensuality.* Amsterdam: Rodopi, 1986. Interesting study of how Green's difficult search for his sexual identity is reflected in his prose works.

Stokes, Samuel. *Julian Green and the Thorn of Puritanism*. New York: Columbia University Press, 1955. An excellent exploration of the spiritual background of Green's works and of his religious evolution.

Graham Greene

Auden, W. H. "The Heresy of Our Time." *Renascence* 1 (1949): 23–24.

Duché, Jean. "Du rocher de Sisyphe au rocher de Brighton." *La Table Ronde*, no. 2 (1948): 306–309.

Grubbs, Henry. "Albert Camus and Graham Greene." *Modern Language Quarterly* 10 (1949): 33–43.

Kunkel, Francis I. *The Labyrinthine Ways of Graham Greene*. New York: Sheed & Ward, 1959. Good overview of Greene's novels from a religious perspective.

Lodge, David. *Graham Greene*. Columbia Essays on Modern Writers, 17. New York: Columbia University Press, 1966. Short but perceptive essay on the novels.

_____. "Fiction and Catholicism Graham Greene." In *The Novelist at the Crossroads and Other Essays on Fiction and Criticism*, 87–118. London and New York: Ark Paperbacks, 1971. Excellent essay on how Greene's evolving attitudes toward Catholicism is reflected in the novels by a shift from tragic conflict between human/divine values to the fiction of comedy and irony of the later works.

Sharrock, Roger. *Saints, Sinners, and Comedians: The Novels of Graham Greene*. Kent: Burns & Oates University/Notre Dame Press, 1984. Provides excellent cultural background and analysis of all the major novels.

Sherry, Norman. *The Life of Graham Greene*. Vol. 1, 1904–39. New York: Viking Press, 1989.

Stratford, Philip. *Faith and Fiction: Creative Process in Greene and Mauriac*. Notre Dame, Ind.: University of Notre Dame Press, 1964. Perceptive study and comparison of forms of religious faith and artistic technique of the two major Catholic novelists.

Joris-Karl Huysmans

Baldick, Robert. *The Life of Joris-Karl Huysmans*. Oxford: Clarendon Press, 1955. Still the best introduction to Huysmans's artistic and intellectual evolution as seen in the major prose works.

Gertrud von Le Fort

O'Boyle, Ita. *Gertrud von Le Fort: An Introduction to Her Prose Work*. New York: Fordham University Press, 1964. A comprehensive yet succinct introduction to the most important of le Fort's prose works. The best English-language commentary.

Reinhardt, Kurt F. "Gertrud von Le Fort: *The Song at the Scaffold.*" In *The Theological Novel of Modern Europe*, 217–34. New York: Frederick Ungar, 1969.

David Lodge

Wheeler, Edward T. "David Lodge: The Machinery of Illusion and Effect." *Commonweal* 17, no. 16 (1990): 538–41.

François Mauriac

Cormeau, Lilly. *L'Art de François Mauriac*. Paris: Grasset, 1951. Remains one of the best introductions to the major novels.

DuBos, Charles. *François Mauriac et le problème du romancier catholique*. Paris: Edition Correa, 1923. Perceptive study of the problem of complicity in presenting sin and sinful natures in novels by Catholic novelists and Mauriac in particular.

Moloney, Michael. *François Mauriac: A Critical Study*. Denver: Alan Swallow, 1958. Valuable study of the intellectual and spiritual influences forming and affecting Mauriac's fiction and his resulting stance as Christian moralist.

Sartre, J.-P. "M. François Mauriac et la liberté." *La Nouvelle Revue Française* 52 (February 1939): 212–32.

Stratford, Philip. *Faith and Fiction: Creative Process in Greene and Mauriac*. Notre Dame, Ind.: University of Notre Dame Press, 1964.

Charles Péguy

Saint Aubyn, F. C. *Charles Péguy*. Boston: Twayne Publishers, 1972. The best introduction in English to Péguy's life and works.

Frederick Rolfe

Greene, Graham. "Frederick Rolfe from the Edwardian Inferno," "Frederick Rolfe from the Devil's Side," and "Frederick Rolfe: A Spoiled Priest." In *Collected Essays*. New York: Viking Press, 1966.

Muriel Spark

Hosmer, Robert E., Jr. "Muriel Spark: Writing with Intent." *Commonweal* 16, no. 6 (1989): 233–41.

Kemp, Peter. *Muriel Spark*. New York: Harper & Row Publishers, 1975. Excellent thematic and stylistic study of the major novels.

Lodge, David. "The Use and Abuse of Omniscience: Method and Meaning in Muriel Spark's *The Prime of Miss Jean Brodie*." In *The Novelist at the*

Crossroads and Other Essays on Fiction and Criticism, 119–44. London and New York: Ark Paperbacks, 1971.

Whitaker, Ruth. *The Faith and Fiction of Muriel Spark*. London: Macmillan, 1982. Provides excellent analysis of all the major novels with an emphasis on the religious dimensions of Spark's fiction.

Jean Sulivan

Gormally, Patrick. "Jean Sulivan: Un pseudonyme d'origine cinématographique." In *Le Sacrement de l'instant présence de Jean Sulivan*, 23–31. Paris: Albin Michel, 1990.

_____. "Jean Sulivan, écrivain chrétien: Une nouvelle conception du rôle de l'écrivain." Ph.D. diss., Université de Toulouse-le Mirail, 1980. Very solid and detailed study of Sulivan's novels as reflectors of his essential religious beliefs and aspirations as novelist.

Sigrid Undset

Bayerschmidt, Carl. *Sigrid Undset*. New York: Twayne Publishers, 1970. Valuable introduction to the author and her works.

Winsnes, A. H. *Sigrid Undset: A Study in Christian Realism*. London and New York: Sheed & Ward, 1953. Provides excellent and perceptive treatment of Undset's spiritual vision and literary commitment and production as a Catholic novelist.

Evelyn Waugh

Heath, Jeffrey. *The Picturesque Prison: Evelyn Waugh and His Writings*. Kingston and Montreal: McGill–Queen's University Press, 1982. An insightful and very detailed presentation of the major novels viewed thematically as the author's means to escape from modern society.

Lane, Calvin W. *Evelyn Waugh*. Boston: Twayne Publishers, 1981. The best and most succinct introduction to Waugh's life and novels.

Littlewood, Ian. *The Writings of Evelyn Waugh*. Totowa, N.J.: Barnes & Noble Books, 1983. Solid study of the thematic and stylistic components of Waugh's novels.

General

Amery, Carl. *Capitulation: An Analysis of Contemporary Catholicism*. Translated by Edward Quinn. London and Melbourne: Sheed & Ward, 1967. Important essay strongly critical of modern German Catholicism. Amery includes an epilogue by Böll supporting his charges that the Church in Germany had gravely compromised its mission in order to be politically correct.

Brée, Germaine, and Margaret Guiton. *The French Novel from Gide to Camus.* New York: Harcourt, Brace & World, 1957. One of the best introductions to the existential novel in France.

Calvet, Jean. *Le Renouveau catholique dans la littérature contemporaine.* Paris: Lanore, 1927. An early work on the Catholic renascence in France that is flawed by the author's narrow doctrinal views and rigid categorization of authors deemed Catholic. (He excludes Bernanos and Mauriac from his list.)

Demetz, Peter. *After the Fires: Recent Writing in the Germanies, Austria, and Switzerland.* New York: Harcourt, Brace & Jovanovich, 1986. Excellent study and overview of German literature after World War II.

Dru, Alexander. *The Contribution of German Catholicism.* New York: Hawthorn Books, 1963. Good intellectual and cultural study of German Catholicism up to the end of the nineteenth century.

Fowlie, Wallace. *Jacob's Night: The Religious Renascence in France.* New York: Sheed & Ward, 1943. An excellent study of precursors, theorists, and authors (Péguy, Maritain, Mauriac, Green, et al.).

Friedman, Melvin J. *The Vision Obscured: Perceptions of Some Twentieth-Century Catholic Novelists.* New York: Fordham University Press, 1970. Important collection of essays on 11 modern Catholic novelists drawn from England, France, Germany, Italy, and Spain.

Gilman, Richard. "Salvation, Damnation, and the Religious Novel." *New York Times Book Review,* 2 December 1984, 7, 58–60.

Griffths, Richard. *The Reactionary Revolution: The Catholic Revival in French Literature, 1870–1914.* New York: Ungar, 1965. A solid study especially good in its treatment of the political and cultural background in and against which the "revival" developed.

Guardino, Romano. *The End of the Modern World: A Search for Orientation.* Translated by Joseph Theman and Herbert Burke. New York: Sheed & Ward, 1956. Very influential work announcing the end of traditional forms of belief and exploring approaches to interpret Christian Revelation in a postmodern period just beginning.

Kellogg, Gene. *The Vital Tradition: The Catholic Novel in a Period of Convergence.* Chicago: Loyola University Press, 1970. An important study of the development of the Catholic novel in France, England, and the United States from the nineteenth century through modern times and up to the period of convergence after Vatican II. Especially valuable in its study of the background differences and opposing currents existing in the three societies.

Kurz, Paul Konrad, S.J. *On Modern German Literature.* Translated by Sister Mary McCarthy. Vol. 4. University: University of Alabama Press, 1977. Although the focus is German literature, this volume provides three very perceptive essays on the Catholic novel: "Why Is Christian Literature at an End?," "The Priest in the Modern Novel," and "The Contemporary Novel about Jesus."

Lodge, David. *The Novelist at the Crossroads and Other Essays on Fiction and Criticism*. 1971. New York: Ark Paperbacks, 1986. Includes perceptive essays on Greene, Chesterton/Belloc, and Spark.

_____. *The Modes of Modern Writing: Metaphor, Metonymy, and the Topology of Modern Literature*. London: Routledge & Kegan Paul, 1977.

_____, ed. *Twentieth-Century Literary Criticism: A Reader*. London: Longman, 1972.

Majault, Joseph. *L'Evidence et le mystère*. Paris: Le Centurion, 1978. Significant study devoted to the reevaluation of what Catholic literature is and what forms it assumes in the post–Vatican II period.

Maritain, Jacques. *Art and Scholasticism*. Translated by J. F. Scanland. London: Sheed & Ward, 1923. Formal articulation of the author's Thomistic art and aesthetics; his commentary concerning the purity of art is especially interesting.

Moore, Harry T. *Twentieth-Century German Literature*. London: Heinemann, 1971. A good general introduction to modern German literature containing substantive references to German Catholic novelists and writers.

Norman, Edward. *Roman Catholicism in England from the Elizabethan Settlement to the Second Vatican Council*. Oxford and New York: Oxford University Press, 1986. A succinct yet admirably detailed study of the intellectual and cultural history of Catholicism from the reign of the Tudors to the present.

O'Brien, Conor Cruise. *Maria Cross: Imaginative Patterns in a Group of Catholic Writers*. London: Burnes & Oates, 1963. Still the best synthesis of major elements of Catholic literary inspiration in the works of the major novelists of the classical period.

O'Connell, David. *Michel de Saint Pierre: A Catholic Novelist at the Crossroads*. Birmingham, Ala.: Summa Publications, 1990. Valuable work not only on this major contemporary French novelist but also on the state of the Catholic novel in France before and after Vatican II.

Orwell, George. *Inside the White Whale and Other Essays*. 1957.Hammondsworth: Penguin, 1975. Offers a pessimistic outlook for future freedoms in society because of passive acceptance of authoritarian principles.

Percy, Walker. *The Message in the Bottle*. 1954. New York: Farrar, Straus & Giroux, 1979. An important study (especially the essay "A Novel about the End of the World") on what the religious novel has become in the postmodern (Death of God) period.

Peyre, Henri. *French Novelists of Today*. New York: Oxford University Press, 1967. Valuable study of the existential novel in postwar France with many references to similar forms in Europe and America.

Prévost, Jean Laurent. *Le Roman catholique a cent ans*. Paris: Fayard, 1958. An interesting but somewhat selective "state of the genre" at mid-century;

gives only superficial coverage to authors who are not French (with Greene the exception).

Reinhardt, Kurt. *The Theological Novel of Modern Europe: An Analysis of Masterpieces by Eight Authors.* New York: Frederick Ungar, 1969. Interesting work analyzing theological concepts and themes contained in the works of six major Catholic authors (includes essays on Dostoyevski and Camus).

Sonnenfeld, Albert. *Crossroads: Essays on the Catholic Novel.* York, S.C.: French Literature Publications, 1982. To date the most significant examination of the Catholic novel as a literary subgenre. Especially valuable in its study of the changing forms and emphasis the novel has undergone in recent times.

Vogüé, Eugène de. *The Russian Novelists.* 1887. Translated by Jane Loring Edwards. Freeport, N.Y.: Books for Libraries Press, 1972.

Index

The Author

Theodore P. Fraser received his B.A. from Fordham University and his M.A. and Ph.D. from Brown University. In 1956–57 he was appointed French government assistant at the Collège Moderne de Garçons in Grenoble and has taught at the Lawrenceville School, Tufts University, Bates College, and Bucknell University. In 1968 he joined the faculty of the College of the Holy Cross, where he has chaired the Department of Modern Languages and Literature (1971–80 and 1990 to the present) and founded the Studies in European Literature program, of which he is currently director. He is the author of *Le Duchat, First Editor of Rabelais* (1971), *The Moralist Tradition in France* (1982), *The French Essay* (1986), *Readings in French Literature* (1975), and *Le Pot au feu* (1975). He served as literary editor of the *French Review* from 1986 to 1990.

The Editor

David O'Connell is professor of foreign languages and chair of the Department of Foreign Languages at Georgia State University. He received his Ph.D. in 1966 from Princeton University, where he was a National Woodrow Wilson Fellow, the Bergen Fellow in Romance Languages, and a National Woodrow Wilson Dissertation Fellow. He is the author of *The Teachings of Saint Louis: A Critical Text* (1972), *Les Propos de Saint Louis* (1974), *Louis-Ferdinand Céline* (1976), *The Instructions of Saint Louis: A Critical Text* (1979), and *Michel de Saint Pierre: A Catholic Novelist at the Crossroads* (1990). He is the editor of *Catholic Writers in France since 1945* (1983) and has served as review editor (1977–79) and managing editor (1987–90) of the *French Review*.